Number 4
Stewart Burton

stewartburton73@gmail.com

https://www.facebook.com/yp90760/

First Completed in 2018

This Edition 2019

Stewart Burton

stewartburton73@gmail.com

Thank you to all those who supported me through the process of putting this to paper.

This book is written in honour of the friends and their families who suffered from the darker side of Hong Kong.

And to my sons who I have thought of every moment of this journey. You have been my strength and continued inspiration.

And yes you can read this book when you're old enough.

This is a true story.

It's hard for me to believe when I look at my life now.

Prison is supposed to be a punishment for your actions and to correct your behaviour.

It certainly did that for me.

But my release was only the beginning of my journey.

The books chapters are written out of order. Chapter 1 later than Chapter-1. It should all become clear as you read.

Chapter One

Jail!

I'm sure it was an old school bus that we were in. I was sitting right at the back, handcuffed to my neighbour. It was freezing cold outside, and black. All the windows were open, but nobody tried to close them. Nobody was moving, talking, doing anything. We all knew better. Although I didn't know the language the threat of violence from the guards was obvious. I didn't know where we were going.

When the bus finally stopped it had pulled up at a set of large gates that looked two or even three stories high. Prison gates. You couldn't see but could imagine the huge walls running away from their sides. I didn't know what I was expecting, I didn't know anything, I was so filled with dread, that for a moment the pain I was feeling right through my body was a dull ache in the background. The gates opened slowly like they were going to consume us, and they did. The bus drove through them into a vast room where it stopped. My whole body tensed with anticipation, some more guards came onto the bus. They walked up the bus like the devil's own air stewards, counting their unfortunate passengers who were heading to hell. The bus then drove through into the prison compound.

When the doors opened a guard stood up and shouted something and all the other prisoners stood up and start to get off the bus, I followed. As we got off the bus they made us stand in a line and then a guard came and removed our handcuffs. We had been chained two by two and when we were separated we were made to stand in single file. I couldn't tell if I was shaking from physical pain or psychological terror. I was shivering from head to toe. I looked up and tried to take in my surroundings.

It was dark and the whole place was covered in a thick fog. There were orange lights shining through it which gave off enough light for me to make out high fences surrounding me on two sides, there were buildings in front of me that I could just make out through the darkness and fog. I also noticed grey fences leading off in different directions. As my eyes started to adjust I could see the source of the main lights. There were turrets on top of the walls. They were spotlights manned by armed guards, I could see their guns. The guns barrels shining in the dark, moist from the rain.

We were lined up facing a door. All I could make out was an orange glow coming from it. There were guards shouting orders at each of the prisoners and they walked through the glow, one by one, into the room beyond. One guard came out; he was wearing a white coat and an officer's cap. He was coming down the line shouting at everyone he passed. He pushed a few of the others in front of me and I could see their bodies were rigid with fear as he approached them. Some he seemed to recognise, he would talk to them quietly like an uncle, and then without warning, he would punch them in the stomach. They would try not to show pain, they would stand as still as they could. It was as if they showed any reaction he would do it again. A couple of times he did.

He finally got to me. He stood there looking at my sorry sight, shivering in the freezing cold. He came right up close to me, so close I could smell him. I was scared, very scared. He whispered to me in a very heavy Chinese accent in English,

"I can help you".

For a fleeting moment, I believed him. I think that I wanted to believe him.

He said, "Come with me".

I followed him past the others to the bright orange glow of the door. Now I could see inside. It was like a doctor's waiting room. Three of the guys who were in the queue in front of me were already in the room, they were naked. There were three big men in white coats at different corners. At each one there was a guy totally naked. I slowly started taking it in. I was terrified. I was pushed to the left. The guard laughed and shouted at me

"See I told you I could help you, now strip"

I stood there; he came right up to me with his baton and rammed it into my stomach. I nearly crumpled to the floor.

He shouted

"Strip"

And then he started ripping at my clothes.

"Do you not understand me gwai gi (foreign devil boy)?"

He shouted.

I just had to do it, I had no choice. I took my clothes off. I stopped at my underwear and he shouted

"Everything"

I took them off. I was standing there naked and freezing, I felt ashamed and scared. My shivering was now a mixture of the cold and of fear. I was then grabbed by one guy in a white coat. He had surgical gloves on and grabbed my head. He pulled at my hair and my ears. He pulled my mouth open and looked inside; he grabbed my

arms and raised them over my head. He told me to spread my legs and pull up my testicles. He grabbed my penis and told me to pull my foreskin back. I could hear other guys going through other treatment but I daren't look round. I was then pushed over to another white coat. There was a chair next to him; he shouted something in Chinese I couldn't understand. I stood there. He punched me in the stomach. He shouted again, this time pointing at the chair which had its back to me, I went to turn the chair around, and I was punched again. He shouted in English
"Bend over"
I was now truly terrified if I thought that I had already been assaulted but it was about to get worse. I was pushed over the chair, another guard grabbed my arms and pulled me forward, my legs were kicked apart and I was held there. The guard came round and looked me in the eyes. He also had surgical gloves on. He put his hand into a large pot and pulled out a handful of grease. He slowly rubbed the grease into his hands, smiled and walked round to my back. I started struggling but the guards just me down. I felt his hands cold against my buttocks. He spread them apart and slowly pushed a finger up my back passage. It was agony but I couldn't cry I daren't. He pushed deeper and deeper and started feeling about. Then he whipped his finger out, I was let go of and then pushed to another table. I felt that I had just been raped. I had been degraded to my very core. Nothing could have been worse. I could have died right there, it would have been a relief. I wanted to die right there. Little did I know that this would happen to me many times over the next few years? Every time I left the prison and came back from anywhere the same thing would happen. This was true hell. This was the day before my 18th birthday. At the next table, I barely heard what the guard said. I was in shock. He was asking if I had any health issues I just kept saying no, no. I was then pushed into another room. It was a small dark room that stank of damp and sick bodies. It stank of misery. There were about five rows of wooden benches at which some prisoners were sitting. They all had clothes on and I looked down. In front of me, there was a large wicker box full of clothes I was told to get dressed. I found some trousers and a shirt. They stank and were covered in stains; they were a light blue colour and made of a material that scraped my skin. No underwear. Next to it was a pile of plastic sandals. I found a pair that fit and was then pushed on to one of the benches. My body ached. I didn't know it but I was going through withdrawal symptoms.

It was like a serious bought of flu. Every bone in my body ached. My skin felt so thin so that when I sat down it felt that I was sitting on a bare bone. I was then told to come forward pushed against a wall and had a photo taken. Then I was pushed back to my bench. Some of the guys were having their hair shaved off. We sat there until everyone had been processed. There was no talking. Nobody even acknowledged each other. There was so much depression in the room you could feel it, smell it. After what seemed like an hour a guard came in and started shouting us forward one by one.
"Gwai gi hai sun" (foreign devil boy get up)
He shouted whilst looking at me.
I copied what the other guys did. Got up and went forward.
He gave me a small card which had my photo on it, my name, the letters YR and the numbers 27343.
"Yee chat sam say sam, cho die" (27343 sit down)
He shouted at me
I looked at him, blankly.
"Yee chat sam say sam cho die"
He shouted louder and shoved me back to emphasise the point.
I sat down.
 We were then told to get up and move outside. We were made to stand side by side. There were new guards now. Everything that they said was in Chinese. I couldn't understand anything. The guards came to each one of us when they were shouting the orders, they got right in our faces shouting at us, spit flying out of their mouths onto our faces. We were then marched two by two into the fog. Gate after gate was opened and closed behind us. We walked through open corridors of grey metal high fences. In the distance, large buildings started to come into sight. We moved towards one of them. It was four stories high, a large long concrete building. It was hard to see in the dark as there were big powerful lights shining at us. We were moved inside. Everywhere was concrete. The guards continued to shout at us. We were led up some cold concrete stairs up to the second floor. There were two prisoners squatting next to two large blue buckets. We went up to them one by one any were given a yellow mug of brown liquid and a plate of rice with a fish head on it. I was immediately repulsed by the sight of it. But I took the mug and plate offered although I knew there was no way I could eat it I was obeying orders already. We were then pushed around a corner to a gate that opened to a long corridor. On one side were dirty slated

windows, the floor was concrete along with the ceiling. On the ceiling, every few metres hung a dull light. On the other side, there was a long line of bars. I was moved down the corridor. After a few metres, I was stopped and pushed through a gap in the bars. The bars were slammed closed behind me. I was standing in a cell. Although there was a light on the ceiling I couldn't see at first, it was so dark. The dark was heavy, thick. You could stretch your arms out and touch each side of the cell. The walls were cold concrete. On one side was a wooden plank on a metal frame, a bed. I walked further in. On the back wall, there was a metal sink encased in concrete and next to that, behind a low concrete wall, a hole in the ground, the toilet. I was brought back to reality when the noise started. The only previous noise was a metal clanking of cell doors being slammed shut. Then there was shouting from the guards. But then our lights went out and whatever tiny amount of light we had before was gone. There was just the low glow from the lights outside my cell. That's when I broke down. I wanted out, I was trapped. There was a button on the wall I started pressing it furiously. A guard came down, I pleaded with him to let me out, I wanted to go home, and I shouldn't be here. I was crying uncontrollably. I was shaking with a panic attack. He shouted at me and left. As soon as he left me shaking alone the other noise started. It was if the whole building erupted into life. There was shouting, banging: a thousand Chinese voices all shouting at once. The noise was deafening. Then the screaming started, it was me.

Chapter -1

Self-harm

My mum always said that she couldn't get me a birthday cake or card for my "special" day because it was just after the New Year and all the shops were shut. I do remember getting presents sometimes, but the parties didn't really happen because I had been born at the wrong time of the year. Nothing could have been done about it. And because of the time of year I was born I was also always the youngest in my class at school.

There isn't much that I can remember from before going to school. One thing I do know is that I could read before I started school. It was my solace and still is. I had read the Encyclopaedia Britannica Children's Edition by the time I was 5. It was somewhere I could escape to. I was an easy child so was left to my own devices most of the time. My father was in the merchant navy and was away from home for many months at a time so it was left to my mum to raise us.

I do remember the first day at school, well not all of it but really one specific event. We were all sitting at our desks and I looked over to see this boy crying. I remember being confused by it and found myself getting up and going over to sit next to him. I didn't know the boy and didn't know why he was crying. I just stared at him, I think and asked him questions about what was the matter.

I was then shouted at by one of the teachers and told to go back to my seat. I think I must have said something back to the teacher and so got a mouth full from them and was told to go and stand in the corner. That corner and I got to know each other very well over the next few weeks up until I was promoted to being sent to the office instead. This was probably my first attempt at connecting with someone of the same age and it was met with punishment. For someone who had huge social difficulties, this one incident on the very first day of school taught me that showing concern for others was frowned upon.

The next event I remember was one day taking my school jotter and drawing faces all over it. Every page was full of round heads, two eyes and a mouth. The only thing that was different on each picture was the mouth. I had a couple of friends next to me that was laughing so I kept drawing and drawing until the entire jotter was full of these emotions. This was my first attempt at understanding the human condition. I have been studying you ever since. I have since come to learn that I have prosopagnosia which is face blindness. Making it difficult for me to recognise people. Adding this to my inability to read emotions on people's faces was probably the main instigator in this artwork. This behaviour was an office offence. Anytime I was sent to the office a huge wave of panic would start to overwhelm my body, but it never stopped me. Individuals with ASD find it very difficult to break the rules. We enjoy rigid and fixed instructions. This helps us feel calm in a world of constant change. However, I believe I kept on with my poor behaviour because I was getting the attention that I never got at home.

After school, I would always go home and go straight to my room to read.

Soon I was getting letters sent home with me detailing the misdemeanours that I had committed that day including flooding the bathroom by stuffing toilet paper into the plug hole and leaving the tap running, and by wetting toilet paper and throwing it on the ceiling.

I was very easily led. I thought that by doing what my friends suggested was how friendships worked. But I was always the one that got caught. I really struggled with the social side of the school. I didn't know how to make friends. I tried to copy others behaviours but it never seemed to work for me. I was only 5 at this point but I was already struggling deep down inside. I didn't play with the other kids all the time, I didn't really know how to. Previously I thought this was because I didn't have a father figure at home that played with and taught me the rules. Whenever my father came home he just did jobs around the house and then sat and watched the TV whilst drinking a bottle of Bacardi whilst my mum drank her whisky. But that wasn't all that he did. For 8 to 10 months of the year, we lived by my mum's rules. Hardly ever sat at the table for dinner, always sat at the TV and she served us whatever we wanted to eat. Never a vegetable or even a piece of fruit in sight. However, when my father came home all the rules changed. He would make us sit down with him one by one and go through what we wanted for breakfast, lunch and dinner for the two or three weeks that he was home. It would last for hours.

"What meat do you want two weeks on Thursday, what vegetable do you want with it"?

He would write everything down and stick it to the inside of the kitchen cupboard. And when it came to two weeks on Thursday and you were served the chicken and peas that you had ordered, you had to eat them. I had to stay at the table until I had finished everything on the plate. My younger brother got away with it and my older brother ate everything anyway. But I was left at that table on many an occasion until ten o'clock at night with cold vegetable staring at me, and me trying to hide them under my knife and fork.

"You asked for those bloody peas, so you better bloody eat them".

I also didn't know how to physically play with my peers. They would have rough and tumble games that I would try to join in with. But unfortunately, I didn't understand what was going on and often became too physical. By the age of 6 or 7, I was completely depressed. I was wetting the bed almost every night. I wouldn't tell my mum and would sleep in the same bed covers until she changed them after a week. She would always say that it was because I was naughty and dreaming of naughty things. This continued for many years up to my teens. I found the school completely horrible. I would get up each and every morning filled with dread that I had to go to school. I would follow the same routine every morning but always try and leave the house by myself and make sure that I didn't find myself walking with anyone else. I was bored in class and never did any homework or anything the teachers asked me. I was sent home with punishment exercises nearly every week that had to be signed by a parent. I learnt to forge both my parents' signatures at this time. We were always given lines to complete. You know like write 50 times

"I must not talk in class".

It didn't take me long to create a device where I connected 10 pencils together so that I could write 50 lines very quickly. Each pencil had to have a slightly increased weight stuck to it so that the pressure was correct. After a while, some other kids were paying me to do their lines for them. Which was great. I would be really happy when I saw someone get lines because I know they would pay me and I would go and buy cigarettes, as I had started smoking by 7.

I can't remember the reason, but at 7 I tried to kill myself for the first time. I was so miserable that I took my bicycle lock and tied it around my bed and my neck. My mum came upstairs and found me hanging there. It was a combination lock and quite a sticky one so it took her some time to get it off. She must have thought I had been mucking about because she just told me not to be so stupid and to not do it again and left.

After that failed attempt I started self-harming. I had quite a repertoire of self-harming techniques; one of them was by trying to knock myself out by head butting walls. I also learnt how to increase my blood pressure in my head to make myself pass out. I think a teacher must have spotted what I was doing and added along with other behaviours they finally called in a specialist to check me out.

So an educational psychologist was brought into the school and put me through a series of questions over a few days. And you know I really enjoyed it. The questions gradually got more and more difficult. I felt really good that I could answer the questions. I got a buzz out of working these pretty intense questions out. Sometime later my mum was called into school to hear what they thought about me. What happened next really was a huge turning point in my life. The conversation that followed between psychologist and my mum would have a profound impact on my life for many years into the future. Of course, I don't remember the full conversation, just this one part of it. The psychologist turned to my mum and said

"You don't have to worry about him; he'll go straight to university".

Bam! To say that to a parent that had already proved that she wasn't that bothered about her son was beyond comprehension. Now she had an excuse not to worry or care. My mum was told that I had an exceptionally high IQ and that they would be implementing a new teaching plan for me. I was taken back to my classroom. A desk had already been put at the back of the class and on that desk was my very own edition of David Attenborough's Life on Earth. I loved that book and had spent many hours reading it. The teacher told me to sit down and said

"As you're so clever, study that".

And that was it, at 7 years old I was told to self-study.

As I'm writing this today I am quite horrified to think that professionals who were supposedly dedicated to the welfare, education and growth of children could act in such ways. To think that any of my children would be treated like this fills me with anger.

I have tried to get access to my school files but have been told that they were destroyed years ago. It would make very interesting reading. However, we have to remember that this was the late 70's early 80's so knowledge of developmental issues with children was very limited.

Chapter Two
Junkies Remorse

The whole night was spent in pain, delirium. All I need to do is get out and get one bag and I would be fine. They could then put me back inside; I would be ready, prepared. Just one bag. I spent hours thinking how I could get out. Feign illness, escape. People escape from prison right? This place was run by the stupid Chinese, wasn't it? It would be easy to escape from them, from here. But the pain. The bed was a plain wooden plank and every part of my body that came in touch with it ached as if I was covered in bruises, head to foot. My asthma was bad, I pushed the buzzer, but nobody came this time. I kept pushing it and pushing it. That's what it's there for, isn't it? If you push it they have to come. I needed my inhaler. The panic started rising again. Every so often I would hear heavy footsteps coming down the corridor. I would get up, a guard would walk passed, I called to him, and he always ignored me and walked passed. He kept walking into the distance then I would hear a click click click. Then he would walk passed. I asked for help, he ignored me and walked passed. The footsteps fading into the distance again. I had to breathe through my clothes, calm myself down. I needed the toilet in the night but I couldn't see. The night never ended.

A loud noise suddenly filled my cell. It was a radio with some Chinese guy shouting from it. It sounded like something from an old film, with some old Chinese guy shouting at his troops before they went into battle waving their stupid red books. It went on and on, I had no idea what was going on. I tried to go back to sleep, pulled the horrible covers over my head. Then there was shouting. Coming closer and closer to my cell. Along with it came a strange, loud metallic rattling noise. It would stop every so often and then a guard would start shouting. I recognised my first bit of Chinese.

"Diu lay lo mo, chow hai" (fuck your mother, smelly cunt)

Would be repeated and repeated. Then the rattling would begin again. It got to my cell, whack! Right on the top of my head.

"Diu lay low mo, hai sun..... Diu lay lo mo" etc. etc. (fuck your mother get up)

My covers were pulled off. I jumped up. A guard was standing there, truncheon in hand. He had hit me with it; this was the noise I heard. He was running his truncheon along all the bars of the cells to get everyone up. I got up. He shouted something at me then walked away to the next cell. I could now take in my cell properly. It was filthy, really filthy. I went to the toilet and nearly puked. It was caked with shit, it stank of stale urine, and it was only a hole in the ground with two feet holes either side of it. I had never even seen one before let alone used one. But I needed to go. I stood over it, pulled my trousers down and tried to squat down. Luckily there was a small concrete wall in front of me, for privacy? To hold on to. I held on to it and did what I had to do. It wasn't the most comfortable experience I had ever had. I pulled the small metal handle that stuck out from the wall and it just spun round in my hand, no flush. That's why the toilet was so bad. How was I going to live like this? I had just had a severe bought of the runs and I couldn't flush it away. I didn't even have any toilet paper. I went to the sink to fill up my plastic cup with water to use that to flush it. I pushed the tap, no water. Suddenly a huge thirst came on; I felt the panic again building. How can I live this? I didn't know how long I was going to be stuck here. It was eerily quiet with only the guards shouting in the background. I lay back down on my bed. It wasn't for long. More shouting erupted at the end of my corridor. I got up and looked out. There were dirty windows on the other side of the corridor. They led out on to a rubbish-filled courtyard and on the other side where more windows leading to more corridors and cells. I could now for the first time get an idea of where I was.

A guard came to my cell started shouting something and unlocked my door. I stood there for a moment not knowing what was going to happen next. I cautiously moved towards the open door like a frightened rabbit and poked my head outside. I looked left then right. All the other prisoners were leaving their cells so I followed. As I stood outside my cell it felt like I was free again, but only for a fraction of a second. Then the guard returned shouting again and as I watched all the other guys turned and started walking towards the end of the corridor. I fell into line, like a robot already programmed for this event. We were led outside and made to stand two by two in a line. We were then marched away from the cell block. I had no idea what time it was. The whole place was covered in a thick layer of mist but this time it was light grey. It was freezing cold. Every now and again a wisp of wind would send the light grey cloud scurrying in different directions. The place looked like it went on forever. Through the veil of cloud, I could occasionally see the outer wall. A huge concrete structure that had a round top. As my eyes followed it around I came to see a watchtower. And standing on it was a guard with a very large gun staring right back at me. I tried to follow the wall around but it again disappeared into the mist. We finally reached another building where we were being led into one by one. I managed to look through a window and saw it was full of prisoners in blue and brown uniforms.

I got into the building to find that it was a dining hall. There must have been five hundred prisoners inside. The blue uniforms were separated from the brown. We walked along the wall one by one. There were shutters in the wall that was open by only 5 or 6 inches at the most. As I reached the first shutter a yellow plastic mug was pushed out with a brown watery substance with brown twigs in it. I picked it up and moved to the next shutter, a blue plastic plate emerged with a horror show all over it. A mound of white rice with two decapitated fish heads with congealed eyes staring back at me. I nearly through the plate back but by the time I was able to process the vision in front of me I had been pushed out of the line. I was now following the line towards a table. The room was full of metal tables with three prisoners sitting on each side. The weird thing was that there was barely any sound apart from the slurping of rice off spoons. Our table was right at the back of the room. I sat down with the other prisoners and place my plate and cup in front of me. In my horror of receiving the plate, I hadn't noticed the tray of chopsticks and spoons so I sat down with nothing to eat my breakfast. Not that it mattered I had no appetite anyway, I supposed I could have eaten something but with the horror in front of me I just couldn't even consider eating anything. All around me everyone was tucking into their food. In the middle of the table was a big blue bowl that the Chinese where spitting the mashed up remnants of fish heads into. I looked around, across the horizon of black hair and to my delight saw a guy with brown hair. He was quite tall but walked hunched over. Just behind him was a shorter guy with blonde hair. They moved silently towards a table and sat down. They both had brown uniforms on. I felt like an alien wanting to make contact with one of my own. We made eye contact and there was a small nod from both of them then they turned around and got one with their breakfast. By this point, others were finishing their food and throwing their plates into the blue bowl in the middle. So I grabbed my plate and did the same. As the rice and fish slipped into the bowl there was a big groan the came from everyone at my table. I had just committed my first, obvious, prison faux pass. If you don't want to eat you should offer your food to others. Anyway, nothing I could do and quite frankly I couldn't give a fuck. So I gave them all a look to tell them to fuck off. My withdrawals were really kicking in again. It felt like all of my orifices wanted to let go. Puking, shitting and pissing all felt like the right thing to do. Fortunately, my thoughts of painting the dining rooms floor were interrupted by a guard making us get up from the table and leave through a door that I hadn't noticed right behind us. I threw one last glance over my shoulder to the two foreigners that I had seen earlier hoping to catch their eyes. They felt like my salvation in this hell. Someone I could communicate with, someone that could help me survive. We were taking back to the first building that I had been taking too the night before. I was too ill to care now. We went into the building one by one. It had been changed back to its original purpose, a doctors waiting room with a couple of desks with prison officers in white coats. It was now that I realised that I had to be honest if I was going to survive. I was called over to see one of the officers. I sat down and told him straight out that I was a heroin addict. That was the first time that I had admitted it to myself let alone anyone else. He laughed and said why didn't you tell us last night, go and sit over there. I went and sat in another seat. A while later I was led through to another room where an actual doctor had his office. I sat down and went through my medical history. I was then led further up the corridor where there were cells. The door on the left was opened and I was pushed inside. There was a Chinese guy there who led me through into the shower room. I was told to take off all my clothes and another Chinese guy came in with a hose. He turned it on and the water came out at full power. It was cold and stung so much so it nearly knocked me over. He hosed me for what felt like ten minutes. I was then given a towel and told to dry myself. Then the guy with the hose grabbed a bucket with a mug in it. The bucket was full of white powder and they started throwing this powder all over me. It was then that I noticed that they had gloves on. They made me rub the powder all over myself, my whole body including my hair. I was being deloused. I was told to sit on a chair in the shower room and wait. I was stinking of chemicals, it smelt like petrol, my skin started to itch, it was excruciating. After an hour I was allowed to have a cold shower to get the dust off. I was given a white uniform to put on and was led out of the shower room into the cell. It was the first time I was able to take in my surroundings. It looked like a hospital ward; well it was a hospital ward. On the left were two low fibreglass beds with mattress and white sheets and a pillow. The next three beds against the wall were actual hospital beds. On the right wall was one more hospital bed running along the wall to a table. Between each bed was a locker. I was given the second bed on the left. The guy who had been responsible for showering me and delousing me was in the first bed.

I was later to find out that he was the head prisoner in the hospital. He was there because he was diabetic and also a child rapist. Then some of the other patients came to sit down and speak with me. Only two of them spoke any English. The one who spoke the best was a young guy called Danny. I say guy but the reason he was in the hospital was because he was gay. And he looked it with tits and everything. Manicured fingernails, eyebrows tweezed the works. He said he wasn't allowed to go to a hall in case he had sex with anyone. They asked me about myself, it was then I realised that this was my 18th birthday. I told them and the guy sitting next to me went to his locker and got out three boiled sweets and gave them to me and said happy birthday. It was the strangest thing. I was totally overwhelmed; it was the nicest thing that anyone had ever done for me up to that point in my life. Three of his own prized sweets given to a complete stranger. They left me then to my sweets. I collapsed onto the bed. The next two weeks were going to be the worst of my life.

Chapter -2

Literal Bullying

After this event, my self-harming intensified and I withdrew further and further into myself. I learnt that I could rub my ruler on the edge of the desk until it was red hot and burn my arms with it. I then found out that I didn't really feel so much pain on my arms so I started experimenting by sticking needles through my skin. Eventually, I was able to stick a long needle straight through my arm, although I do remember one time hitting something deep inside my arm other than the bone with which I was already familiar with, and screaming in pain. It must have been a nerve, so I didn't do it again for a few days after that. I was smoking whatever I could get my hands on. My social circle was actually a zero. But I kept going to school; I kept functioning as I was expected to function, I suppose. All the teachers obviously knew there was something different to me as I remember one incident that they must have all planned together in the staff room to humiliate me.

One day I was asked to go to another classroom to collect a long stand so that my teacher could hang things on it, I think I must have been about 8 years old. This was quite an honour because it was meant that you were trusted to leave the classroom by yourself and walk the school corridors. So I set off with my head held high. As I walked into the classroom I was met with 30 faces staring back at me. I remembered what I was there for so in a confident voice I asked the teacher for a long stand. The teacher smiled at me, picked up a piece of chalk and drew a big cross on the ground in front of the class and said

"Stand there".

As I moved towards the cross the whole class erupted in laughter. I was made to stand there until just the end of class and then was sent back to my own classroom. No need to tell you how that made me feel. To think that the teachers must have been aware of how literal I was and to think that they must have all been laughing together in the staff room when they came up with the plan of how to humiliate me and how they must have laughed afterwards when their plan had *worked and that they had managed to fool the strange boy who sat by himself.*

The problem was that even though I had been separated from the rest of the class I found it impossible to shut out the teacher's voice. I tried to concentrate on reading my book but couldn't. Although I did find it more relaxing being away from the others I found myself following their lessons more than reading my book. So I did learn what they were doing, well I took everything in anyway. But my social anxiety grew and grew and that's probably what led me to my huge issues at break time when I spent most of it banging my head against the wall.

Chapter Three

Abandoned

Everything that had happened to me in the past 18 years would have nothing on two weeks of withdrawing from the strongest heroin on the planet.

Those two weeks is a bit of a blur to me. No matter how I lay on my bed I could not get comfortable. Every part of my body that had weight put on it screamed in agony. I would wet myself and mess myself constantly. The diarrhoea was the worst. If I did manage to fall asleep I would wake up with my clothes and bed covered in shit. Twice a day a senior prison officer would come round to inspect the hospital. Each time he came round we had to stand up next to our bed. The hospital guard would shout something everyone then would say no sir, and the senior officer would look around and then leave. On more than one occasion when this happened I passed out and found myself lying on the floor somewhere. I was constantly sneezing as if I had the worst flu in history. I had no appetite and would throw up anytime I tried to eat. During these two weeks, the police were building their case against me. A few times I was dragged out of my cell to a visiting room, where the police would be waiting asking me more and more questions. I don't know if I refused to answer their questions or just couldn't. One day I was dragged out and told to put the blue prison uniform on. I was put in a van and driven somewhere. I had no idea what was going on. The clothes that I was arrested in were in a bag next to me and I was told to put them on. They were absolutely stinking and filthy. I looked terrible; I hadn't washed in days and hadn't shaved in a couple of weeks. I was stinking of all sorts not to mention urine and shit. I found myself being pushed into a line up with around five other white guys. They all look smart, clean shaved and hair done. I stood out like the proverbial sore thumb. They did allow me one concession and that was to choose where to stand in the line-up. God knows what these other guys thought when they were looking at me. Anyway almost immediately this Chinese guy was brought in to see if he could pick me out of the line-up. You would have had to be pretty thick not to see which of us had been arrested recently. He picked me out straight away. And then another guy came in but interestingly this time he didn't pick me out. But when he was leaving he turned to a policeman and said he thought it was me. I didn't stand much of a chance, no lawyer, looking like shit. I bet if I had been given the chance to shave and wore some nice clothes I wouldn't have been picked out. After all, all us gwai gi's look the same to the Chinese, don't we? They all look the same to us the black-haired pricks.

During those two weeks, I was also visited by my family for the first and what also happened to be the last time. I was taken to the hospital and made to put on the blue uniform again and marched to the visiting room. It was a long narrow corridor with booths separated by concrete walls. In each booth, there was a stone seat and a thick steel-reinforced glass with a speaker and microphone built into the side of the wall. I waited for a couple of minutes sitting painfully on the stone and then in they came. My mum, dad and wee brother. My mum sat down on their side and picked up a telephone next to her. She didn't look good. Dad just stood behind her angrily not looking at me and my brother stood next to my mum. I must have looked terrible to them. The mundane questions came,

"How are you, how is the food?"

And I answered

"Shit, shit."

Then came the news that they had decided to move back to the UK. They had met my court-appointed lawyer briefly, whom I hadn't even met yet and that he said that he would keep them in the loop with what was happening. My mum said that she would write as often as she could. I asked if she could send me the addresses of my friends as I didn't have any of their info with me and that they may be wondering what happened to me. She said that she would rather not and

"Let's just see what happens."

They asked me if I had seen my lawyer yet and I said no. and that was basically that. When they got up to leave I had no idea when or if I would ever see them again.

Back in the hospital, although in a deranged withdrawing state, I was aware of some things going on around me.

Like the rapist next to me who would do 50 push-ups about 10 times a night. Exactly the same speed that you can count to 50 and right down and up, proper push-ups. Problem was this was all he did and his upper body shape showed it. His upper back actually looked like he had twin humps. And his chest looked like it had been pumped up with air. And thinking that this child rapist was stronger now, stronger than before he came into prison also made me quiver. This was all new to me, and at the time I was going through severe withdrawals. But at times I have thought why didn't I beat him up for what he had done? I came to realise that this was the prison hierarchy. You judge others so that you feel better about your crimes. The murderers had a hierarchy. Killing someone in a fight is okay but killing a granny whilst robbing her is worse. Killing an adult is better than killing a child. Killing a cop and you are the top man. Rapists also have a warped hierarchy too. Raping a woman in the same age bracket as you are better than raping someone younger. For example, a 20-year-old raping a 19-year-old compared to a 50-year-old raping the same 19-year-old. Raping a grandmother is not as bad as raping a child. But please don't think that the prisoners who have committed such grave crimes go around having competitions with themselves. This is simply not the case. They tend not to discuss it. They are category A prisoners and are held at the top of the prison hierarchy anyway because of their length of sentence. The lower category prisoners are a different story. They are constantly trying to gain the respect of others to ensure their safety in the prison. The ones who do not talk are the ones who have mugged grannies or thieves. Thieves are one of the lowest regarded prisoners. They are looked at with contempt and are even thought not to belong in prison because their crime is so pathetic.

Chapter -3

High School

Eventually, I escaped primary school and moved into secondary school. I remember being totally lost in the big school. Every break time I would find a corner of the playground and try to disappear into it.

Each lunchtime I would go into the woods and smoke cigarettes by myself. Sometimes I would go home, but not often.

In my first year in secondary, I was in English class when the teacher asked to stand up and read an extract from a book. Now, this I could do. I always prided myself in being the very best reader in class. I had the ability to scan way ahead of myself whilst reading so that it was always flawless my delivery. I was standing up in front of the class reading away very happy when I came to the word

"Stork".

Now, I was born in England but didn't live there long enough before I moved to Scotland to pick up an accent, I was a baby when I moved to Scotland. But I have a funny accent. I pronounce words differently than other people. The Scottish roll their R's, I cannot. The teacher asked me to say it again, and again, and again. She got me to repeat the word for what felt like 15 minutes. I was again feeling humiliated. At the end of the class, she sent me home with a punishment because she thought I was doing it on purpose. This punishment I gave to my mum. She just signed it and told me not to do it again!

Not long after that, I started drinking. I would go into my parents drink cabinet and fill a small bottle up with a bit of this and a bit of that. I would take my ill-gotten gains into the woods, with my cigarettes, and consume both. I would then stager home and sneak up to my bedroom where I would engage in one of my hobbies.

I was given a fish tank one birthday. Needless to say within a couple of years I had twenty. That was my main obsession for a long time. I would spend hours reading and learning everything possible about the fish I had. I learnt their Latin names, where they came from, the acidity of the water they preferred, and their breeding preferences. The first fish I was able to breed were Zebra Danios. I spent hours monitoring their water quality to ensure that everything was perfect. I ended up with a whole tank of them.

I was devoted to my large fish tank that I had in the living room. In the first year, not one fish died, for which I was very proud. I had a perfectly balanced ecosystem, what fish that balanced one and another out perfectly. My pride and joy were two silver dollars that were by now six inches in diameter. I had almost lost one to a fungal infection that had attacked the whole side of its body. I tried isolating it and medicating the water but that didn't work. So I reread my books and found one that gave me step by step instructions on how to operate on the fish. So with needles, scalpels and scissors, I set to work. It took some time but I eventually managed to return the fish to the tank where it continued to thrive. Months later there was a large fish contest in Glasgow. So I took my two beautiful Silver Dollars along. They were kept in a tank together, at my request, and I stayed with them for hours to monitor them. The contest was over three days. I knew I wouldn't win anything because one of them had a huge scar on its side but I just really enjoyed showing them off like a proud parent. I went in every day to check on them. On the third and final day, I went to pick them up. As I walked towards their tank I couldn't believe what I was seeing. There was a big rosette on the tank. I had won the best fish in the show by a junior, and I got a trophy for it too. I was so proud, beaming I went up to collect my trophy and then took my fish home again on the bus. Years later my parents threw out all my fish stuff including the trophy, but I still have one photo of them together.

School was getting worse and worse. I had very little contact with anyone else in school. The kids I did hang out with would be my friend one minute and then beating me up the next. I went home once after such a beating that my face was all over the place only to be shouted at by my parents to go and finish my paper round. They did ask me what happened to my face and I told them I was playing football and nothing else was mentioned.

Chapter Four

Death by Chopsticks

After my two weeks in the hospital came to an end I was moved back into the general population.
Whilst in the hospital I had been put on what they called ON chaan. That is overseas national food. What it consisted of each day was a piece of bread in the morning with a cheese slice and a cup of tea with milk and sugar. The bread was always really stale and the tea was totally impossible to drink. There was always something floating in it, rice, and hair and probably spit and other things worse. I never drank it. At lunch, it was the same and at dinner, I would get a plate of offcuts of vegetables and a piece of meat. The vegetables were horrific, it was the stuff that you would throw away whilst preparing vegetables for a meal, inedible most of the time and boiled to within a second of it turning into sludge. The meat was, well, let me put it this way leather shoes are more tender. I have no idea what kind of beast it came from. Sometimes I couldn't tear into it. All I had was a spoon to eat with. In the hospital the other guys left me alone to enjoy my meal to myself, they showed no interest in it. However, when I got back to the general population this all changed. When going to the dining hall I was always made to go last. I pick up my spoon, my plate of whatever and mug of shit and then I had to go and sit at a table by myself. The first day I did this was for my evening meal. I had just sat down when a Chinese guy came past me quickly and swiped all the food off my plate. It was gone and there was nothing I could do. I couldn't grass on the guy or I would be beaten or even killed. I had to sit there and do nothing. I had seen violence already. Maybe the second day I was in the main dining hall. It was in the morning around half-past ten. When you are on remand you did nothing all day apart from sitting in the dining hall. Some people had books and magazines to read, there were even chess boards for people to play with. Problem is it was Chinese chess and I had no idea how to play it. You couldn't move around, you had to sit at the table where you had your breakfast. So I sat by myself all day. Talking wasn't allowed but there was some whispering going on that the guards turned a blind eye to. Now there is a hierarchy in the

prison. The top guys are the Hong Kong Chinese, they run the place. They have a top dog in each cell block and dining room. He had his second in charge and everyone fit into their gang at different levels. Then there were the mainland Chinese or the II's (illegal immigrants) they also had their hierarchy but theirs was more makeshift, always changing because they tended not to stay on remand for long and got sentenced quite quickly to 6 months. Then there were the Vietnamese guys. Or Vietnamese dogs as they were called. These guys were the most dangerous of all as they had nothing to lose. They had either escaped Vietnam on a boat with their whole family only to be put into a detention centre or were born in the detention centre. So when they were released from this prison they went back to the detention centre. They didn't care. Some of them had already lost their whole family when their boat had sunk. I later met one guy who watched his whole family drown one by one before he was "rescued" and thrown into a detention centre. I had visited one of these centres a few times when I was at school to play table tennis and teach the kids about computers as a volunteer. Depressing places, yes even more depressing than this place. Later that first morning we were told to get up and were moved outside only to line up again outside. It was lunchtime. We went back in, collected our lunch. I went to my separate table and sat down. I was just about to start eating when there was a huge crash. Two of the Vietnamese dogs had jumped on top of another guy. They had chopsticks in their hands and they were stabbing him ferociously in the back and the neck. It happened so quickly, the guy had no chance. They took him from behind, just as quickly an alarm went off and all the guards started running towards the fight. They grabbed the two guys off the other and started beating them up. Very quickly we were told to get up and leave the hall. I turned back to see the other guy still sprawled out over the metal table with blood slowly covering it and dripping off the edge.

I never found out what happened to the guy.

Chapter -4
Hatred and Depression

I hated my life and truly believed that most people hated me. For the last couple of years, I tended to hide in corners, not knowing how to be part of a group. All the friends I had, well, all three or four of them didn't go to my school. They were basically misfits from their own schools and we had happened to join together somehow along the way. For the first few years of secondary school I would go every day even though each morning, as I woke, it hit me with a huge surge of anxiety that I had to go. I would walk to school in the morning in those early years doing all sorts of superstitious stuff to try and make sure that I survived the day. I really thought that one day I would be killed in that school. No one had ever come to me with a knife or anything but I felt myself watching, being alert and ready for the attack that would come one day. It felt that one day everything would just explode and I would die. I never had any urges to hurt anyone else, I never planned any attack. I had just given myself up to the torture that was Eastwood High School. Our school was in a nice area of Glasgow on the south side. The primary I attended was directly across the road. However, although the primary took only kids from the posh and middle-class area the secondary took kids from further afield. These are the kids who could quickly make a name for themselves in an area that wasn't their own by throwing their weight around, I often caught that weight. It seems strange to think how meek I was then. I had no self-belief at all. Even though I was bigger and stronger physically than most kids in the school, even from my first years there I didn't recognise this. I would generally just stand there when someone punched me or threatened me. I haven't really worked it out but the teachers usually took their frustrations out on me too, I suppose when you are younger you don't see the same weakness in adults. They too must have thought I was an easy target and therefore also had a go at me when they could. My only safe place in the school in the last year was the common room table tennis table. Any break time that's where I was and as there was a strict rule about the best player staying on, that was where I stayed. I would never go into the common room if the table was busy, as I just wouldn't know where I could sit. No one that I could join

comfortably. I know that a few of my fellow students did try and bring me into their fold but I was just so sociably awkward it never worked. If the weather was okay I wouldn't walk along the road to school, hopping over cracks, counting everything up to five, timing my arrival with pinpoint accuracy for the school bell, I would head across the field at the bottom of my street that had a stream at the far side and a wooded area that backed onto our schools rugby pitch. There I would go early in the morning and hide in the woods. I would make invisible dens where I could sit and read books and smoke the Benson and Hedges or Silk Cut cigarettes I had nicked from the cupboard in the kitchen.
I the last year of school, 5th year, I was there more and more. I was actually for the first time bunking off school for long periods of time. I had never done it before. Even when some kid had threatened to kick my head in the next day I would still go to school. I hated breaking rules, yes I would do naughty and silly things but actually planning to break rules was something I really struggled at. Always worried about being caught and my parents being called even though I knew they wouldn't do anything and wouldn't care, I still didn't want to go through the shame. But I didn't need to worry because even if I hadn't done anything wrong I would end up getting blamed anyway even though it way more than obvious that I was the victim. One day my younger brother and I were mucking about in the local golf course. We tended to sneak on with clubs, play a couple of holes when no-one else was there and hunt for lost golf balls. Never did any damage, always respected the course. 3 lads from my year in school turned up. These were the biggest lads in the year, the roughest boys in the class. They were perfectly friendly and we shared clubs and balls with them and played together for a good hour or so when one of them walked up to me and punched me in the face. This time I went down, got up and got hit again. It wasn't a full-on attack but just target practice. Every time I got up one would knock me down. They would sometimes say sorry man just having a laugh we will stop now, so I would get up only for one of them to run over and smash me again. My brother may have been 9 at this point and was totally traumatised, just standing there in shock, unable to say anything or move. One punch sent me down a hill, head over feet, down and down until I hit the bottom in a heap. At this point, I decided enough was enough, called my brother and we legged it. My problem was that when we got home my wee brother told my mum everything and it

must have been during one of her more clear periods as she called the school the next day to complain to the deputy principal what happened. So we were all called in. I stood there as the deputy asked the 3 other guys what had gone on. They said that I had provoked them by calling them all names. That was it, their excuse for an hour's long assault on me witnessed by my brother. I told the deputy that it wasn't true. He believed them. These 3 hulks of boys had been so traumatised that I had been able to beat them all up and hurt their feelings and that I was a monster. The fact that my face and their fists were black and blue meant nothing. I was suspended for 2 days and had a huge punishment exercise to do. Unfortunately, when I got home my mum had lost her focus and didn't do anything in response so I just had to get on with it as usual. It wasn't the first time I had been beaten up for fun and it wouldn't be the last. That last year I was barely in school. But no-one seemed to notice my absence. Whether the school contacted my family or not, I never found out. I was still getting beaten up for fun quite regularly. One entrepreneur in my class was now paying me a couple of pounds every now and again to get beaten up. If someone wanted to have a fight with someone, I would get paid, turn up at the given spot and time and engage in a fight with them. One time the guy held me down and head-butted my face for about ten minutes. My face was barely recognisable. When I got home my mum asked me what had happened and I said I was playing football my dad then shouted at me to go out and finish my paper round and that was that.

Chapter Five
Choices and No Choice

The days blurred into one and another until the day came of my trial. The police had come in a few times asking questions. Who did I get the heroin off, where was I going with it? Who did I do the robberies with, who were my accomplices? If I gave them names they would see if I could get a lighter sentence. A lighter sentence, what, a death sentence? The prison was full of triad; you wouldn't last long if you were a grass in here.

So the trial came, I plead not guilty, they looked at the evidence, they found me guilty.

After a guilty verdict and before you are sentenced you get placed in limbo in the prison. You have nothing, you do nothing. They put you in the detention centre part of the prison. You get a grey uniform and spend your whole day in a small room crammed with fifty other guys and made to sit all day, all day, all day. No exercise, no reading, no TV, no this, no that. I didn't have to wait long, only a month. Some guys are in that limbo for months. One good thing about the Hong Kong prison system is its speed. From arrest to sentence had only been three months.

When I went back for sentencing I was surprised, shocked and embarrassed to see my old form teacher in the court, Mr Forse. I didn't get a chance to speak to him. The judge sentenced me to a total of six years. At that point, I couldn't remember hearing anything else. It was only when I returned to the prison that I found out that the sentence was is multiple parts and he had run all the sentences together so my total was only three years so I would be released after spending two-thirds of it. So my release date would be 2 days before my twentieth birthday because 1992 was a leap year. So because I had already spent 64 days in prison I had 666 days to go. That was as long as I didn't have any time added on.

Young Prisoner 90760

When I returned to the prison I was given my much sought after brown uniform. I was led up to the cell block that held convicted prisoners. The whole place was clean. The hallways, the bars on the windows and cells. The cell I was shown into was a little bit dusty but everything was working. Water in the tap, the toilet flushed, and

the bed was sturdy, the mattress was still the worst part, absolutely stinking. That first night I thought to myself,
"This is where I am going to spend the next 2 years of my life".
Something changed in me that night. Something that wasn't good. I had crazy dreams that I was going to take over the prison. That I would take control of all the Chinese because they were stupid Chinese after all. They wouldn't be difficult to control. They were all morons. They were all petty criminals that didn't have any smarts amongst them. I would start tomorrow as soon as I got out of my cell. I would put on an attitude that I was the boss and not them.
I had flipped. My brain had gone into meltdown.

Chapter -5

The next fight was my last.

I was heading towards the back gate of school one fine day when I heard a lot of footsteps behind me. They weren't walking but running. I turned around and there was Alex. I had known this guy my whole life. He was a wee guy but a very fast runner and good at football. We had been friends at different times of our lives but since secondary, we had become distant. Anytime I met him we would always interact as good friends if he was alone. It's funny; he's probably one of the guys I would have done anything for. I would have helped him and supported him anywhere, anytime. He did have aggression about him I don't know exactly why, family stuff, and the fact that he was shorter than the rest, anyway something made him hostile. He came up to me and said those immortal words of the Scottish playground. The word that I had heard said to me, the word that I had chanted on many occasions when I wasn't involved. The word that could send shivers up and down your spine.

"Fight!"

I looked around me; the crowd had drawn a circle around the combatants. In their eyes hunger for action and also a grateful expression that they weren't involved. I looked at Speedy, as that was his nickname, and realised that I didn't want to fight him. This was for a few reasons. First of all, I was actually worried that I could hurt him, I didn't want to. My reach was so much longer than his and I must have weighed at least half again his weight. He was an old friend, I liked him. The fight would be unfair, I knew he was fast, but I had been smashed so many times in the face and body I tended to be able to take even the biggest hits. I said to him that I didn't want to fight but he just said it again,

"Fight."

He pushed me, I stood there, he pushed me, again and again, I just stood there. The crowds baying getting louder and the numbers were building as others heard the playground jungle drums.

"Fight, fight, fight"

He then went to punch me. I had to think about what to do, where to hit him. I needed to put him down with the least damage to him possible. I wanted it to end quickly so that he would be okay. I took a load of his hits and then found my moment when I swung with my left fist hard into the underside of his right lower jaw. I knew this was a good place to cause a jarring of the vestibular system and possibly cause a knockout. I connected beautifully but not beautiful enough because although he was sent flying to the ground he was helped up and ran at me again, fists flailing. Okay, I thought, maybe not as easy as I hoped, what should I do next? I was thinking all this whilst fending off his blows and holding him back. He was getting tired so I decided to give him a huge jab to the diaphragm to wind him with my left and then a big uppercut right under his chin. The second punch wasn't needed as the body blow sent him flying, gasping for the air that had been ripped out of him. As if in slow motion I was realising that this was the end of the fight. I would be able to walk away and get on with my day. He was lying on the ground and I moved towards him to help him up. After all, I had no bad feelings towards him at all and I was just saying sorry when I was grabbed from behind. It was the first time in my life that I had gone flying backwards because someone had grabbed me. It was a weird experience and a totally incapacitating experience as well as you have no means to counter it at all. As my back slammed into the ground ten black school shoes came flying towards me. I was getting absolutely pummelled by the initial group that had joined Speedy in the beginning. It was a total set up. No matter what happened they had planned for me to get a total kicking. And why? Don't know. Just for kicks and power. You would have to track them down and ask them because I have no idea. However, this wasn't the first time I had been set up and not the last. It had happened on a scouting trip once when the older lads made me fight a smaller guy, whom I refused but they made me do it and then kicked the shit out of me because I had won that fight too. I knew I had to get out of there with or without my dignity. One well-aimed boot could have ended it all. They weren't trying to kill me but it could happen. Did anyone have a knife? I was out of there in 5 seconds. I managed to throw them all back and legged it out of the school. No one followed me, I was alone, I had escaped, I would never go back, and I would never see most of them again

Chapter Six

666 Days to go.

When I woke up it was still dark. I lay on my bed trying to think, trying to remember all the crazy dreams I had during the night. There were brief flickers of dreams. One I could remember was just giving up to everything and killing someone, anyone who annoyed me. To become an animal in prison, to give up all the societal norms that I had learnt over the years. I thought of my friends, my life outside, where I had gone so wrong. That thought was the one that would stay with me and be a constant companion over the next 12 months of the hell that was about to follow.

I had thought that I would be joining the population today but I was in for yet another surprise because all newly sentenced prisoners had to go through a week of induction. Basically, we were made to clean the prison. From sun up to sun down we were scrubbing, sweeping. Everywhere we went I was getting stared at. Prisoners getting moved from one place to the next would all be staring at me. We were made to eat our food separately from the rest and I was made to sit separately even from my induction group. Each morning we were marched silently into the dining hall. I was always made to be last. When I got to the first shutter a guard would shout

"ON chaan"

And a dirty yellow mug of milky, sweet tea with all sorts of extras floating in it would be pushed out. I then walked to the next shutter and a plate would be flung out with a thick piece of stale bread and a cheese slice on it. I would then go to my table and sit and look at what I had. The other prisoners got black Chinese tea and a plate with a huge pile of steaming rice and a couple of fish heads. I never could drink tea. I tried a few times when the thirst was overtaking my senses. It was always cold and disgusting, with rice, hair and other identified objects floating in it. The bread was always dry but with the cheese slice, I managed to force it down. I lost a lot of weight in those early weeks. For lunch, the Chinese guys would get either sweet green congee or rice soup. The green congee always smelt amazing and I longed for it. I got the same as breakfast. At dinner time the others got another plate full of rice with vegetables and occasionally some bits of chicken wing or other indescribable meat. They would also get an orange. An orange! I never liked them before but how my mouth watered when I saw them. When they all started peeling them after finishing their rice the smell filled the whole dining hall. It was so intoxicating. Mine was tea and a plate of what you would normally throw away when making dinner. Potatoes that had more black parts than white, the offcuts of vegetables, you know the root of a cabbage, the ends of carrots, and a piece of meat that was tougher than any leather shoes I had ever owned. It may as well been shoes because that's what it also tasted of. We were so hard-worked during the day that I was so hungry I would have eaten the plate if I was allowed to. I was never a big vegetable fan outside but in the evenings I managed to force everything down. The other prisoners continued to stare at me all the way through meals as well. I felt a deep foreboding. The only reason why nothing happened was because the guards ran the place so strictly and anyone who caused the slightest bit of noise would be dragged from their chair and battered by a group of them. No talking, stay in line, do exactly as you are told or suffer the consequences. There were some definitely mentally challenged prisoners amongst us and the guards used them for their own amusement. Sometimes they would call one of them over and then give them a beating because they had gotten out of their seat. There were fights sometimes, probably over the slightest things. The fights didn't last long because of the pleasure the guards got in wading in and swinging their batons around. It had been a long time now since I had spoken to anyone. No one spoke to me in English, even though most of the guards wore the red flash under their number to say that they could. I bumped into one other prisoner once and without the aid of language we got into a fight when a simple argument could have solved everything. That time we weren't seen by the guards so we got away with it but that was the last time I did.

The week of the induction came to an end and I was finally allowed to eat with everyone else. The prisoners were split into two groups. Group A and group B. The two foreigners that I had seen before were in group A and I was put into group B this meant that I was never able to be with them.

Chapter -6

In the Navy

I ran away from school and straight to the train station where I got the train into Glasgow and found the Navy recruitment office and decided to join or runaway to which was more appropriate.

It wasn't quite as easy as that of course. I had to sit a lot of tests and be interviewed. The tests reminded me of the ones I had done when I was 7, and I found them even easier than before. I was then sent home with something for my mum to sign as I was only 16. She signed it without much said, and that was it.

A few weeks later I headed off to England and then I headed down to HMS Raleigh by train and started what was to be, up to then, the most stressful but easy 6 months of my life.

You would have thought that the Navy would have been the worst possible place for an Aspie (person with Aspergers) to be, but you'd be wrong. Routine, routine, routine. It was great. I knew where I was going, what I was doing, when I woke up, when I slept, it was heaven. The difficult part was the other people. And I thought I was crazy. The Navy is full of dropouts. You can't make it in the real world well join the Navy, should have been their advertising campaign. It's all about teamwork. Teamwork whilst we're actually doing something work-related and intense is okay for me but when you return to your dorm and people are hanging out together, I just couldn't hack it.

My first home leave was coming up and I wouldn't have anywhere to go as I couldn't head to Hong Kong where my parents and younger brother were now living. I asked if I could stay on base but they refused and said I had to go home. So off I trundled a few weeks later back to Glasgow where my older brother was now living with his girlfriend in the house as he had decided to stay when my mum and dad and wee brother moved. I got there and nobody was home, so for the first 4 hours of home leave, I was sitting on the front step waiting for him to come home. When he did get back and let me in I went up to my bedroom which was now a dumping ground for all his stuff. No room at the inn. So I decided to sleep in the garage. I was glad to leave a week later to go back down to Plymouth.

Our passing out parade was coming up, which is when you all dress in your finest uniform and march in front of dignitaries and family and friends to celebrate you completing your basic training. I started having stress-related events in the run-up. These caused me to be held back so that I didn't pass out with my own class. The first event I woke up in the morning completely blind. I lay there on my bed for what seemed like an eternity trying to decide whether I was awake or still asleep and whether I was going to blind forever. Eventually, my sight came back, but that was one scary moment. The next thing to happen was my right knee froze. I couldn't straighten it. For that I had to go to the medical staff that put me on restricted duties for a week, so that ended the possibility of me passing out on time. It didn't stop me from taking part in the passing out parade. Afterwards, I decided enough was enough and put in a request to leave called a PVR, or premature voluntary release. They couldn't really stop me leaving as I was still only a kid, so off I went back to Glasgow. I didn't stay with my brother, so went between different couches for a couple of weeks until my parents agreed to put me on a flight to Hong Kong.

Chapter Seven
Double Murderer

I was allocated the television repair workshop. It was a long narrow room with workbenches along each side and one long one in the middle. I walked in and had 50 pairs of eyes turned on me, with not one smile amongst them. They just sat there and stared as if sizing up their quarry. I felt vulnerable; we were locked in the room with just one guard who was called master, See Vous. He was a strange little fellow, bulging eyes and a humped back. But he was the only person to smile at me for months and welcomed me. He actually seemed happy to see me. It almost caused me to well up, almost, but not quite. Showing weakness here I reckoned was the same as showing fear to a dog, I would be bitten. He showed me around the workshop, showed me where I was to sit. So I sat. There was no talking out loud, but whispers back and forth between the other prisoners all the while never taking their eyes off me. I watched see Vous fixing a TV with another prisoner who seemed oblivious to my presence. So we sat there all morning, me watching See Vous, they watch me. Then it was lunch and we were marched to the dining hall where I collected my tea, cheese and bread and sat down. 500 pairs of eyes watching me eat my lunch. I noticed that today it was white congee for lunch and hardly any of them took any. For them to not eat it, it must have been bad. Then I noticed that they weren't just staring at me but they were staring at my food as well. What was unsatisfying for me was something they hadn't had in a long time, and they wanted it. At the end of lunch, they walked passed me to take their cups back if they had had congee. They walked as close to me as possible. There was some muttering under breaths as they passed. I couldn't make most of it out but there were some words I did understand.

"Diu lay gwai gi" Fuck you, foreign devil
 Was unmistakable.

In the afternoon, I was taken to the classrooms. As this was a younger offenders unit you had to go to class once a day. Each class held about 15 prisoners and one teacher/guard. As I walked down the corridor the small barred opening to the classrooms were full of staring faces. I was taken to the last classroom. This classroom I soon found out was for the second-highest security prisoners. The serious badasses. I was put into it because I was deemed to be a big

risk. Although my charges and convicted offences were only category B I was seen as a category A prisoner due to the prisons risk assessment. We were all kept away from the extremely serious crazies, the ones who would bite your face off if they got a chance. It was a lucky break for me being put in with this lot. They were the very long term prisoners; the shortest sentence was about 15 years so they had been in for a while and were a lot more subdued rather than the short term guys. I sat down next to one guy. He was about the same age as me but there was an air of depression surrounding him. He hardly ever looked up from his desk. We all sat at desks but only a few were doing any work the others were just sitting talking. This was the only place in the whole prison that you could sit down and have a conversation with the other prisoners as it was classroom and talking was permitted. A skinny little Chinese guy walked over to my table and said
"I speak English, I double murderer, I double murderer"
He seemed pretty pleased with himself. His English was pretty poor but with my crap Chinese I was able to work out that he had robbed a travel agent and stuck a screwdriver through the throats of both the members of staff. Seemed that there was no need to do it but he found himself doing it anyway. He even did it after he had got the money. He had been sentenced to a full life sentence but was waiting for his appeal. Others were in for acid attacks where they had thrown acid onto their ex-girlfriends or even just girls that had refused their advances. There were a lot of murderers, my new deskmate whose English name was Stephen was also doing a full life term for murder. It was then that I discovered murderers are the least cause for concern in a prison as their act is mostly out of the blue or under the influence of drink or drugs which isn't available in the prison.

His story was really sad, and you could see it reflected in his whole personality. Two schools met up to have a fight, as many do around the world. An argument that he couldn't even remember had brought them together. Then the fight happened, a few kids got hurt but everyone went home. Unfortunately, one went home with a head injury and died 3 days later. Stephen had hit him over the head with a stick and caused a blood clot on the brain. Because Stephen had taken the stick with him to where the fight was going to take place he got done with premeditated murder. Although he had a full life term because he was 15 at the time of the offence he was hoping to be freed after 18 years. Fuck, on one hand, you've got a twisted fuck like Mr Double Murderer and then you have Stephen. The whole room was full of these kinds of stories. But most important for me the classroom was the only place that I felt relatively safe.

I was going to be here for at least two years so maybe I should try and do a course or something. Get myself qualified for when I am finally released.

At the end of the day, we marched again to the dining hall for dinner.

Chapter -7
Arriving in Hong Kong

I sensed the start of the decent more than felt it. The tone of the engines changed; there was a slight change in the angle of the plane. It had been 15 hours this flight from Heathrow. I had sat there most of the trip not moving. I had done the usual check of the pocket in the back of the seat in front. Slipped the aircraft's magazine out first. It had its usual short stories of places of interest. Interest-only for the airline as I don't think I'd ever read about a place in an airline magazine that said airline didn't fly to, and I had been on a lot of planes. I was 16. Then I had taken the complimentary headphones and plugged them into the armrest and listened to some radio, but it was too much of a distraction. I needed to be alert, there was so much going on around me. I had a window seat, which can be good and bad if you are anything like me. Good because you have two angles at which you can put your head, not just the one if you are in the middle seat. The first angle is straight ahead. It doesn't really give you much to look at apart from the person in front of you, and if that's an annoying kid who then starts to think you are playing a game with them and they start peeking their "oh so cute face" between the seats and over the top at you, you are in trouble. And if you are behind a chair recliner well you are fucked because then you're looking very closely at an airline headrest. This is not a good idea because it is only then that you start to notice how disgusting the plane really is. You notice hairs on the coloured napkin thing on the seat rest that don't match the person sitting there. You start to think I thought they would have changed them after every flight, and then you start to look around. Your senses go into overdrive. Not only is your hearing stretched to breaking point because you are listening to every creak of the aeroplanes structure and the hum of the engines, because in your world you are an expert aviation engineer and the slightest changed in engine hum means definite disaster, and also listening to every conversation around you because when you open your hearing up to the plane you can't then turn off the background chatter. You are also listening to the bells or buzzers that tell the cabin crew what the pilot is up to etc. etc. But if you then start using your other senses you start going into break down mode. You are looking for dirt and grime and you start seeing it but at the same time, you start to realise that the interior of the aircraft

isn't as well maintained as you thought it should be. You start to wonder if that loose panel just to the front and right of you, above the overhead lockers, could contribute to the overall destruction of the aircraft. Then there's a bit of turbulence and you see the panels moving, oh shit they're not secure!! The gap starts to open up, you hear a bell ping twice, and that must mean trouble, no seat belt sign, why why? The pilot hasn't had time to put it on, and then another bump shit the port engine has changed, it's about to explode..... Then you start to smell things too. It's strange because I thought on a plane you couldn't smell anything, you can but it's just a little bit more difficult. I find myself doing some sniffing, and some more sniffing, but then I stop as it sounds like I've got a cold, and there is nothing worse than sitting next to someone on a plane who's got a cold. Your nose starts to run, you feel a sneeze coming
" I will not sneeze, I will not sneeze, I will not blow my nose because that s me admitting I've got a cold or the FLU!!!"
You wipe your nose, secretly, don't let anyone see you, look the other way, which would be impossible if you're in the middle seat as there is no other way and you would feel the glare of two complete strangers from both sides. So I'm at the window so I turn to the window and lower my head into my left hand as if resting, all the time listening to hear if anyone is talking about my sniffing. Then when I think the coast is clear I wipe my finger across my nose. Damn didn't get it all, and now I feel a sneeze coming so I lower my head more until my nose is now resting on my hand, I squeeze it, secretly between my fingers to stop the sneeze,
"Shit made some snot come out."
Now I have to wipe my nose and hold it at the same time to stop the sneeze. I will do anything not to sneeze and we all know that just makes it worse!! Eventually, you have to do the inevitable and go to the bathroom before you have a sneezing fit. You try to start pumping adrenaline around your body to give you the strength to turn to ask your two neighbours to excuse you. When you've mustered up the strength you turn to the first one and find the fucker asleep!!!!!!!!!!!!!!
You have to decide whether to wake them up and try to squeeze by them and then you run the risk of waking them up in a startling way. But if you wake them up first them they will have to stay awake until you get back from the toilet, so thus limiting the time you have in the toilet. Coz just because you have to blow your nose just now you should make use of this once in a lifetime opportunity to do all the

normal toileting activities. Pee, shit, wash your face, check for spots, maybe wash your pits if you have to. Then the next thing you have to check is whether the person in front of your neighbour is a pesky seat recliner, because if they are you've got to make sure that when you go past and put your hand on their chair for leverage you don't pull their hair, I've done it before and had it done to me, not fun. Now you're in the aisle. Shit, you just remembered that you sensed the plane descending, any minute now the fasten seat belt sign will go on. You look around people are looking at you, if you give the game away they'll all be up. Look cool, relaxed, shit a sneeze that won't stop, it's coming, my nose is dripping, well it feels like that, I must look like I'm going to throw up, then you sneeze, get your hand to your face quick!!! Then where do you put your hand, coz the people in front of you are watching, if the planes not too bumpy you can walk down easily. If there's turbulence and you try to walk down without holding on you know you're going to land in someone's lap. The pressure the pressure. Somehow you make it. Empty your nose, bowels, and bladder. Wash your face, armpits, and hands. Discard of paper towels in correct receptacles. Do you wipe down the toilet seat after use as they ask you to do for the comfort of the next passenger to avail themselves of these fabulous facilities after you, do you fuck! Back in my seat, I look out of the window, it's cloudy with a few breaks. The captain comes on. Yah nice to have been your captain yah, it's now time for me to perform a skill all of you think I must be a superhero to perform. Love to you all. God bless the queen. I look out of the window the fasten seat belt sign goes on. We are going down. Through the first layer of cloud as smooth as silk. I had never been here before. I was staring trying to get my first glimpse of the place. I hadn't physically been here before but I had dreamt it. My parents and younger brother had moved here about a year ago, I hadn't seen them since. Two years ago I had had a dream. My mum came into my room in the morning and said she had something to tell me. I said I know we're moving to either Manchester or Hong Kong. She just stared at me for a moment and then said. We're moving to Hong Kong. She didn't ask me how I knew, nothing more was said about it. It hadn't ever been mentioned before. She must have got a late-night call from my dad telling her that his company was promoting him and that meant an office job in Hong Kong. Then through the clouds, I got my first glimpse. It was a Chinese Junk ship in full sail; it was beautiful, right down there on the vast ocean. Then it was gone again in the clouds. Now I had flown many times before. At least twice or four times every year for holidays, and just after I was born in Somerset up to Glasgow, but what happened next scared the shit out of me. I'm used to wee turns left and right on a plane, but this was different. The whole aircraft violently turned to the right. We were virtually on the wingtips. I felt my whole body stiffen, the vice-like grip of anxiety gripped my stomach, and my chest felt like an elephant was sitting on it, my sphincter grabbed on for dear life. But I always felt like this so I assessed the situation, everyone else was calm, there was no look of worry or panic on anyone's face, no screaming apart from in my head, no announcement to take up the brace position. By the time I had gone through my checklist, the plane righted itself and then the most amazing sight came into the window. High rise buildings, we were flying right past high rise buildings. No, not past them but through the middle of them. I could see washing hanging on lines, air conditioner units strapped to the side of them like some sort of futuristic parasites. Then I could see people in their flats. This was all whipping past quickly, we were in a 747 after all, but I could see it all clearly. Then we were lower I was looking at a rather grey scene, a concrete jungle. Then we were down. That was crazy, I thought to myself. After disembarking I followed the crowd and retrieved my luggage. My family was going to be there, weren't they? I didn't have much money, only what was left from my last wage from the navy, but I did have their address, Conduit Road Mid-Levels, so I knew I could get there if I had to. It was then that I noticed that I was starting to shiver, the air-conditioning was crazy. I had left a chilly Scotland in October and arrived in a roasting Hong Kong. I remembered that when we got off the plane it was sweltering but now the air-conditioning in the arrivals hall was starting to send me into some sort of shock. Once again I was following the crowd; we came to some big sliding doors that opened dutifully when we approached. It was the meeting point, the final point of arrivals when you are free to enter the country. It was a long slope downwards with railings on either side with people hanging onto eagerly waiting loved ones, or not. And then I saw the familiar faces of my family, well not all of them of course. My older brother had elected to stay in Scotland and by the looks of it, my dad has also elected not to be there. Not that I thought he would be there of course. Firstly I had left his beloved navy after just 6 months, I had quit. Didn't like it, did everything that I was supposed to do, passed everything, even got an exceptional commendation sent to my mum, I never saw the letter. I just didn't like it. But apart from that, he was never there. My wee brother and my mum were there to greet me. Hugs and stuff followed and then they led me outside. The heat hit me like a blast furnace. Air conditioning is good until you go outside and then you realise that some idiot had it on too cold. We went to a long taxi queue and stood in line. They asked me a lot of questions, I looked about. We got into a red taxi, just like a New York taxi but red. I clambered into the front seat and used the only Chinese I had learnt,

"Nei ho ma." (How are you?)

The driver replied he could have called me a prick for all I know with a deceptive smile, I would have probably done the same. Then we were off. The first thing I noticed was the cars. Hello there. The first one that is in the lane next to us was a Porsche 911 turbo in full body kit. Beautiful. Then there were Mercedes, Rolls Royce, Bentleys, Ferraris I kid you not it was a wet dream.

The rest was a bit of a blur. We went through a tunnel and then we were on Hong Kong Island. It felt that I was watching a roll of postcards going passed the window. Every view was amazing. Now my dad had gone to Hong Kong a few months before my mum and brother to get settled in and find somewhere for the family to live. His new company was paying for the flat, just like most other companies in Hong Kong. You work for them they pay for your accommodation, kids school fees, and even your medical fees. So my dad had found the most skanky flat he could. We got out of the taxi and into this building on Conduit Road. We walked down some stairs and into the flat. It was a dump. Built into the side of the mountain you walked straight into the main living area. The lounge and kitchen were combined. The kitchen must have measured four square foot and the lounge was really dark and dingy it had a window at the back that looks into somebody's nice flat downstairs and their garden. We didn't have a garden. There were a disgusting toilet and two bedrooms. My wee brother's room was filled with a bed and a wardrobe. It also had a window that looked out into a main, all I can call it is an open sewer from the top of the building to the bottom where water dripped continuously and it contained some probably undiscovered insects. My mum and dad's room was just as bad. The whole place stank of damp. So this is the high life, is it? From Newton Mearns, a nice suburb south of Glasgow, to this. So I slept on the couch that was my room. My mum said that because I had joined the navy they didn't need an extra room.

After I had dumped my bags I was full of energy so we went out for my first real Chinese meal. It just wasn't the food that was amazing, it was the whole atmosphere. The waiter was really friendly. Chatting away in broken English. We tucked into the best Chinese feast I had ever had, every dish was completely different from what I had before. The flavours, smells and textures filled my senses. At the end of the meal, I got my first ever fortune cookie.

"Persevere and you achieve",

If you believe in omens this one looked good.

We took a taxi home. I had a quick cigarette out the back door where I found more cockroaches than I thought existed on the whole planet. As they ran across my toes I took a deep breath.

"Things are looking good"

I thought to myself. And for a while they certainly were.

Chapter Eight
For the Love of Biscuits

The first wage I got was HK$2 and I was able to buy a packet of biscuits. It was the first real treat I had had in months. It was a small packet of 6 round biscuits with a cream filling. They were called Ci Ci Sik. To hold that prize in my hand was just amazing. I sat in my cell that night and handled the packet for about an hour deciding whether to desecrate it by opening it. I just couldn't wait any longer. I was imagining the taste, the feeling of the biscuits and cream in my mouth. I tried to smell them through the packet and dreamt that I could. I opened the packet a tiny bit at first and immediately brought it up to my nose. The smell filled and emptied my stomach in a moment, I'm sure jets of saliva shot out my mouth, and perhaps I even became slightly aroused? I opened the packet more, slowly making sure that the ends that had been heated together were peeled apart so gently as so not to rip. To rip this packet would be abusive, abusive to the upcoming joy. If the packet had ripped the whole experience would have been slightly damaged as if I had disrespected the moment, the encounter with this sweetness. Once the end of the packet had been perfectly separated I sat back on my bed and had to make a tough resolution. Do I bite through all three layers at once? Feeling the top biscuit breaking against my top teeth, the lower biscuit crunching with my lower teeth and eventually feeling the cream through the rubble of the broken biscuit? Or do I pull the two top layers apart and take the cream first by tonguing it gently? I had to decide before I could take this fondant filled orgasm out of its erotically decadent packaging. I sat back again, I just couldn't decide. You have to remember that this was the only biscuit I had that year, for 6 months and I would not be getting any again for another month. These indescribable ponderings were painful. I was also considering that at any moment my life may be brought to an end. The sharpened point of a chopstick rammed into my cranial areas. A sharpened piece of toothbrush with perhaps a razor blade melted into it dragged purposefully across my neck opening my throat and gullet wide enough to feed one of these delicious-smelling ci ci sik biscuits down. That was it if they are going to kill me then I should just go for it. And with the passion of a wild animal that has scented the opposite sex and is greedy for lust-filled rutting, I grabbed the first piece of joy and I shoved it into my mouth. Full, complete, and I crunched it as if I was a grazing animal and it was my grass. Every crunch throwing shivers of orgasmic passion through my body. My mouth cumming with saliva. It was a multiple orgasm, waves and waves of pleasure coursing through the facial area. Nerves endings dancing with joy with this intrusion. I fell back on my bed spent. That biscuit was crunched expertly for the longest any biscuit had before and will have in the future. Every piece of it was admired, loved and thanked for the joy it brought me that dark night in my dark, damp hell-hole. I was not just thankful to the biscuit I was thankful to myself. For putting so much effort into the act of mastication, so much thought. I would never do so again. That would be the peak of my mastication efforts, the finest thing that I will ever put in mouth. For it wasn't just a biscuit it was what it stood for. It stood for hope; it stood for effort, earnings, energy spent. It stood for survival and saying fuck you to all who had tried to kill me or make myself kill myself or even others. I had control back. I could decide whether to crunch or pull apart and I decided that I would no longer pull things apart; I would tackle them head-on. I would stick a whole biscuit in my mouth as a sign of defiance. This is all I thought, going through my head like a steam train. I was having a sugar rush that was giving me delusions of grandeur that would not last. Finally, the light went from my cell again, I remembered where I was but most importantly that I had 5 more biscuits left!!

Chapter -8
New Opportunities, a Teenagers Dream

After my last experience of school in Scotland, school in Hong Kong was a completely different experience altogether. And one that I was completely unprepared for. My mum took me for a meeting with the principal at Island School. The school was mixed and had the Cambridge Education system in place. However, the principal was a bit concerned that I had missed so much school and the year had already started a couple of months prior to my arrival. It was looking as if I wasn't going to be allowed to join the school. But as I was sitting

there I was analyzing everything around me. This is something I have always had the ability to do. I see everything and I am able to add all this information together pretty quickly. So, just as my mum was about to get up and say thank you anyway I said that I was good at sports. I could play rugby, table tennis, cricket and chess and that I had done so at a high level in Scotland. It worked. I had worked out by looking at all the trophy's, medals etc. on the wall and that I had read about these kinds of schools, that they were always interested in what they call "jocks", athletes. The principal looked up and said well okay then I think you can join the school!

I was up really early that the first day. I had ironed my shirt and trousers the night before so only had to shower, shave and have breakfast before I went up to the road to wait for the school bus with my brother. The shower was cold but I barely noticed due to the huge apprehension of my first day at school. I'd been through a lot in my short life so far but it didn't stop my anxiety creeping up on me. I decided to keep quiet and not talk. I would try to take everything in and not get engaged with anyone so as not to draw too much negative attention to myself. I was a lot stronger now having spent the last 6 months training in the Navy so that I knew I could handle myself. I had decided that no matter whom the first person was that gave me trouble on my first day I would hit first to let them know who I was and that I wouldn't put up with any shit. It was going to happen and I had to keep my wits about me. I wouldn't be at this school for long, maybe only a year until I had finished my exams and left school once and for all to get a job. I could keep myself to myself for a year. Keep my head down, do my work, maybe make some friends but most importantly discover work opportunities in this amazing city. I didn't know exactly what I was going to do but it was a place that you could make money and a lot of it.

I waited for my brother and then we went out together, climb the stairs to the main entrance to our building and walked across the road to wait for the bus. We were the first there, standing outside number 7 Conduit Road. We were too early. It wasn't for another 10 minutes that the next school kid turned up. From 1st year to 5th you had to wear the school uniform but in 6th and above you could wear whatever you wanted, within reason. I was never any good at clothes shopping and tended to choose the same things over and over again. This time I looked as if I was still in the Navy, in the clothes that I had bought had a remarkable resemblance to the number 8 uniform, blue shirt and blue trousers. And unfortunately, it was pretty close to the school uniform a well. This was also causing my anxiety to go up. My brother had told me about two bus prefects, older students who were in charge of the overall behaviour on the bus. One of them was alright he said but the other was a dick head. Eventually, the bus turned up at 0715. An old-looking thing that said school bus as soon as you looked at it. I didn't know what I was expecting, maybe one of the green and white minibuses that did the route from HMS Tamar up here. But no it was a full-size bus. We climbed on and I surveyed the scene. There were a couple of younger kids already on, staring out the window. Nobody took any notice of us. We went halfway towards the back of the bus and sat down. A younger kid sat in front of us and started talking to my brother who informed them that I was his brother and was starting school today. It was a weird feeling. Here I was sitting on a school bus after being in the navy for 6 months. I was carrying a school bag and not a sterling machine gun. Travelling in comfort and not in the back of a big truck with wooden benches. I'd seen pain and destruction now I was staring at kids with bunches and rosy cheeks!! However, it was still a scary experience. Just like the battle scenarios we had completed at basic training. All that training was going on inside my head as these 12-year-old kids were making pleasantries towards me. The bus stopped again soon and some older kids got on, still a year or so younger than me but I surveyed the threat and consciously prepared myself for combat. This was one of the first bus prefects. He stared straight at me and came up to me

"Who are you, you're not allowed on this bus?"

Confrontation immediately. I jumped up, spun him around, put his head into the crook of my left arm, grabbed the top of his hair and smashed his face into the window across from me, sending younger kids screaming and diving out of the way as his whole body was sprawled across the seats.
Well I did that in my head and whilst I was thinking of that my brother said
"It's my brother, he starts school today and he's paid for the bus".
"Well, I'm in charge of the bus......"
He trailed away, I was just sitting there staring at him still thinking of how I was trying to push his face through the window. He must have seen something in my face so he just walked away and sat down. Our apartment was halfway up the hill that was Hong Kong Island. The roads carved their way around it like a dragons tail, all running parallel with each other as they snaked this way and that and joined each other at points due west or east so that the roads and homes sat on the side of the hill as terraces cut into the side. This meant that bus took a long time to get to the school as it wound through all of these roads slowly filling up with a multitude of nationalities. It took about 45 minutes until it finally made the slow, gear grinding trip up Bowen Road and then onto Borret Road where it stopped at the back entrance to the school. Here many more of the same types of bus, but painted different colours, were depositing their cargos. There was also a school opposite ours filled with only Chinese students so there was a huge hubbub of noise and movement. However, I knew where I was going as I had been asked to report to the principal's office first thing. My brother showed me how to get there from this back gate and I arrived just before the first-morning bell went off. I sat there in that same waiting room that I had sat a few weeks earlier with my mum. I once again looked around at all the trophies and medals. I also took in a lot of the photos as well that dotted the wall with their groups of smiling students and teachers with a smorgasbord of views and backdrops. I was kept waiting there for what seemed to be a long time. My anxiety rising as I didn't know what was going to happen next. Another teacher passed me and went into the principal's office then I was called in. As I walked into the office the atmosphere was heavy, or was it just my imagination? Sitting behind his large desk was the principal and standing by the side was a teacher I hadn't met. He was quite an imposing figure.

Tall, with a stern look. He had wavy dark brown hair and a beard. His eyes were locked on mine as if he was telling me
"I'm in charge here".
"This is Mr Harding".
I said the polite good morning then the principal began.
"Look, we know that you have been in the Navy and that worries us. You have also missed the first term of the year so you are already way behind in your class. We will not tolerate any bad behaviour or anything that causes disruption to this school. We will also not tolerate any reports of bad behaviour outside of the school, is this understood?"
"Yes," I said.
"Okay, then I wish you the best of luck. We have had a couple of new students recently that you will get to know Melanie and Andy and they have settled in well. We have also arranged for you to have a buddy who will show you around. If you have any problems speak to them or see Mr Harding. Mr Harding will now take you to your first class"
And with that, I was dismissed. Mr Harding and I left the office together and went up a flight of stairs to the next floor where my class was and I was to be introduced to my new school buddy who would look after me. Just after we had turned into the corridor to go to my class the loveliest girl I had ever seen in my entire life came bouncing down the corridor with blonde hair flowing. I thought she was going to run past me and I was transfixed by this vision of beauty. But she stopped, right there in front of me. I had to check to see if my tongue was hanging out, my jaw was definitely hanging loose.
"Hi, I'm Kylie".
Those 3 words came to me as if separate, separated by a period of time so that I could interpret what was happening to me right at that moment.
"Hi".
She was talking to me. She was being friendly to me. This was something I had never experienced before. In my previous life, I had been mostly ignored, for the entire length of my being people had never said
"Hi"
To me in that way before. It meant that she wanted to interact with me on a level I had never experienced before. That singular

"Hi"
Was the most incomprehensible
"Hi"
I had ever been part of, and the next word seemed to have been spiritually put there to amplify the first.
"I'm"
She was introducing herself to me; she wanted to form a relationship of communication between us. She was also giving me her complete attention. Her body language was open and her eyes, and my God what blue eyes, were piercing like sharp bullets into mine. I could almost feel the sight receptors at the back of my brain starting to burn.
"Kylie"
Never has a name had such an impact on me? It summed her up perfectly. It was only just then when she uttered her poetic name that I was able to work out that she had an Australian accent. Every adolescent in the UK had been hypnotized by the antics of another Australian Kylie twice a day, once at lunch and once after Blue Peter just before the news at 6. As her alter ego Charlene Robinson, Kylie Minogue had our blood running red hot for the last few years as she frolicked about in the paradise of Australia. And here I was standing in front of the most dazzling girl I had ever met, her bronzed, athletic body turned towards me. Her glimmering head of sunshine hair with her deep-sea eyes looking right into mine whispering romantic poetry into my ears and only for my ears
"Hi, I'm Kylie".
That moment was the most beautiful of my life and would be, well probably forever.
"I'm your buddy and I'm going to look after you".
Had my entire existence up until that point been purposefully bad so that I would experience the joy of those few seconds at the highest level possible? Any higher and my heart may have burst right there and then. But it was just that and never anything else. Having spent the previous years of my life searching for belonging, searching for love and affection that moment I was experiencing was just that. There was nothing sexual about it at all. I didn't fancy Kylie; I never would, but that moment was still beautiful. It made me feel, well perfect. I had always tried to mirror other people to try and fit in. I had done it so much that I now did it without thinking. And so to mirror Kylie right there and then, well that meant I was beautiful too,

didn't it? Kylie took me to my class where I was introduced to everyone. Debbie, David
"Bet you don't know my nickname"
"Eh, is it Del"
"What? How did you know?"
Mathew
"Everyone calls me Blakey"
The first break time at school I had a huge group of people surround me all wanting to introduce themselves to me. It was intense. At my previous school, new kids were left by themselves hiding in corners until they slowly made friends. That is what I had had to do for the last few years. But now I seemed to have a hundred kids all wanting to be my friend. To be honest, it was a little too much for me, I was overwhelmed. During that melee of meeting new friends, I was invited to a birthday party that was happening that weekend. How I had longed to be invited to a party. I was usually a hanger-on. Turning up to a party because one of my friends had been given an invite and they took me along. Parties were so complicated to me. I stressed for a long time before going. Who did I want to be at the party? I had no real identity. Always trying to be someone who others would enjoy being in their company. The clothes were a nightmare and how bad would my acne be. I tended to get drunk before any party event. But I never stuck to any limits. It was the only thing that I knew to do. It gave me something to do when I was feeling uncomfortable. Problem was that I always drank too fast so was always having to get myself another top-up so that I wasn't standing still long enough for someone to try and engage me in conversation. How do you talk to people? What is the cool, polite, nice thing to say to someone who approaches you? I always felt such a twat on these occasions and my drinking habits helped me to become that twat quite quickly. Negative attention is what I got. I had been raised on it and I carried it on. You had to be popular; there was no other way to be as a teenager. And to become popular I did the things that made people laugh and therefore remember me. I got drunk, acted an arse, did risky things and basically became the party fool. All I needed was the pointy hat and tights and I would have fitted the role of jester just perfectly. So here I was surrounded by all these cool, foreign, gorgeous kids who wanted me to come to the party that weekend and they didn't even know me. This was an opportunity for me to reinvent myself. To become the cool person that everyone liked.

Maybe even girls! It wasn't even just a normal party, it was a boat party. I learnt that we would all meet up and head down to one of the piers at the harbour and go on Chinese junk that would head out into the sea towards some island somewhere. These junks are amazing vessels. I had seen that one when we were coming into land. This was going to be the best party I had ever gone to in my life. When the bell went I followed my class to the next lesson. Staying as close to Kylie as possible but with Blakey at my arm at all times. I really liked this guy; he reminded me a lot of myself. He was about the same height as me with blonde hair. He told me he was from Wales but had lived in Hong Kong for a long time. He had a really kind smile and told me to stick with him and he would keep me right. I scanned around the school on my way up to class. All the corridors were on the outside of the building, open to the weather. There were a few different buildings that were connected with open walkways that students were walking back and forward over. There were open playing areas with lines painted on the ground for a multitude of different sports and next to them was a large area of steps whose purpose was really for everyone to be able to sit down on and watch games that were taking place or chat whilst they were eating and drinking what they had got from one of the tuck-shops. If you like your Chinese food well these tuck shops were just amazing. The chicken noodle soup would be the best I had ever tasted and they also did polystyrene boxes of rice with pork and other delicious things. Blakey shouted at me to get moving, so I turned from my exploring to see him moving towards a set of stairs towards our next class. At lunch Blakey took me to our house room. The students were split into different houses, I was in Rutherford. The older students all had their own common room, one for each of the houses which were Rutherford, Einstein, Da Vinci, Wilberforce, etc. They were a place for us to hang out during break or to "study" during free periods. On entering our common room there was a bank of lockers on the left. Blakey told me to get a padlock and claim an empty one. "I've got 3 lockers for all my crap"

He said looking pleased with himself. The rest of the room was filled with chairs to lounge around in. There was a stereo playing music. Good music too, rock music. I was introduced to everyone in the room. Not everyone was enthusiastic about coming to meet me, but most were.

The rest of the day I went from class trying to see how much I would have to catch up with everyone else. Not much it would seem. Although I was three months late joining the class I had a good back round knowledge from all the reading I had done to understand what was being taught. In I didn't really need to do much remedial studying at all. I was pretty up to date and even ahead of some in the class. The week went well; I got to know more and more people. The person who I clicked with more than anyone else was the girl that I was told had also just started, Melanie. Tall, slim with strawberry curly blondish reddish hair that always smelled amazing, Melanie was drop-dead gorgeous. But she was also very grounded. She seemed to have effortlessly melded into the social structure at the school. The first time I met her it was break time

"Hi I'm Melanie, do you smoke?"

"Yeah," I said

"Come with us".

I followed her and a couple of others up a set of stairs that I hadn't seen yet. It took us up to part of the roof that led to the football nets that were up there. My God what a view. Looking down from halfway up to Hong Kong Island directly towards the harbour. The postcard that most people will know of Hong Kong. Looking down over the gleaming skyscrapers it was almost an unbelievable sight all the way over the harbour and the mainland beyond. The view was shimmering in the late autumn heat with waves of mist caused by the humidity swirling around the peak of the island. I turned to see Melanie and a couple of lads sitting down leaning against a wall and pulling out their cigarettes. I accepted a Marlboro red from Melanie and sat down with her. One of the other lads was Andy, who had also just started school. Both of them were from England and even a blind man could see the flirting going on between them. If they weren't going out already they certainly sure would be soon. It was an exotic experience sitting up there just below the roof overlooking the harbour, almost romantic.

"Are you going to the boat party this weekend?"

"Sure, I'm definitely going. It sounds amazing"

"We usually go to Thingummy's on a Friday night then there is the beer buffet at Inn Place later, do you fancy coming? We all go every week".

"We meet at the corner of Pedder Street, do you know it, anyway we meet next to the ATM's and then all head over to Inn Place together, some go to Thingummy's first, you wanna come?"

"Definitely".

We finished our cigarettes and headed back downstairs. After that first experience of the smoking on top, that is where you would find me from now on. At the end of school, I met up with my brother.

"I'll show you where the school bus is"

"No it's ok I'm heading into town with some of the others".

I met up with a group that was heading down into the town. Across the road was a lane that took you through the woods towards the other lanes that would eventually take you down across all the winding main roads and eventually you would arrive in Central. There was a long wall which had a load of kids hanging around, some smoking and the others talking. I joined the groups of smokers and was introduced to kids I hadn't met yet. I felt the centre of attention and it felt great. All the lower and upper 6th students could wear what they wanted and, most of the girls looked fine. The climate was a big help as most had loose-fitting clothing over their tanned healthy bodies. Pretty, pretty, preeeety they all were. And they were all talking to me. I didn't know where to look.

After a cigarette, we started to walk down through a series of lanes and paths through the bewildering array of buildings, down through the humidity and towards the bustling metropolis below us. Before I knew it we were walking into McDonalds. This would be a treat. McDonald's was not cheap. In Scotland, it was a few pounds for a meal. I didn't have enough money with me to buy anything so I didn't know what to do. I didn't want to have someone buying for me so when I got to the service counter and looked at the prices I was staggered to see I could afford everything. A big Mac was 80c. Result! I bought 2 and went to sit down with my huge new group of friends. I sat back and ate whilst listening and watching. This was amazing I was part of this dynamic straight away. No-one was giving me a hard time. No comments threw towards the new guy. The feeling of acceptance filled me. I was overflowing with happiness.

Back home that night I lay down on my bed, the sofa, and tried to take it all in. The weather, the location, new friends and the girls. It was the perfect dream but reality. Had all my previous worries built me up to this wonderland of love and friendship, opportunity and my *future? I decided to write a letter to my couple of friends back in Scotland. Maybe I was gloating, I don't know, but I wanted to tell them all. Maybe even to say to them that there is a brighter world out there and Glasgow was just a pit of despair and that the rest of the world was different.*

Chapter Nine
3 Square Meals to Starvation

The days continued for a few weeks. Nothing really changed. Then one day I was sitting in the dining hall after just getting my dinner when a Chinese guy ran over and stole my plate. I was in a state of stunned shock. First of all how come he got away with it and second of all if I did something in retaliation what would be the result. So I just sat there, dumbfounded. I went back to my cell and tried to work out what to do. The guy who had taken my plate was a guy that was always hanging around the top guy in the prison. He was called the big brother. And the other guy, the little brother. These terms were triad related. The guy who took my plate must have known that the guards wouldn't have done anything as he was the little brother. I imagine that everything had been planned for days.

The next morning at breakfast the same thing happened again. He sneaked up behind my seat and stole my bread and cheese. I was already starving from not having anything to eat the night before. This time I couldn't hold my rage back, I leapt to my feet but before I could reach him the guards jumped me and held me down for my first official beating. I was dragged to the floor and they laid into me with their batons. I was then dragged to the governor's office where I was told that I wasn't allowed to get out of my seat. I considered telling him what happened but I knew that was grassing and my life would not be worth living. So I said nothing, took the telling off and went to my workshop. At lunchtime, I could just tell that something was coming. Standing in the queue waiting to get served a Chinese guy deliberately knocked into me. I turned around and squared up to him. He screamed something in my face and pushed me. I had nothing to say and pushed him back, harder. But before anything else could happen a guard appeared between us.

He pushed us apart. Sent me to the back of the queue, and let us continue to get our lunch things. But this was it, I had a feeling that this was coming. They were starting to size me up. I looked over to the table where the big brother was sitting and stared at him. He was staring back with the little brother talking excitedly in his ear. The big brother nodded and the little brother got up and walked towards my table. I looked around and saw that none of the guards was

looking but every prisoner was. As he neared my table I readied myself for an attack. It didn't come but as he passed me he whispered in English
 "We gonna kill you"
I believed him.

Chapter -9
The Inn Place

So here I was 16 years old and getting ready to meet my friends and go to a club. Not an under 18 disco, but a proper club. Looking in the mirror, I smiled to myself. I put my best on and headed out. The night was dark and I was leaving too early, but I couldn't help it. I was going to walk down to central for the first time at night on my own. I decided to go via crunch alley at the back of our apartment. A dark alley so filled with cockroaches every step was met with a satisfying crunch of half a dozen of their bodies. It led down a dizzyingly steep set of stones steps most broken and cracked down into the darkness at the back of poorly named Emerald court towards Robinson road which ran parallel but a good hundred foot further down the side of the island. Across there and through another dark alley. Across a road to a dark alley again and again, until the gait of my walk moved towards the flat land I came out onto the busy streets of Central District. I wandered through the high rise buildings one out of thousands heading towards their destinations. I knew Pedder Street well as my dad's office was located halfway down it, just past the cigarette seller and one of the many entrances to the MTR. Right at the top of the street was a couple of ATM's belonging to the Hong Kong and Shanghai Banking Corporation and right next to them was a low ledge, I hopped up on it and waited for my friends to arrive. Pedder Street acts as a funnel for the slow-flowing traffic trying to get from the higher part of the island to the lower part towards where you get the ferries or buses to the rest of the colony. The flow is nonstop with red taxis, buses and luxury cars all fighting for their own piece of tarmac. On each side of the road are the people all seeming to be travelling in the same direction. With the landmark shopping mall on the other side and with the MTR on my side, this pavement is always busy. I sat there almost invisible to it all. Able to hide away without anyone paying me any attention. I was early and it was a good 30 minutes before others from school started to arrive. Everyone was dressed to impress. There was an even mixture of guys and girls, and I have to say that all the girls looked gorgeous.

"*So is this a normal Friday night in Hong Kong?*"

I thought to myself. As we waited and chatted, everyone coming up to introduce themselves to me, I thought back on my previous life and realised that I am only really appreciating what's happening now because my life back then was so shit. But I would keep that to myself. At the allotted time we all headed towards the local MTR station and bought our tickets to go to Tsim Tsa Tsui. The last MTR was around 1 am so that's when we would be coming back and heading to Thingummy's to finish the evening.

We all jumped on the first train that came into the station. We practically filled the carriage. Some were already drunk having started drinking earlier and were dancing and singing in the carriage. A lot of the local Chinese were quite obviously disgusted by our behaviour and moved as far as possible away from us. I just sat there smiling and talking to some of my new friends. Arriving in Tsim Tsa Tsui we all pilled out and danced and sang all the way up to the street. The Inn place was just off Nathan road on Hangkow road. When we got there I could hear the music coming up a set of stairs where a big neon sign had signalled our arrival. At the bottom of the stairs, the beat of the music was filling my every sense with excitement. There was a big English guy sitting there and we handed over our 50 bucks and he either gave you a voucher for two drinks or a stamp on the back of your hand for the beer buffet. I took the stamp and walked up to the bar with the gang, showed my stamp and the young Chinese guy behind the bar filled a pint glass with San Miguel and we were away. That was my pint glass and I had to keep hold of it because as it was a buffet I could go up to the bar and fill it as many times as I wanted all night long! Mental, looking around there was absolutely no-one over 18 years. It had the look and feel of an under 18 disco, but it was a nightclub with drink as much as you can, beer. So we drunk we danced we laughed and we got drunk, inebriated to the point of having to go to the toilets and throw up. I got to know the staff behind the bar really quickly. The guy who kept serving me was called Ricky and the gorgeous waitress who was hanging around in her white shirt, short black skirt that framed her amazing arse and tits was called Eddy. I spent a lot of time talking to Eddy, she was just fabulous. She may have been 5 years older than me but we hit it off really quickly. Towards the end of the night, I found myself staggering over to a seat and looking around.

"Whatever you do," I thought to myself

"Don't fuck this up, you're in heaven buddy".

"Last MTR!"

Went the shout. It was a call for the gang to get together and stagger up the stairs quickly to get the last train. If we missed it we would have to pay for a taxi to get back over to the island through the tunnel and I had been told that the taxis didn't like changing side of the harbour at this time of night and would charge double. How we made it up the stairs let alone to the MTR station I have no idea. Everyone was pissed. I mean really pissed. There were kids puking in doorways, others latched onto each other, with faces that may never be pulled apart. Hands down trousers, with penises sticking out, hands up skirts with hands frantically looking for buried treasure. It couldn't just be a normal Friday night, could it? And to think that tomorrow night was an actual party, a birthday party on a Chinese junk. I was too drunk to feel overwhelmed. I just followed the crowd to the station, stepping over vomit. When we got on the train the pissing, vomiting and mutual masturbation didn't stop. It was like an orgy. My head was rolling about, trying to see through unfocused eyes, and now we were off to a place called Thingummy's.

Chapter Ten
Revenge, well maybe?

"He kill 2 your friend"
One day sitting in the classroom on the first floor the Cat A's walked passed our door as usual. Acid Boy leaned next to me and whispered,
"He kill 2 your friend"
I said
"What"
"He kill 2 your friend"
"What do you mean?"
I said
"That guy who walk past kill 2 foreign school kids with his friend, long time back"
It suddenly clicked in my brain. Could he be serious? It made sense though. I was in the maximum-security prison and the Cat A's are the worst of the worst. What he was saying was that one of the guys who walk past our classroom twice a day was responsible for the brutal rape and murder of 2 kids who went to my school a few years ago. My instant thoughts went to retaliation. It was the most powerful feeling I had in months, finally drowning out the fear of attack, the intense depression of loneliness, the lack of any sort of control I had in my life. My mind went straight to how I could get him. It was nearly impossible. We were always locked up when they were outside. Kept safe from the sadistic killers that were housed in a block, the prison within the prison. Twice a day they would walk past, and the next time I would get Acid Boy to point out exactly who it was.
I waited, staring at the door for the rest of the day. My focus on seeing which one it was. My mind planning how I would avenge in some way the terrible event that he and his other animal friends had perpetrated. I didn't even know the kids he killed, but that didn't matter. They went to my school, my friends had known them. The school still remembers those events clearly.
I knew the time was coming when they would be taken out of their segregated classroom and back to their high-security safety. I got Acid Boy to sit next to me and to point him out to me, my prey.
Then I could hear the footsteps as they approached, my skin started to crawl. Thinking that I am going to come face to face with one of the monsters. As they went past acid boy pointed and said,
"Him"

He looked into our classroom, our eyes locked, and my intense hatred flew across the room in my glaze, and he saw it, he knew.
From that day onwards his face was burned into my conscious memory. I would see him at least twice a day, sometimes more. He always looked at me glaring at him. I felt that I could feel, sense his discomfort. He knew that I knew. He understood that my only goal in life now was to get the chance to attack him, to harm him. I had no concerns for what would happen to me. What the guards would do to me, what sanctions I would get. I would happily spend the rest of my sentence in solitary confinement just to get one chance to get my hands on him. I would hurt him as badly as I could. I would have mere seconds to attack. I couldn't risk a weapon, I didn't want to get caught with one and never get the chance to attack him. The chance I would get would come out of the blue. I would be unprepared for it as it would have to happen by accident, a hundred different circumstances all coming together at one moment when me, a Cat B prisoner would mistakenly be in the same area as the Cat A prisoners. So I waited, I glared every day, week, month. I would be ready for the chance when it came.
When it came, the chance, I wasn't in the classroom. The police had visited me again. To ask me questions. A waste of time. Other crimes committed by a foreigner that I think they just wanted me to take the rap for as I had already been sentenced. Somebody had stolen a TV out of a shop in Wan Chai last year!! I think I know who did it, it actually sounded like him, but it wasn't me. So I was being taken back to the classrooms. I was with a bunch of remand prisoners who the police visit quite regularly so we were taken through the dining hall so that they could be dropped off first. I was led to the back door of the hall and stepped out into the small courtyard there; right into the path of the Cat A's coming down the stairs.
I don't even think I saw him I reacted that fast, just the knowledge of the time and the location, who he walked with, where he was always placed in the group. I had studied him for months, his height, build, who he walked with. I was on him before anyone could have realised their mistake. He fell back onto the stairs, I had scattered everyone in front of him and he fell hard on his back, his head hitting the stone stairs behind him. I grabbed the front of his shirt and picked him up and hit him back again his head making a great noise as it hit the stair just like a boiled egg being cracked. I fell forward and my knee went into his stomach, just missing his balls where I was aiming. All I

saw was him; all I heard was my breathing. I saw his teeth, those teeth that had marked the skin in his crime against two innocent, defenceless kids. I punched those teeth, once, twice, and then I was in the air, falling upwards away from him. I spun around and was at the bottom of the stairs, I wasn't looking at him anymore but I only saw his face. I had done it; satisfaction overwhelmed me, drowning out the sensation of batons raining down on me. Unable to feel the weight of the officers on top of me, unable to hear anything apart from the joy of achieving a goal. Taking control, completing a task, getting some of our own back against a guy who had destroyed so much.

There was a buzz amongst the officers. At first, I was dragged to the governor's office where everyone is taken when there has been a fight, but instead of waiting there for hours before finally been seen by him and given my sentence I was dragged off straight away to solitary. I was thrown in a dark cell and the door slammed shut. I lay on the floor for ages. Not wanting to move until I could tell that there were no officers around. It was then that my senses started awakening and the pain from the beating I had taken started to fill every part of me. I was sick, soiled myself and wet myself. I could not get off the floor I was so weak. I don't remember how long a lay there but the unmistakable noise of many boots came down the corridor and my cell door was opened again. They swarmed in and all started taking their best shots at me. I crawled into a ball trying to protect myself but they pulled my legs one way and my arms the other and let fly with their batons into my stomach. They were all screaming at me, I couldn't understand but I had obviously pissed them off. They had made a mistake and were in the shit and the way they wanted payback was from my pain. They let me go and I crawled into a ball, tears and vomit flowing from my face. The door shut and I was left. I lay there for hours, I couldn't move, I was racked in pain, any movement sent waves of pain through all my other injuries. I finally reached up and grabbed a blanket and covered myself, I lay there until the next day. I dreamt. I dreamt of the two kids he and his friends had murdered. My dreams took me to that hillside and I watched them do it. I witnessed the whole event in my mind. As the event was happening I looked into the kid's eyes and they looked back at me. It was as if time and space had mingled. They knew what was happening; they knew what I was going to do and what I had done. We connected for a brief, fleeting moment and then I was back in my cell, on the ground, stinking but at peace. It's strange but that morning I didn't feel triumphant. Why would I? I was happy with what I had done but it didn't change anything. Yes, I had got what I felt was a bit of rightly deserved justice for those two kids but my mind started to play tricks on me straight away. What if I had actually attacked the wrong guy? I only had acid boy's finger point to decide who out of a group of Chinese guys I would attack; who I believed was guilty of a heinous crime. But never mind, whoever I had attacked was a bad guy anyway. He wasn't in here for stealing someone's roses, was he?

Chapter -10

Thingummy's

Walking towards the small roads that start at the bottom of the island that ends at the peak, I stared at all the neon signs declaring the finest accoutrements the modern man and women need. Rolex watches, Benetton clothes. This was the high-end shopping district of Hong Kong. It was like walking through a modern cavern with buildings seemingly leaning over us as if they were touching; they were at such a great height. We walked up to a long street on the right and followed it's shop windows, some with fish tank walls where a restaurant hid behind and you could choose only the freshest of fish. This started to become a little bit grubbier. The side street off the glamour. A Street that I was more used to, recognizably grubby like Glasgow. At one point all the unfamiliar odours gave way to something that was all too familiar. The smell of urine. Yuck, I thought someone has been using one of the many tiny narrow alleys that ran off the street as a toilet. I would be wrong to think that, the stink was coming from an open doorway, and above that doorway was a sign that welcomed us to Thingummy's. Now through my drunken haze, even I could recognize a shit hole when I hadn't even seen one yet. But looking around at the well dressed and somewhat naïve fellow students, I had to trust my gut. If this was Glasgow there would have been no way I would have entered such premises. In Glasgow, these places only mean one thing, drunken violence, sectarian singing, and more drunken violence.

As I entered the dark hallway I became aware of something sticky on the ground immediately under my feet, the carpet. I walked forward and in the gloom, I could see the top of a staircase that curved downwards to my left.

"POW"

The hit came from the right-hand side, I had been too slow to respond, I had been stupid, it was a trap, the hit knocked me into the wall to my left, and plaster flew everywhere. I gagged as I realized that it wasn't a hit made of matter it was pure gas. I strained through my tear-stained eyes, trying to rub the stench off of them, and could just make out two toilet cubicles, wood rotten, doors hanging off.

"Don't go in there, mate"

One of my new friends uselessly informed me. As I managed to crawl past the crossfire of putrid outpouring from the death chambers I reached the top of the stairs. It was only then that the noise from downstairs could permeate through the stench. Like chemical warfare the two senses fought for prominence, now sound won.

As I walked down the spiral staircase the hum of voices joined in with the music. I was descending into some sort of Dickensian fairy tale, a bar filled with only teenagers. No, not a bar, a cave, not a cavern but a cave. I passed an old black telephone on a small shelve and looked over the scene below me. To the left was a curved bar where an old Chinese guy stood in front of various drinks on optic. There were actually adults in here as well. Three sitting at the bar. But the rest of the view was filled with teenagers all sitting around on old seats with no discernible colour. Each group was in small alcoves, curved cushioned seats with tables. There were also seats lining the walls of what looked liked panelled wood but was difficult to make out with the explosion of a multitude of graffiti marks left by visitors over the years. It looked like over hundreds of years. In one corner was an old jukebox that was responsible for the music that filled the small space along with a thick fog of smoke that had been expelled by these teenagers. It was in anyone's eyes a dump, but it was a dump where smartly dressed kids could come and fulfil their desires which not only included alcohol, I could only guess. We all got pints of San Miguel and squeezed into spaces that others made for us. I spent the rest of the night trying to read the graffiti, meeting new people and settling into, although I didn't know it, what was going to be my home for the next few months. I was happy, drunk, and comfortable. I had a family of friends around me like I had never had before. These were my new family. Away from the real family that I had felt I had never been able to fit into, and into this new one. I felt safe and loved for perhaps the first time in my life. This is where I wanted to be.

Chapter Eleven
Breaking Down

Solitary is rough. They give you as little contact with others as possible. My clothes were in a mess but they never came to give me a chance. Later the first full day I managed to get myself off the floor and onto the hard fibreglass bed. It wasn't any more comfortable than the floor but did give me a little insulation from the cold hard concrete. My food would come, late, cold, and little. Almost inedible and served without a smile. That night was bad, my body was trying to heal but every time I moved I hurt. It reminded me of the physical pain of withdrawal. Every nerve that had been injured screaming when any pressure was applied to it. The next morning I managed to get up. I stumbled to the small sink at the back of the cell to check to see if there was water because sometimes there wasn't. This time I was lucky. I took off my soiled clothes very slowly trying not to retch at the stink because each time I did my ribs would ache. I washed my clothes as well as I could and looped them around the bars at the front of the cell to try and get as much water out of them as possible. I swung them around my head after that to try to dry them. It was cold in the cell, the only heat source coming from the very dim light bulb in the ceiling. Eventually, I just had to put my clothes back on. I couldn't heat myself up the usual way by exercising because my body was now starting to seize up. That night I was cold and damp. I started to shiver and that actually helped my pain a bit. As if giving my bruises a little massage.

Every day I would get up expecting to be taken out of the cell to the governor's office to get sentenced for my crime of assault, but no-one would ever come apart from to throw me some food now and again.

Each day I lay there in the near dark, listening to the sounds of the prison but seeing nothing of it. I was supposed to get out an hour each day for exercise but when I suggested it to a guard he just laughed. So I just lay there thinking. My thoughts were of hopelessness. I didn't regret what I had done in the fight but I regretted being here in the first place. I went through my whole life, recounting all the sadness that I had survived. All the feelings of loneliness, self-hatred, fear, loathing. I cried a lot. I thought of my family. How I felt that they all hated me, and quite rightly so. I thought of friends and how I had let them all down. I felt sometimes that the best way to go would be just to kill someone in here and then spend the rest of my life in solitary, slowly going insane like an animal trapped in a too-small cage. I would stare out of the cell, trying to make out shapes beyond the barred windows of the hallway. It looked out onto a wall. I would count the bricks; start making shapes with my mind. One day I lay there trying to contact people I knew through thoughts alone. I thought that I would be able to use the power of my brain to contact them and that they would hear me and say hello back. I spent hours doing that, days doing it with no-one answering. Sometimes I thought that I had been forgotten about, that the only orders given to the guards on duty were to feed me. I believed that I was going to be in here forever. Some prison rule that I hadn't been told about would cause me to take on his sentence and he was to be freed and I was to be in here for life. I was slowly going crazy but didn't realise it. You don't realize it. Because it is your everyday living, your normality. I thought back to the time when it was evident I had lost my mind just before prison. I was sitting on the steps of a building in Causeway Bay pretending to be in a music video. Singing my favourite songs whilst being filmed by a secret film crew. People would be walking past staring at me as I would very animatedly sing to an invisible camera. At the time I thought it was brilliant. What a great video, all these unsuspecting Chinese people not knowing that they were in a music video of a famous western singer. But in reality, I was a crazy guy sitting on the steps singing to myself in the middle of the day.

The days and then weeks passed until one day they let me out. I was taken to reception where I was given new clothes and then taken to the dining hall. My eyes burned with the sunlight. I had no idea what time of day it was. When I got into the hall it was full of my group of prisoners. I was glad to be with them again. I got my food and sat at a separate table. I ate and then was taken out of the hall first by myself. Everyone was staring at me, I even thought I got a couple of smiles, but I don't know. I was taken back to my cell where all my belongings were. I made my bed, lay down and cried. When I heard the other prisoners coming I got up, picked up a book and sat on my bed. This time they just walked past, no spitting, and no name-calling. They just stared at me. Nothing was mentioned about the fight by anyone. But the Cat A's never walked passed our classroom again. We never really saw them again, only at a distance when they were in their exercise yard.

Chapter -11

My first boat party

My first thought when I woke up the next morning was
"What am I going to wear?"
My wardrobe was pitiful. I had only managed to bring so many things over with me in my one case, and as I'd never really gone to parties before, and had never been interested in fashion so I was a bit worried. I found a pair of jeans and a t-shirt and decided to wear them. The whole day I was wracked with nerves. I had never had so many people want to be friends with me before. How should I act with them, what should I do in conversations? I ended up having to go out for a walk. There was no privacy in the apartment. I walked all the way down to central and back trying to calm myself down. When late afternoon finally came. I got dressed and waited on Conduit Road for the small white and green minibus that would take me all the way down to the final stop outside of HMS Tamar. It was a really regular service. Not one with a timetable. The bus would wait until it had enough people on board and then set off. The roads down the hill were steep, and it sounded like the gearbox would explode at any moment, sending shards of fragmented gears flying through the air. But with gears and brakes screaming we did make it down the hill. I was glad I was getting off at the last stop as I hadn't mastered the "lee do, m'goy" (here please)
This is what you needed to shout at the driver when you wanted off.
The pier where the boat would be leaving for the party was a two-minute walk from the bus stop, opposite the Hong Kong City Hall, Queens Pier?
As I turned the corner onto the paved area that ran along next to the harbour wall, I immediately saw a large group of teenagers, but my eyes were taken to the boat. Wow, It was a full-on Chinese junk with massive brown sails. It looked incredible; I couldn't believe that after only one week in school I was going to a party on that. I joined the group, and at the command of the birthday girl's dad, we all climbed aboard.
There were buckets of beer everywhere. There must also have been food, but I didn't see it. The Junk manoeuvred itself away from the quayside and into the mass of other boats, large and small that swarmed over this part of the harbour. We headed west. Most of the

others were chatting, laughing, and downing beers. I was leaning on the rail staring out at one of the most stunning views on the planet. It was a mixture of organic and non-organic. The huge skyscrapers lit up with the mountains just a faint but always present hugeness behind. Small wooden boats that had whole families living on them. Dad at the bow with a long bamboo pole with a net picking up anything recyclable, beer cans thrown by some of my shipmates and plastic bottles. Halfway down the tiny craft mum was hanging the washing and under a canopy at the stern a couple of children doing their homework, oblivious to the rich kids sailing past throwing their empty cans at their father for sport.

As we left the main part of the harbour the view opened out so that you could see many different islands dotted around. Some having lights so you knew they were inhabited, some not. One of these was a prison I was told. How terrifying that must be as all the islands looked foreboding. Covered in thick jungle, jagged rock faces. We passed some huge container ships, anchored and waiting their turn to enter the harbour and pick up containers full of Christmas gifts that would sit under millions of western Christmas trees. Kids excited with their new toys for a day or two. Wonder what the kids living on the wee wooden boat would get?

The night turned into a drunken mess. Kids getting thrown off the Junk from time to time. I ended up so pissed I ended the trip throwing up in the toilet. There was a mess everywhere. It was a proper Junk party after all.

Chapter Twelve
Psychosis

Something had changed in my mind. No, not just my mind. I could feel the change in my whole body, in every cell. The cells fizzing with this new sensation. I was going to fight back. I had finally lost my mind, but I didn't realise it. I was not going to sit there and be attacked; I was going to attack first. It wasn't quite hearing voices, well I don't think so, but I was telling myself,
"Attack, attack, no more Mr Nice Guy, I'm gonna die here but I'm taking you with me"!
I would get up early, before the radio and work out. I had to be strong when the time came. I would dream of all the scenarios of how I was going to do it, where I was going to do it and what the outcome would be. I would find myself dying over and over again in my dreams. Smiling, looking upwards, and shouting out
"Sorry mum".
There would be bodies all around me, blood in pools around the lifeless bodies of the prisoners I had taken with me. Officers in the distance running towards me, in slow motion, with truncheons held high. I would be feeling the life slowly leaving me; it would be peaceful, almost tranquil. This was me preparing to die, to be at peace. I would dream about how people would react to the news. People from my past aghast at the brutality I had afflicted on people.
I would shower and clean my cell, sometimes I would have to sit for what seemed like an hour before the radio even came on. The night officer would sometimes go past and tell me to go back to bed because it was only 4 am! But I wouldn't I would continue with my plan. I had the look of the mad. I would stare at everyone with this look of pure evil in my eye. I could see them stop and take a second look, they would appear to take a step back from me, and I was exuding such evil, malice and threat.
As we were being lined up outside in the morning I could hear the others whispering about me.
"Watch out Gwai Gi is crazy"
"Gwai Gi will kill us"
"We have to be safe".
The voices where in my head, they were like a thousand whispers all mixed together.

I would growl at people if they looked at me. In the dining hall, I would keep a low growl coming out of me when picking up my food, whilst sitting, whilst eating. Whilst sitting at my table I would put my left hand around my food and drink, lower my head over my plate but with my head tilted up towards the others while I ate. Like a snarling dog. They all just sat there staring at me. In the workshop, I would pace up and down at one end and they would sit at the other, staring at me. I would be muttering to myself and they would be speaking in hushed tones. This happened in the classroom as well although there I took a chair and put it with the back to a wall facing everyone and the door. The cat A's didn't walk past anymore but I was watching for them.

Chapter -12
A new life

Each day after school I would head down the hill to McDonald's, I would rarely go home straight away now. There was a group of us that followed the same routine. McDonald's, a walk around central and then up to Thingummy's. By the time we got to Thingummy's there was just a handful of us, and then sometimes just me. But by the time I had got downstairs, there were always a bunch of friendly faces. Peter would pour me a pint when he saw me, speak to me in Cantonese, I would smile and shake my head and go and sit with my friends. There I would stay most of the night with a few outings to 7/11 to get something to eat, noodles, tuna sandwich, but always head back to Thingummy's. If it was a friend's birthday we would head up to one of the pubs or clubs in Lang Kwai Fong and spend the night there. These were the weekdays but the weekends we usually headed to one of the beaches where we would take a carry out of beer and dance on the beach until we either got the last bus home or all shared a taxi.

Chapter Thirteen
Retribution

"What the fuck are you all looking at?"
"Fuck off the lot of you"
"You want some, come and get it pricks"
I picked up a table and threw it. A chair was next.
The rest of the class was huddled in a corner. The alarm was ringing. The officer was shouting at me trying to calm me down. Tears were streaming down my face. The voices in my head had finally formed one maelstrom of thunder. Everyone had been whispering about me, they were all taking little sideways looks at me. I had had enough. I jumped up and started screaming. The classroom door flew open and 5 officers ran in and pinned me to the ground. Blows of feet, fists, knees and batons poured down on top of me. I was screaming, I shit myself, pissed myself, everything just released out of me. I was dragged out and down to the governor's office.
They finally got off me when I had calmed down. I managed to stop sobbing and pulled myself up and tried to stand as proud as I could be in my shit and piss-stained uniform.

The governor decided that because of all the agro I was to be kept apart from the other prisoners. He refused my request to go to solitary. Every morning I was to be taken out of my cell last and every night I was to be put in first.
That night I was marched by myself to the cells and put into my cell before the others came upstairs. My cell was the first on the landing. The first prisoners to go past were the Vietnamese dogs. As they went past they started hurling insults at me. I reacted and ran to the front of my cell where I was met with an onslaught of spit and fists flying. I went mental, screaming and ripping off my shirt. I was clawing at the cell door wanting to rip it open so that I could grab one of them and beat them to death. After they passed the Chinese then walked past. They all stared at me and cursed at me, issuing obvious threats. I didn't run forward again in case I was spat at again. I just concentrated on working out. Doing push-ups trying to ignore their threats. It was like this every morning and every night for the next few weeks. I tried my best to ignore it by turning my back and doing push-ups and sit-ups. But every day I was becoming more

and more mentally damaged. I was starting to lose it again. At night my dreams would be full of me being murdered in the prison. The different ways it would happen. Sometimes I would go out in a blaze of glory the others I would be set upon by a bunch of them and be stabbed more times than I could count and slowly die there on the ground staring up to the sky.

One Sunday we were taken to the football pitch for the first time. This had been a moment I had been dreading ever since the trouble began. I remember the days at school playing football when if someone didn't like you they would kick you to pieces. This is what I was expecting to happen today. I was never any good at football. I was always chosen last at school or even after school when we played in the fields at the bottom of my street. I usually ended up playing in goal where I was actually quite good because of my size and for my ability to save the ball from any angle. I don't know how I just seemed to be able to judge it for some reason.

As the teams were being selected I noticed that the big brother was talking to one of his lieutenant's. I was put into the II team and went into the goal. It was very clear from the whistle what was going to happen. The lieutenant that the big brother had been talking too was their best player. He had been given instructions not to score past me to get the ball near our goal where he was to kick the shit out of me every chance he had. It really was schoolboy stuff and I was prepared. I had gone to school in Glasgow and I was English and everybody knew it. I was also very bad at socialising with people and was bullied continuously at school. Most of it was my own doing, well so said my teachers and family. I had been attacked both on and off the football pitch all the way through primary school and secondary. It was nothing new to me. From the very first kick of the ball the lieutenant was given the ball and ran straight towards me. He had too many thoughts going through his head about how he was going to get me that as soon as he was close I took the ball off him before he had time to decide. He ran back to the big brother who was not happy with him. Time and time again he came at me, from every angle and every time I took the ball off him without him being able to touch me. He was getting more and more frustrated. He began to even forget about the ball and just tried to get close enough to either kick or punch me but every time I managed to get the ball and even some times take him out whilst doing so. I would go down low, throw my body at him, knock him flying and stand up with the ball. By now

the big brother was screaming at him and instead of being 11 a side it was now just one against one and I was playing the game of my life. I was enjoying it, I loved it. I don't know who won or whether it was a draw but I know that they never scored against us. As the final whistle blew they were defeated. They looked defeated and were walking defeated. As we were leaving the pitch and I had my chest pumped up. The big brother walked over to me and said.
"This is China"
And walked off. I knew what he meant. But for the first time, I realised that this bunch of fierce prisoners were nothing more than a bunch of bullies, school dropouts that were scared of the guards and had to come up with pathetic attempts to get me instead of just an all-out assault which would get them into trouble. I wouldn't find out until much later that that wasn't the case and I was actually being protected by forces unknown to me at that point and that any attack on me had to be sanctioned by someone a lot further up.
The next week we went out to play again. This time I wasn't in goal. And this time I was chosen to be on the same side as the lieutenant. I was in the same team as the big brother too. Maybe winning a football game was more important to them. We played well together, maybe this would be the turning point I had dreamed of. I played a fantastic pass from the right wing. It curled into the box right on the end of the lieutenant's foot and he drove the ball into the net. I turned around and jogged away knowing that no one would come up to congratulate me. In the second half, the game continued from where it had left off with me playing on the wing and crossing the ball into the lieutenant for him to score. I was running down the left wing after a ball, totally relaxed now, not looking out to see if anyone was going to attack me when it happened. They had played a good hand. I was totally relaxed. Concentrating on the game on the ball when a tall guy came thundering into me. He took me mid leg with both his feet. He went straight through me. I went flying and skidded along the ground for a few feet before I came to a stop. The adrenalin was pumping through me and I jumped up straight away ready for any afters and then I fell down. I didn't understand what was going on. I tried to get up again but fell straight back down. I then felt hands on my shoulders pushing me back down onto the ground; it was one of the guards. I stared at them over my shoulders and then looked at the others as they started to come round me. I then looked down and the bottom half of my leg was all wrong. The rest is a bit hazy. I was

taken to the hospital and a short time later I was in an ambulance being driven out of the prison. I don't know if they had given me pain relief but my head was swimming. I can't remember how long it took but we eventually arrived at the hospital where I was wheeled into the reception. I was handcuffed to the trolley to make sure I couldn't jump up and run away. I was a bit out of it and remember looking at all the people around me in the waiting room and saying things like crazy foreigner and making strange noises. I was then taken in a lift where there were some frightened-looking normal people in it too and I was making strange faces and noises whilst they were staring at this strange foreigner handcuffed to a bed and surrounded by prison guards with lots of guns. We eventually got to the prison ward which was in the basement of the hospital where I was wheeled to a large cell that had 8 hospital beds behind a wall of bars. I was taken in and dumped in one of the beds. I then fell asleep.

Chapter -13

Lennon

The first time I met Lennon was in Thingummy's.

I was sitting in my usual spot getting drunk with some friends. I had just given the duke box key back to Peter so that I could add free credit and choose some of our favourite songs. When a young Chinese guy came and sat next to our group. He was older than us, didn't say anything but laughed when we laughed and acted like he was part of our group. He was a big lad, looked like he worked out, but a nice guy. After a while and a few more beers, he nudged me.

"I'm Lennon"

"Hi"

I said.

"I want learn English, you help me?"

Well, me being me I said,

"Why not"

And that was that. For the rest of the night, we chatted and I shared some phrases in English with him. He picked it all up very quickly, his English wasn't that bad.

At the end of the evening, we said our goodbyes.

The next night I was in again, must have been the weekend, and there was Lennon. He bought me drinks all night and our friendship continued. So that was that. A brief description of how a triad made friends with an ex-pat. Little was I to know that he had plans.

Chapter Fourteen
Hospital Dungeon of Death

I don't know how long I was asleep for but when I woke up I was a bit dazed and confused, it was then the pain hit me. My leg was bandaged from the groin to the ankle with a huge bandage and it was in agony.

As I looked around the room little did I know that this would be my home for the next two months as I waited for an operation that would be continuously cancelled because someone else who was not a convicted criminal would need an operation before me?

It would also be the last time I would ever take heroin, but that was all to come. The first few days I was off my head on pain relief, I didn't really take much in. Eventually, on the third day, I became fully conscious. My room had actually only 6 beds and they were all full. The guy next to me was an older guy who had tried to kill himself when he was arrested. He had murdered his wife and then taken the knife to himself. He had stabbed himself in the stomach and when that hadn't worked tried to cut his throat. Looking at the wound he very nearly succeeded. It was quite grotesque and would open a little sometimes if he laughed or coughed. Two of the other guys just lay there and stared into space, dying of some sort of disease that I never found out what. But they looked like they were about to die and in both of them did a short time later and were taken out without much fanfare and replaced by another two who looked like they were also about to kick it, but at least the sheets were still warm for them as the staff hadn't changed them. Breakfast lunch and dinner were a lot better than the prison. It arrived in polystyrene pots and was just like the street food I used to buy at the little roadside cafes. Sometimes it was delicious. On the third day, I tried to get out of bed because I really wanted a shower but when I tried I just fell on the floor, pain shooting through my leg and then the rest of my body. I didn't really know what was wrong me and would never find out. I mean I know there was something wrong with my leg, but was the bone broken, ligaments, dislocated. I had no idea, and nobody was about to tell me. On day four I eventually worked out how to operate my bed and managed to sit up properly. I was then able to see that there was another cell straight across from us and at that very point I witnessed a very strange complaint. There was an old guy standing at the bars in his underwear with what could only be called one gigantic testicle hanging down through his shorts! It was hard not to stare at such a sight and I started coming up immediately with strange songs to the same tune as Hitler only had one ball, but it was huge!! A short time later a new patient was hauled into our cell and was plonked on a rattan matt on the floor. After quite a long attempt at communication as he was an II from somewhere in the north of china we found out that he had woken up on the morning unable to feel anything below his waist, he was paralysed. But he also had 12 fingers and 12 toes which was just as interesting. He just lay there on the floor. A short time later someone in a white coat came in. I would have called him a doctor in any other hospital-related drama but I really couldn't be sure. He spent the next 30 minutes with a needle torturing this guy on the floor by pushing the needle into lots of different parts of his body to see if he was acting or not. The poor guys had wee pools of blood all over his legs but also on his arms and body because they wanted to make sure that he registered pain in other places. They started shouting at him for wasting their time and that they would just throw him back into prison because they didn't believe him. They let him slump to the floor again and walked out. The wee guy's expression never changed. I don't know if his paralysis was psychological but he definitely appeared to be paralysed to me. He just lay there for days and then one day they came in and carted him off to who knows were. After about a week of being confined to my bed, I finally saw someone who appeared to be employed in the medical profession. Three in white coats came in. unwrapped my bandages. Poked me and bandaged me back up again and went out. The next thing I knew I was told to come to the cell door. Okay, I thought I am going to do this. I had pissed in a bottle all week but today I am going to get out of bed. The most difficult and painful part was putting my leg lower than the rest of my body, it was when the blood going down into my leg caused so much pressure the pain was almost too much. But this time I was prepared and managed to get my leg down and put the pain out of my head. I hopped and slithered over to the cell door where I was told to put my hand through and they were handcuffed together. Obviously to stop me sprinting away! The cell door opened and I was ushered out to the middle of the room outside the cells where a person in a white coat was standing with a catheter set. I knew what it was; it wasn't my first time in hospital. I actually felt quite excited I was going to be operated on at last and have my leg fixed. I hobbled over to the white coat that had everything laid out on a hospital cabinet. He took my right hand and started to insert the needle of the catheter. In it went, and back out it came. In it went again and back out it came. Where's the vein hiding I thought trying not to show any pain on my face. Even now I didn't want to show any negative emotion. Not wanting to show any weakness. So there I stood on my, I don't know how smashed up, leg with a white coat sticking a needle into the back of my right-hand time and time again trying to get a vein. The back of my hand was a bloody mess with bruising starting to add to the horrid discolouration. He gave up with that hand and started on the left, thankfully after only 5 or 6 events, he managed to find a vein and successfully inserted the catheter. He looked at me with beads of sweat on his brow and I stared right back at him. He honestly looked as if expectedly me to kill him. But I just turned around and hobbled back to the cell door which was opened and allowed me to hobble back to my bed. I only sat on the side of the bed and then asked to go to the toilet. I was vertical for the first time in a long time so what was the point in wasting that effort. I went to the bathroom and found it to be pretty clean with a row of showers, behind a separate door I found to my great delight a bathtub. Oh my god, I was going to have a bath as soon as these bandages come off. I went to the toilet and decided to have a half shower as well as I was filthy. It was the best as I had to keep my bandages clean but it felt good. By the time I got back to the cell and had the cuffs taken off again another white coat came in and stuck a needle in the catheter. This guy actually told me that he was giving a pre-op. Thank God for that, at last, I was going to get fixed. Within the next hour, the op was cancelled. This happened so many times that I never got excited again. However, after about a month the day finally came where I was given the pre-op and 30 minutes later they came for me. I was handcuffed to a trolley and taken up to the theatre.

I was back in my bed when I came too, leg bandaged again but this time with a completely different feeling and covered in blood.

I fell back to sleep.

The next day I was actually lying in bed and woke to find a doctor, yes an actual doctor next to me talking to someone else with a white coat, but then he was off. I nearly found out what they did to me but not quite.

Over the next couple of days, I managed to get out of bed more often. I even managed to get a shower or two without getting my bandages too wet. That night I was lying on the bed when something extremely interesting happened. One of the older prisoners was at the front cell bars keeping watch whilst another was calling up a tiny gap between the wall and the ceiling. He was shouting out instructions to someone above. Then after a minute or two, a small package started to appear and slowly came down towards the guy's outstretched hand. He managed to grab it, and the string disappeared again only to reappear with another package. This happened four or five more times. Then it was over, all packages were received. They quickly undid the packages. There were cigarettes and small wraps. When they opened them I saw straight away that it was smack. The instant I saw it I wanted it. After all these months spending hours alone in my prison cell thinking about how I had ended up there. Thinking about how I had to change. How I never wanted to be in this position again my first thought was that I wanted some. I last had smack the day I was arrested, not before my arrest but after. I had been in the police station for hours being questioned over and over again. I said nothing to them. I had been warned, you say anything and you are dead, simple as that. They repeatedly asked me about my family, their names, phone numbers, address, and I refused to say anything. Eventually, though they tracked them down. During the formal interview when both my parents were present, they brought out the smack that I had in my pocket for personal use. When they brought it out some spilt on the table. Now it was probably not noticed by anyone else but because I was starting the withdrawal process the small bit of white powder that was on the table was the biggest thing in the room. I slowly moved my hands towards it, rubbed my fingers over it and then rubbed it on my gums. Nobody noticed and this was the last time I had any. It was now more than 8 months later and I was still an addict even though I hadn't touched it. It shows you how strong addiction is. The prison system had another part to it for lesser offences committed by drug addicts and that is a six-month treatment programme that they must complete at a drug treatment centre. But here I was after all these months still an addict. The guys quickly made a couple of cigarette joints and lit them. They licked the outside of the cigarette so that it would burn more slowly. After they had both had a few puffs each it was offered to me and I took it straight away and inhaled deeply. I took a few puffs and passed it back. And that was me. I climbed back into my bed and drifted off. I awoke the next day wanting more, but there was no more to be had.

That was it. I was mentally craving it but had no physical withdrawals. I hadn't had enough to be physically addicted again.

A couple of days later my bandages were taken off and I could see for the first time what they had done to my leg. It was a huge surprise that I saw only three small scars on my knee. Unknown to me I had actually received a quite good new treatment. They had performed keyhole surgery on whatever was wrong with my knee. I now knew it was my knee that was the problem, didn't know it before just thought it was my whole leg. I was helped out of bed and with some basic hand signals was told to try to bend it. It was extremely painful. I was given a bit of paper written in Chinese but with some pictures showing me some basic exercises to do. It was never translated for me but I could work out from the little Chinese that I had picked up over the last eight months, namely written numbers that I had to do the exercises three times a day. So I did and did them a bit more. Each day I would get out of bed and practice walking then I would start the bending exercises. Then one day I was allowed out of the cell to have a shower. I hobbled straight to the bath and filled it with hot water and slowly sunk into it. I felt like Cleopatra with her warm asp milk bath! It was a huge luxury; I stayed in for as long as I could.

Chapter-14

Prom

Acting the gentleman I bought Rosie a corsage and got a taxi to her house to pick her up. She was in my law class and I had asked her to the Prom. She was very pretty with curly brown hair and really smart. She wasn't one of the party crowd either, which was just perfect.

This was a big deal. I would have to meet her family and be very polite. However, this was no big deal for me, because deep down that who I really was. She looked beautiful in a dark blue dress with puffy sleeves, tight waist with the hem filling out down to her knees. Beautiful indeed. I was feeling very dapper in the tuxedo Blakey had helped me pick out to hire. We got into a taxi and went straight to the Hilton Hotel where the dance was taking place. What a sight it was. All the guys in Tuxedos and all the girls in amazing dresses. We danced all night, stuck by each other's sides. Twirling and jigging. At one point there was a dancing competition so Rosie and I jumped onto the floor and danced away. I wasn't really paying much attention to anyone else I was simply enchanted by how gorgeous Rosie looked. At one point I looked around and there were only a few couples left on the dance floor. Others had been randomly chosen to leave the floor to let us that were remaining dance it out to see who would be crowned king and queen of the prom. Up until that moment I had been completely relaxed but now with the light on us I started to freeze, but Rosie expertly calmed me down and we started dancing together again as if we had been born dancers. To my absolute astonishment, we were suddenly the only couple left on the dance floor with huge cheers going up all around us, Rosie and I were king and queen of the prom. I couldn't take it in. from being the most despised person in my last school to being the king of the prom within the same year. We had to go up to the DJ and accept our prize which was a lunch for four at the Hilton on a Sunday.

What a buzz. When the dance finished Rosie had to go home but I decided to stay on with my pals and ended up going to Lan Kwai Fong where we all danced away looking amazing in our prom outfits. It was a great night. One I won't forget. The night when I was made a king.

Chapter Fifteen
Sleeping with the dead

I had been in the hospital for about 2 months now and was actually dying to get back to prison. Some people around me were actually dying and it was never fun sitting in your cell with a dead body whilst they organised to have it removed. I remember this one guy, one of the first I saw in my hospital cell; well he died shortly after I arrived. It was at least a couple of hours when they finally came to take him away. He just lay there uncovered dead until they ordered us to our beds whilst they picked him up and dumped him on a trolley and wheeled him out. I don't know how many died or what they died of but there were a few. Some had died in the night and had probably been dead a number of hours before anyone took any notice of them. Some were old and other young. Some looked terribly ill, and others not so much. I suppose a lot of them had been inside for many years and this was to be their last cell. At least they died outside the prison if that was any consolation.

Eventually, I was met by a physiotherapist who gave me a walking stick and taught me how to use it. After a few days of getting used to it, I was told that I would be leaving to go back to prison. At least I was leaving this place of death alive.

Chapter -15

Missing in Action

The partying got harder and harder the closer to Christmas we got. I had met many people now who had their own flats so had been spending a lot of time staying with friends. There was little point going home. No bed to sleep in made a bed at and my friends somewhat of a better proposition. And when my dad was home it was just horrendous. I thought that his promotion may have made life a bit better. But now that he was home most of the time instead of working away, his drinking was a constant as well as my mums. The times I tried to stay at home in the evening, sitting there watching TV with them drinking their Whisky and Bacardi, was just not fun. Even if I was tired I couldn't go to bed because my bed was the couch where they sat for at least 6 hours every night drinking. Then because he was hungover in the morning he would come into the living room and start shouting at me calling me a lazy bastard and to get out of bed and get to school, whilst my mum, bleary-eyed, would stagger into the kitchen to try and make breakfast. She would be so all over the place, and the kitchen so small so I couldn't get in there to make myself anything, I usually left the house without having anything to eat at all. Sometimes I had to take money out of her purse just so that I could buy some food at school and pay for my McDonalds and time in the pub later. I now could run up a tab at Thingummy's. I paid it once a week when my mum gave me some money. But there was no life at home anymore, and I just didn't want to be there. My brother had his own room, so he could hide in there, but I know it was affecting him too.
So on Christmas Eve this year, I didn't go home. I didn't go home until 3 am on the 5th of January. I collapsed on the couch only to be woken by my dad.
"Shit, here we go"
I thought. Thinking that I was going to get a complete battering from him. I suppose it would show he cared, so that would be positive. But no, I was wrong.
"You have to get up at 7 am because you're playing cricket"
He and his friends had organized a cricket match at the Kowloon cricket club and I had to play. That was it. I hadn't seen him since the 24th December, hadn't spoken to my family, and that was it? No

mention of where I had been, all I had to do was not let him down by playing cricket for his fucked up drunken mates.

New Year

But before that, it was New Year. I had been staying at different friends houses. You see so many of my friends had families with a lot of money. They didn't just have a bedroom most of them had a separate part of the house with a lounge and everything so it was easy to crash at theirs. Also a lot of them their parents worked away so the house was empty, so party. Some of their families had even left them in Hong Kong whilst they went home to their own countries for the holidays, leaving my friends in the capable hands of the amah's (Filipino housemaids) and drivers. Sometimes the drivers would come and pick us up in the families limo and drive us about, McDonald's, 7/11 Lan Kwai Fong, where ever we needed to go. And my friends had money, not just money, but a lot of money. It would seem that most parents chose to deal with their guilt of not seeing their kids by giving them tons of money. On Christmas day itself, Rosie and I went with our friend onto his dad's company's yacht. His dad was the president of HSBC so as you can imagine the yacht was amazing.

I can't remember all the parties that I went to. But I didn't see Rosie at all during this time, and to be honest we had pretty much split up by then. So on New Year's, we all headed to Thingummy's to start the night's celebrations. It was incredible. That was a night that I became a man, I think. I kissed so many girls that night, 6 I think I remember. But not only that within the first hour I was screwing this redhead from a different school in the rat-infested alley next to Thingummy's, as I said incredible. No condoms were discussed just casual sex. And she wasn't the only one. By the end of the night, I had sex with three different girls and snogged I think at least 6. I wasn't the only one to be doing this. It was mental. I remember at one point walking up to 7/11 to get more cigarettes and practically having to step over two teenagers who were on top of each other in the middle of the street. It was mental. We left Thingummy's and staggered up to Lan Kwai Fong. Then someone shouted
"You want to Tria Fuck"
"What"
I said rubbing my ears
"Tria Fuck, you wanna go Tria Fuck"

Still looking confused one of my mates said
"Friar Tucks"
A pub around the corner on Ice House Street.
Laughing we headed towards this new pub with the hilarious name.
As soon as I stepped inside I saw her.
She was sensational.
I don't know what it was about her, but she shocked me sober.
She took my breath away; I just stood and stared at her. She was the most beautiful person I had ever seen in my life.
She turned and saw me. She locked her eyes on me, and what was this, she was coming towards me, smiling. She took my hand and led me over to a table, and kissed me. What the hell, what was going on? This couldn't be possible.
"You don't know me, do you?'
She asked between breaths and kissing.
"I know you, I was there at the prom trying to get your attention, and you don't remember seeing me do you"
"No, I don't sssorry?"
She kissed me again.
"You want to know my name?'
"It's Allison"
And she started kissing me again, she wouldn't stop. I don't know if I got a drink in the pub but soon my friends were telling me we had to go. I was being wrestled out of the door with Allison still stuck to my face.
We were on the street before she let go.
I just looked at her, in total shock as my friends dragged me away. What was I doing, I was going away from heaven. At 16 years old I was overcome. Overcome with her energy, her amazing energy. And then I was around the corner and she was gone.

Chapter Sixteen
Back Home

When I got back to the prison I went through the normal routine of a full search. I had gotten used to it a bit by now but by no means was it a pleasant matter. I was taken straight to the prison hospital and admitted because I still wasn't able to walk very well. But before I was fully admitted to the hospital ward I had to wait to see the doctor. I quite liked seeing the doctor as he was the only person who actually spoke English to me. Even though he didn't actually speak directly to me as he was a little odd he would only speak in English so that I always knew what was going on.

When he eventually appeared I was sent into his office. He was sitting there reading my notes. I couldn't make out everything he said but I picked up medial meniscus, ligament damage. It was the first time I had heard what was wrong although I didn't really understand what it meant. He then said the following "won't be able to run again or walk uphill without assistance"

That floored me. It wasn't said to me, there was no clarification towards me. No discussion about what was to be done. And as always I wasn't allowed to talk so could ask no questions.

I was then admitted back into the ward. Back into the ward with this huge weight of what he just said. It didn't sound right, it couldn't be correct. It didn't feel that bad but was it. No, I couldn't believe it. And I at that very point was determined for it not to be the case. But all that had to wait as I had to deal with all the new faces in the ward. I had to size them up. See who thought they were in charge, see what the hierarchy was and see how I was going to fit into it.

The first thing I noticed was that the child rapist was not in the first bed anymore. A small fat strange, poking out eyes Chinese guy was now the hospital boy. He brought me my white hospital uniform. All the beds were filled with new guys. I had to take the only free bed which was next to the wall at the far end. It was a proper hospital bed so was quite nice. One of the new guys had his hand in the most amazing of devices. Connected at his wrist a claw of steel was coming out with bits of wire attached to each finger. It looked like a new injury as it was in a bit of a state his hand. Huge red scars covered his hand. I found out later that when he was being arrested he put his hand through a window. Another guy was a young triad. He was covered neck to feet with tattoos. The most amazing tattoos I had ever seen. Although not coloured they were amazing. His whole body was one tattoo really. A snake a dragon and a phoenix covered and wrapped their way around his body until their heads met at his stomach where there was a ball representing the sun. But what was more amazing was that he had the most chopper wounds to his body that I had ever seen someone alive with. They were everywhere from his head across his chest, his right arm was nearly halved at the elbow, on his stomach and both legs. He had been in a real fight and unbelievably had survived what must have been a horrific attack. He was also only a small guy but must be one tough mother fucker. But was no risk due to his injuries. The other two were nothing to talk about, I've forgotten about them.

We spent the days as we had before rolling out toilet paper for the rest of the prison. Each prisoner was given four squares of toilet paper a day and it was our job to divide the toilet roles into the four-piece rations that would be handed out in the evening.

I had developed a method where I could roll out a whole roll on my bed with each four squares slight offline with each other so that I could finish a whole role and then just gently pull the paper apart. It sped up the process and I had normally finished my quota before anybody else and would usually take some of their quotas to help them. Danny the tranny and one of his pals would be brought to the ward on a daily basis. Danny had been released from his last sentence and was back in again on another petty theft charge, something like stealing makeup from a shop. He had been taking more of his hormone injections so his breasts were quite impressive now.

I settled back into the hospital routine, I was actually quite high up in the hierarchy in the hospital. I was known and I suppose a little respected. I got into my push-ups and sit-ups even though it was still quite difficult because of my leg but it wasn't long before I was up to 50 push-ups again without much bother. Different prisoners came and went. One I remember was a cannabis addict. One of the most addicted individuals, I had met and ever will. He came in and it was obvious he had been living rough for a very long time. He was stripped and his body was caked in dirt. It was so thick you thought that it was actually part of him. He was painfully thin and his hair was crawling. He was thrown into the shower room and had the hose turned on him. It really was a sorry state to see. After a few minutes, it was obvious that the dirt wasn't coming off so he was given a hard bristled brush to scrub his body but he was so week that he couldn't even do that so the guards ordered the prison orderly to go in and scrub him. He was screaming out in pain but it had to be done. Eventually, he was clean and then it was decided that his hair had to be shaved but because he was so wet a dry razor had to be used. After he was mostly bald with just a few patches left he was dried off and covered in powder. He wasn't allowed in the main cell so was put into one of the side cells where the really damaged prisoners go. He was there a week before being moved out. He never made a sound as if he had never been there.

Chapter -16

Love

The first day back at school the front hall was filled with students. I can't remember why but there were names on boards in the hallway, it could have been for exams or something. But the whole school seemed to be filling the space. People were greeting each other after the holidays and there was a huge noise from all the excited voices. It was difficult to make yourself heard. I was looking around for my friends when something magical happened. As I turned to my right it was as if on command all the students in front of me started parting. First the ones right next to me then the next ones and the next like some kind of strange human domino effected. I stood there staring at what was happening. Then it was as if a bright light shone from nowhere and there she was standing right in front of me. It was as if I was seeing an angel. My whole being turned to jelly, it was an overwhelming feeling. She was standing there smiling at me, and I started smiling back. We moved together as if on a moving walkway, hers towards me and mine towards her. And then we were together. No words would come to me; I stood there in amazement and awe at this incredibly beautiful girl standing in front of me giving of all the energy that I was feeling. She was as I was. We were the same. I couldn't speak, she couldn't speak. It was her, it was Allison.
Then one of her friends whispered in my ear
"Ask her for her number'
Beverly said
"Can I have your number?"
I barely got out
"Yes its'........"
And she gave me her number, and then the crowd started closing in on us again and the school bell went and she disappeared.

Chapter Seventeen
Suicide

The next prisoners to go into that cell are a completely different story, an extremely sad story. Because of the newspaper censorship in prison, I never knew the true extent of their crimes.

Anyone who is sentenced to a life sentence spent their first night in one of these side cells for observation. Even though most will be expecting the sentence it is always a huge blow when it happens.

This day two boys of about 15 were brought in. they had just been sentenced to life for murder. Something that they had both been involved in and sentenced together, that's all we could gather at the time. They were obviously very down and looked like two of the saddest people I had ever seen. Now there they were. At lock-up at 7 pm, all the cells are locked and we are allowed free time until the lights go out at 9 pm. All the prison keys are taken to the gatehouse and locked away as I knew when I had to wait a couple of hours whilst I was having an asthma attack in my cell one night. Anyway, this night after lights out and we had all gone to bed we heard the noise that after being in that prison long enough you know exactly what it meant. I had heard the noise many times before and had learned by the commotion from other prisoners who had also heard the noise I quickly learned that it meant that someone had stood on their chair tied a self-made rope as high as they could and had tipped the chair over to hang themselves. There was never another explanation for that noise. That noise always represented a hanging. In each of the side cells, there was a fibreglass table and chair along with the bed. Because there were two of them an extra mattress had been put on the floor and an extra fibreglass chair had been put inside. The noise is the scraping of the chair across the floor then it hitting the ground.

A hanging.

I and the orderly jumped out of our beds and ran to the cell door where there is a square gap in the solid metal with bars. You could see across to the other cells and see right inside as the door was fully barred. What we saw will stay with me forever. The two boys were hanging there, choking, clawing at their necks. Eyes wide spit coming out their mouths. The orderly hit the in cell alarm and I shouted for the night guard. I shouted and shouted as they had a habit of just ignoring you. The orderly came and started shouting in

Cantonese. The night guard then came running, but as he had no keys he was off again. By this time the other prisoners were at the door trying to get a look, the orderly had seen enough and moved aside for someone else. I just stood there watching them, I watched them die. Both of them with different twitches and spasms then one of them would find some bit of energy and start flailing again but stop abruptly. The guard was back in a few minutes, a few minutes too late with another guard, but with no keys yet. It was what seemed like another 5 minutes before the keys arrived. By this time they had shouted at us to get back to our beds. It didn't really matter that the keys had arrived and in all honesty, if they had arrived when the second guard arrived it was probably too late. I tried to sneak another quick peek but there were too many guards and I didn't want to get another bollocking so I went back to bed. There was nothing to say, nothing to do, so we all went to sleep. I bet we all had strange dreams that night. I just thought of them both deciding to go out together. When had they decided? Was it during their trial? Had they made a pact that if they got found guilty they would do it or was it a spur of the moment action? Whatever they were not there in the morning and nothing was ever shared with us. And we knew we wouldn't be reading about it in the newspapers.

Of course, we mentioned it together a few times but over the next few days, there was a quiet calmness in the hospital. We got on with our normal daily duties and that was that.

Chapter -17
The Deal

It was Friday night. It must have been some kind of holiday because everywhere was jumping. I had been in Thingummy's all night and was now standing on the street outside with a large group of friends. We were all in a heated discussion of where we were going to head next. All of us a bit pissed and standing in the middle of the streets holding pints. The whole street had groups of teenagers hanging around. Some sitting on the steps on the pavement others in the middle of the road. I spotted another three that I knew from the year below me, or two years, I couldn't remember. They caught my attention because they kept looking up towards us whilst they were whispering. They were planning something, I didn't know what, but I was on guard instinctively. I may have had no problems here in Hong Kong but that didn't change who I was after years of being attacked and beaten in Scotland, I was always on edge.

"What are you guys up?"
I thought as I tried not to be obvious that I had seen them looking at us. I turned back to my group of friends and joined the conversation,
"Beach hut"
"97"
We were back to discussing which club to go to when there was a pull on my sleeve.
I look round and then down to the girl who had been with the two other guys who were whispering.
With a big bright smile, she said,
"Do you know where we can buy some grass?"
Firstly, I had never seen grass
Secondly, I had no idea where to buy it
Thirdly, I wanted to look cool as she had come up to me to ask, so I didn't want to admit that I didn't know and
Forth, I didn't really think that they should be taking drugs. They looked drunk already. It had only been quite recently that I had to look after a young girl who was so drunk she was unconscious. She was lying on the street outside Thingummy's, dumped by her pals in a short blue dress with drunk old Mr lee trying to pull up her dress. She was going to be raped, no doubt about it. I picked her up and took her to the park across the road and put her on a bench. I sat with her

that night for 5 hours until she sobered up enough to go home. So I thought for a moment and then said,
"Wait here"
I headed up into the same park, where I had sat with Lucy that night. I took out 3 Marlboro lights from the packet I had and then removed the film sleeve from the packet. I open the three cigarettes and put the tobacco into the sleeve. I held it up to the dim light that illuminated the park into hundreds of shadows. I was totally in the dark w whether it looked anything like grass. But I shrugged my shoulders to myself and headed back out onto the street and nodded for the three kids to come over. I said,
"20 bucks"
They handed me the money, and I handed them the "drugs"
"Be careful, it's really strong"
I told them.
They nodded and scurried away towards the 7/11 to get rolling papers. I went back over to my friends and joined back in with the drunken discussion.
"Where do you want to go?"
"I don't mind"
"Where do you want to go?"
"I told you I don't mind".
We decided eventually to go and get something to eat before we went up to Lan Kwai Fong. We were all really drunk so thought 7/11 noodles would help us last the night; I used the $20's that she had given me to put towards our noodle bill.
An hour later we were back outside Thingummy's at the same spot waiting for a few others to come up from the cave below. When they climbed out of the darkness and joined us we all turned and headed towards clubland. To my right, I saw the three kids from earlier. The two boys were sitting on the pavement rolling around whilst the girl who had taken the "drugs" off of me was swinging around a lamppost, head flung back.
When she saw me and managed to focus her eyes she said'
"That was really good shit man, thanks a lot"
I nodded to her, trying to hold myself together, as soon as my group walked around the corner I started laughing,
"What's your fuckin problem man?"
I told them what had happened, and everyone started laughing.

I kept laughing at the 3 kids stoned from 3 Marlboro lights without using a filter as we headed toward the noise and the lights, clubland, for a night of full-on dancing. I had no idea then how much that one interaction was going to devastate my life.

Chapter Eighteen

Physiotherapy

One day I was in the ward and my number was called out.
"90760, choi sam" (Get dressed)
Get dressed. Now, this shout by a guard was very unusual for me these days. In the beginning, it happened quite a lot and meant that I had a police visit. But I was now convicted so if it was a police visit I was in deep shit. Had they discovered a crime I had committed that I hadn't been sentenced for already? I didn't think so, well I hoped not, because some of them could carry a hefty sentence. So I got dressed and stood next to the cell door like a good boy with my walking stick. The door was opened and I was told to sit in the waiting room.
"Gwai Gi cho di"
I waited and then was told to get up, was handcuffed, which meant using my stick was very difficult and taken outside. In the prison main gate area, there was a high-security prison van, the ones used for very serious offenders. I had never been in one before so this was an interesting experience in some regards. The van had 6 doors that ran down the sides of a central corridor. Each door led to a tiny room that had a seat that was just big enough to sit down in. but because I am tall my legs were right up against the wall in front which for me with a bad leg was extremely uncomfortable. I managed to squirm sideways in the seat to get somewhat comfortable. I wasn't comfortable at all and that was when we weren't even moving. As soon as the van started driving the movement sent waves of pain through my leg. We then stopped for the obligatory check-in at the main prison gate hall. I was the only one in the van so it was over quickly and the main gates opened and we were off again. A journey to I didn't know where in a tiny box stinking of what I did know. It stank of piss, shit and body odder. The walls had been engraved with a thousand names and stories. Numbers were predominant I didn't know what they meant but some of them looked like the length of sentence, 10, 15, 30 were common figures. The box had a heavyweight of depression lingering as if thousands of souls were still trapped inside. I could feel it all around me. All most taste it and smell it. It was thicker than the smell of human waste. It was the smell of human waste as if part of their souls had been discarded in this box as punishment and would live here forever to torment the individual for the crimes they committed. But with everything, there

is an opposite. This is china and yin and yang is everywhere. So for all those rightfully convicted of their crimes the opposite must also be true and that some of the discarded pieces of souls were from those convicted of crimes they did not commit but were destined to spend 10, 15 and 30 years in prison for. There was a tiny slot window but it had been gratified so much that it was only letting in a tiny bit of light and would not allow the viewer any scene from outside. That was irony. The countless souls who had put graffiti on the inside, displaying their despair of being removed from the outside world, damaging the window so much that any last look at the world outside was stolen for those who came after them. Was it done purposefully but subconsciously so that they could have some of their despair shared with others to lighten their own burden? I would never know but without the view, I had all this time to think of it. I had to think of something. That was my safety net. Fill my head with thoughts of my own choosing so that my mind never for one moment had a time of emptiness that could be taken over with my own thoughts of despair. It was probably what had kept me sane so far. When you are blindfolded and on a journey to an unknown destination which is an unknown distance away and what awaits you is unknown, slipping into despair and even panic. This box had witnessed all of that over the years. Maybe it had formed its own soul net to capture the damaged souls. Maybe it fed off them. The van stopped. The door to the box opened. It was then that I had realised that throughout the whole journey I had forgotten the pain in my leg. I thanked the box as I painfully straightened my leg and the pain came back. I thanked it for helping me forget. I hobbled up and caught myself from falling with my walking stick and shuffled down the corridor to the back of the van and immediately winced at the bright day outside. When my pupils had finally dilated enough I was able to admire my surroundings. A car park with mown lawns with trees and shrubbery. And behind it, a single-story red-bricked quaint old building. I was taken to the building, through a reception area and then into a large room. I finally realised where I was and what was happening. The room was full of equipment that was being used by lots of people, most of them were old and accompanied by someone in a uniform. It was a physiotherapy centre. I was amazed again at the level of care I was receiving. Nobody looked at me this time as I was taken shuffling to the end of the room and introduced me to a Chinese woman in a uniform who was going to be my physiotherapist. Nobody was interested in me. They were all too engrossed in what they were doing to even notice me and the two prison guards coming in. My physiotherapist Miss Chan was next to a set of stairs that went up and down to nowhere, quite reminiscent of my thoughts during the journey here. She explained to me that she had been tasked to get me to be able to walk up and down stairs unaided. So that's exactly what we did for the next hour. Up and down the stairs. The only stairs that I had attempted recently were the steps into the van and back out again. I hadn't realised how bad my knee actually was. I was taken back to the doctor's office where he read that I wouldn't be able to walk uphill unaided or ever run again. And at that time I said to myself that they were wrong and I would achieve it all. I had said that to myself before I had even experienced hills or even stairs. Now I was coming to realising how difficult it was actually going to be. Because I had not used my leg for over 2 months the muscles were wasted. My knee hadn't been bent in all that time either. At the first attempt, she took my stick away from me and I actually started to panic. I almost fell but managed to grab the handrail that accompanied the steps all the way up and down again. There I stood, with both hands grabbing the same rail, both legs wobbling and then shaking. It was a humbling experience and for once I almost felt my resolving crumble and my eyes welled up with tears that I managed to get rid of quickly. Real emotion for the first time in months, I wasn't going to allow that to happen. So over the next hour, we worked on me trying to lift my leg up to the first step, when that had been achieved, I had to try and put my weight on it. Every time I tried I failed. At the end of the hour, I was feeling pathetic, lost and a complete failure. But Miss Chan told me that this was just the beginning and that I would be coming every week until I had succeeded and that it was her job to make it happen. I stumbled back to the van at the end of the session with a mixture of emotions. First I was going to get out of prison once a week for the foreseeable future, which was a positive even though I would have to go through the whole search procedure when I got back. It wasn't as bad anymore, I had somewhat got used to having it been through it so many times now. It wasn't pleasant and it wasn't my first choice of how to finish a fun day out, but it was worth it. I was going to get weekly what some of the guys inside would only get after 10 or 15 years. The only view that they would have of the outside was the top of a solitary tree that could only be seen at one corner of the wall and only if you were in that part of the prison. I realised that I was going to physiotherapist only because the prison needed me to be able to walk up and downstairs so that I could go back to the general population. So, on the one hand, they were helping me to get better but on the other, they were helping me to go back into hell. I was someone in the prison hospital and no one in general population. I also wanted to get better too. But I was stuck with the previous realisation that when I got better enough to go back I may be sent back to the hospital in an even worse condition if I even made back to the hospital and not out the prison feet first. This was a real possibility in my mind.

Chapter -18
Out!

I was a little sad that my week of work experience at the head office of the English School's Foundation was coming to an end. When I had first been told that was where I was going to work I wasn't happy. I had been supposed to find my own place to spend the week. Most of my friends were going to work with their parents. Asking my dad was not going to happen, I didn't want to be turned down by him again in my life. Anyway, my new party lifestyle had led me to concentrate less and less in school. I only found it possible to sleep at home when my dad wasn't there as well, when he was away was the only time when I could get some sort of sleep on the old sofa in the front room. Although when he wasn't there I had become so entrenched in my new life that I still went out drinking every night at Thingummy's. I would head home sometimes at midnight but mostly 3 am after the clubs. When he was at home I stayed with friends, lots of different friends. Or I would stay out in the clubs as late as I could, sneak home and get changed then head out to school, sometimes without having slept at all.

Anyway, I had enjoyed this week. I had a list of things I had to do in the office each morning. The best was weighing and then stamping the mail in the franking machine. Because when I had finished I was to take all the mail down to the central post office to post them. This gave me the freedom to walk around this amazing city streets, discovering back alleys, short cuts from here to there. This city continually excited me. I would see openings and head towards them to see where they led to. Some of the alleys were so narrow and disgusting that you had to go sideways very carefully so that you didn't touch the sides. I would find entrances to underground caverns where the rain from the monsoon would gather so as not to flood the city. I would go through buildings and find that so many of them are connected above ground level so that you could walk from Wan Chai to central without ever having to go to street level. Whenever a security guard would try and stop me I would show them my red post bag and shout

"Mail boy"

And they would smile and wave me through; I had complete access to this city and started to dream that it was mine and always would be. I was part of its heartbeat, the hidden part that no-one could see.

I ran through the veins to keep its massive organs fed. Without me, the city would fail.

When I eventually got back to the office they would sometimes ask why it had taken me so long when the last guy they had only took a quarter of the time it took me, I just said that I was new here and kept getting lost, hoping that I wouldn't get into trouble from the school.

I was just getting the mail ready for the last time, my last journey with my little red bag when I saw two of the staff from school walk into the office.

"Shit"

I thought. I'm busted. The fuckers have complained to the school about my postman adventures. They looked at me without smiling and went into a meeting room. I couldn't believe that I was going to get pulled up for this. My friends told me that they had been doing nothing all week whilst pretending to be working at the parent's office. Getting 5-star reviews whilst on the beach. At first, I had been jealous of them but as the week went on and I had started to enjoy my "job" I had forgotten about it. Now I was pissed off with them. The lucky bastards. But then that's the law of the jungle, isn't it? If you can get away with it then do it, just like I had been doing with the mail. So well done them, I wasn't going to say anything to save my skin. I had learnt that a long time ago. No point saying anything as it only got you in more bother and nobody ever believed me anyway. I recognized the two staff members but hadn't had any interaction with them before, so maybe they weren't there to see me after all. Maybe I was being paranoid from the lack of sleep, food and too much partying I had been doing. And anyway this was their head office; they could have been here for anything. I tried to gain my focus and get back to the franking machine, shake the negative, paranoid thoughts out of my head, and then I heard my name called,

"Can you come here please?"

A request, a demand, no matter, I put the letter down that I had just franked and walked over towards the meeting room, still trying to work out what I had done so wrong to get this kind of response to the school. I had always been here on time, never asked to leave early, completed all the tasks asked of me, okay maybe a little slowly, but they had been completed. I walked in to be greeted by stern faces; I tried to muster a smile,

"Sit down please"

I sat and listened.
"We have information stating that you are a drug addict and drug dealer. You are using hard drugs and selling hard drugs to students in the school"
The floor opened, I fell, kept falling, there was nothing to stop me, I was spinning round and round, bouncing off every word that came out of their mouths like the sides of a deep cavern ripping my clothes and my skin, each word stinging my nerves as it came to me at maximum velocity.
"What"
I squeaked.
"There has been an investigation over the last few weeks on information received that you are a drug dealer and have been selling drugs in school"
I was in brain coma, a vegetative state, I'm sure saliva was dripping from my open mouth and down my chin.
I had switched off and only heard a word here and there,
"He told us"
"Has witnessed"
"You sold marijuana to"
Boom, wide awake, sitting upright, my pupils gaining control, my cognition coming back online,
"Wait I know what you're talking about, that wasn't drugs that was cigarettes, it was a joke, I don't know where to buy drugs and I've never seen hard drugs, okay maybe I've smoked some grass and hash a few times, but that's it, I swear"
Oops, I went too far, I should have stopped after the first part.
"Who do you buy your drugs off, who do you take your drugs with, and do you take them in school?"
Then there came a list of names,
"Do you know such and such, they said that you did this and that, tell us about such and such"
These were my friends they were talking about, they were saying that these friends of mine had said all this about me, I couldn't believe it. But then again could I. Had they said all these things to save themselves? Rule of the jungle 2, last one in first one out. And then they said
"We've had calls from concerned parents"
I tried to work out what a concerned parent was, I tried to think of going home and telling me " concerned " parents about things

happening at school. Then I thought of kids going home and getting into trouble for something and then trying to get themselves off the hook by saying

"The new guy sells drugs"

I had smoked some hash and grass, I didn't really like it. The first time was at repulse bay beach when I and Blakey had smoked some and ended up lying on the beach thinking we could see pink camels coming towards us. I think that was the first and only time I had seen Blakey smoke it. Some others were more prolific and always seemed to be smoking it, but I would only take a puff or two from a joint or a pipe. I couldn't even roll a joint. I had never even bought it myself from a dealer. I knew a dealer a big guy called Rick, who I would see at the inn place sometimes and he would fill me with tales of going and purchasing big sausages worth of hash from China and selling it here for a big profit. But as money interested as I was I was never interested in that kind of thing. And then it comes to hard drugs, I had never seen a hard drug in my life, didn't know anyone who took them and to be honest would have difficulty in telling you what a hard drug was or even looked like. I was raised by alcoholics, and that was my "drug" of choice along with cigarettes. I thought I was naughty drinking underage and getting caught once by Mr Harding smoking Marlboro on the school roof!!

"Okay, they finished with, please collect all your items and come directly to the school and wait at the principal's office"

With that, they were gone and my work experience week was finished. What else was finished I had no idea, but it wouldn't be long until I found out.

Chapter Nineteen
The Handover

Back in the hospital one day I heard that the guy who had so maliciously attacked me on the football pitch had just returned from his appeal hearing. He had been serving an eight-year sentence for armed robbery. I found out that the appeal hadn't been brought by him and his solicitor but by the prosecution who had wanted a longer sentence, and they had won. He came back with a 15-year sentence instead and had been moved into the prison inside the prison the secure category A unit for the seriously bad guys. This was somewhat of a moment for me to cheer about. At first, I cheered because I had this crazy idea that his sentence had been lengthened because of what he did to me, but also that I wouldn't be anywhere near him again as he was in the nuthouse. The category A block is a creepy looking place. It has an air of the super evil about it. We were in a maximum-security prison with huge walls, fences, gun towers etc. Even the visit rooms were high security with a bomb-proof glass between you and your loved ones where you could only use a phone to communicate with each other. The category A unit was behind another set of fences in a corner of the main prison. It had its own gun towers and the only exercise places for the inmates were separate cages although there was one big cage where they could occasionally play a sports game together if it was believed that they weren't going to try and eat each other! I had heard that they still had the execution chamber in there and that you could see it as it was still in working order just in case it had to be used. They used to hang people in there and still had the ability to reinstate the death penalty if need be. They hung people and supposedly you can see the whole set up minus the rope as it is right next to the TV room and that the prisoners walk past it every day as if to show them how lucky they actually are that they aren't being hung by the neck until death. The problem for a lot of the inmates in that block is that in a few years Hong Kong was going to be handed back to China. It was on a lot of our minds. Even if I spent my whole six-year sentence here I should be released before the handover, however, there was always a real chance that something could happen in here that would cause my sentence to be increased to keep me here until the red army marched across the New Territories and took control once again. No one could trust what china said. It had promised to enter into a 50-

year joint government with the UK but no one was totally buying that. Millions of Hong Kong Chinese were trying to get out. The word on the street was that the UK government was selling UK passports to Hong Kong Chinese for a million pounds each. The joint declaration was signed by the UK and China in 1984 for the handover in 1997 but it wasn't until the terrible events in June 1989 that most people woke up to the reality of it all. You see 40 years before Chinese people trying to escape from Mao Tse Tung's socialist revolutions extermination squads fled to Hong Kong's borders. And many of them had been hiding here ever since. Some of them believed that the Chinese government still had a desire to hunt them down and punish them so they were petrified with what happened on the 4th of June 89, as were the rest of us. I had taken part in protests after the slaughter of students by the Chinese army not knowing how close I may come to being imprisoned by that regime. Afterwards, there was a huge panic amongst Hong Kong citizens and what became known as the brain drain took effect. What it meant was that anyone with the money and contacts to get out of Hong Kong with their family to a relatively safe country elsewhere. Because of that, there was overnight a huge opportunity for anyone looking for a job. Companies were so desperate to hire people that they would give you a minimum of a two-month contract that meant that you would get paid for at least two months before they sacked you. On Saturday mornings the local paper The South China Morning Post had their job section. It was huge, dozens of pages advertising jobs from the president of huge multinational companies down to messenger boys. For even the lowest level employees the salaries were attractive. One of my classmates from school was looking for a secretarial post in an office. She attended 7 plus interviews and turned them all down until she got a job that had an office with a view over Hong Kong harbour!! She was only 17 years old but got an amazing view and salary. One company that we all worked at was called something like World Wide Finance and had its office in central district. It was a sales job. Selling shares, stocks, futures etc. and none of us had any idea what we were doing. After a few of my friends had worked there I went for my interview and got the job on the spot. It had a great wage and no fixed hours to work. Basically, they were hoping that we would go out to our rich parents and get them to invest in the company's portfolio. But none of us ever did. It was open 24 hours a day as they were engaged in stock markets around the world. I sometimes went in after being in the pub to take heroin in the toilets and watch the rolling news come in on the printers. There was a room full of printers that would churn out news from different agencies from around the world, associated press, some French stuff, CNN the BBC etc... I worked there for the allocated two months, got paid and left.

Chapter -19
Black Friday

I got to the school for 12 and waited at the principal's office as directed. I was called into his office at 1215 and by 1220 I had been expelled and told to go and collect my belongings from my locker. I had been given a letter asking my parents to come to a meeting on Monday. And that was that. Instead of going to get my things I went out the hole in the fence next to one of the basketball courts near the back stairs. This was my smoking area of choice after Mr Harding caught us on the roof. I sat there in the woods smoking cigarettes one after the other trying to formulate what happened to me. It had all happened so quickly. They hadn't listened to a word I had said, they had already made up their mind. They believed everyone else and not me. Why? It didn't seem fair. How can that happen? What was the point of coming to ask me anything when they weren't going to listen or even check on anything I said? If those kids had been brought in that I had sold the "grass" to and also the friends that were there that night who I told about the "grass" deal, well surely they would have had to apologies to me and admit that they had their s wrong. And who were the people who said I was a drug addict? What drugs had I taken? What proof did they have? They didn't have any, they just decided to hang me out to dry because one of those kids had got caught doing something so they told their whole story. And wait a minute aren't those kids getting expelled as well? They bought what they thought was drugs. But no, I was the big bad drug pusher when all I had done was try and stop 3 kids taking drugs. I didn't like drugs; I wasn't a drug user and never would be. I drank, that's what I did, and I liked it.
"I wish I could have a drink right now"
I thought to myself whilst grinding out my last cigarette.
I went to my lockers which were actually in a couple of house rooms. The people I met there, I informed that I had been kicked out
"What"
"Why"
"No way"
I had collected my things from the Einstein room and walked down to the ground floor. I saw Allison there, my girlfriend at the time. She had a look of concern on her face; it would appear that it was an

open secret. I didn't know how, but then I hadn't been at school for a week. She ran up to me and threw her arms around me,
"They've expelled me"
I whispered in her ear, that's when the tears came.
Others started to gather round us standing there, friends coming to see what was wrong. The secret was out and being passed around. Kind words being used towards me, tears from close friends. The grief of teenagers for a downed friend. But then I noticed others, not coming to me. I saw the names that had been spoken to me in that meeting room; the names were looking at me sideways as they walked out of school. They didn't come up to me, they walked passed me. The looks they gave me were new to me in Hong Kong but so so familiar from my school days in Glasgow. I couldn't quite understand the emotion they were displaying but it was familiar that look. And usually, bad things happened after I saw that look. Isolation, fear, depression. The look I couldn't work out but the aftermath I could. Those feelings slowly took over the grief that I was feeling, loss taken over by uneasiness. A feeling that I had forgotten for so long in this teenage paradise. A feeling that came with terrible memories and terrible ramifications. I walked with friends down to McDonald's, trying to make sense of what was happening.
"There's a drug bust every year"
Someone said
"Remember it was such and such last year"
Someone else
"But I don't do drugs or sell them'
I said
"Someone thinks you do"
So was that it? For the importance of the school, to keep on the good sides of its powerful parents they had to be seen as taking a hard stance and this year I was the scapegoat? I could understand this logically, but it wasn't fair, it wasn't right and it wasn't fucking true. The next thing someone told felt even worse. I had lies told about me before. Like the time I beat up 3 lads at the golf course and got suspended. Even though I had a witness who saw that I was the one being beaten and I had the bruises to prove it. But this next bit hurt even more. It hurt because it was an untruth that affected my friends. I could handle taking the fall for something but when someone attacked my friends it got me angry. I would always defend my

friends no matter if they were in the wrong or not. I was loyal like a dog in that way.
Many of the others had also been interviewed at the school during the week. They had been told that I had given the teachers their names. I was the grass, I was the informant. But that was just simply impossible. I was the last to be interviewed, the last to be spoken to. How could I possibly have given all their names? Forget that I wouldn't have done that, as that was just my word against the teachers. But the simple of timing would surely stand up in any court. They had come to me last and said that all my friends had given my name. They had spoken to my friends before me and said that I had given their names. Just not possible. And there you have it. It was a setup. My name wasn't the only one mentioned but I was the only one getting expelled. I was the executioner and the executed. My paradise was crumbling right in front of my eyes. I stumbled out of McDonald's and onto the busy streets. I didn't see my city anymore. I was on autopilot. I walked the long walk home, instead of getting the bus. I didn't want to be near anyone. I resolved on that walk to go to Inn Place that night. It was Friday night. What else would I do? Sit at home after giving mum the letter and watch her drink herself into oblivion whilst watching shit on TV waiting for whatever the 9 o'clock movie was going to be on either the World or Pearl channels. I got in the house and handed my mum the letter and as brief as possible gave her my side of events. She got some whisky to calm her nerves, nearly downed it in one and said,
"I'm glad your father is away"
driver's
That was it that was all she said.
I had a shower and got changed. It was early but I decided to go straight out. I would again walk down to central to get the MTR to inn place. I went out the back door, crunching through the thousands of cockroaches. Smoking cigarettes I took a different route than normal, trying to take as much time as possible before I got to the MTR. My thoughts during that walk turned to despair. The feeling that I had left behind, what felt like years ago, but was only months ago. Loneliness engulfed me. Only yesterday I had a beautiful girlfriend, a huge group, no, groups of friends that was always there for me in person or on the phone. Now I was a dirty drug dealer who had been expelled from school, the lowest of the low. All of what I had built up around me was lying in shreds, scattered at my feet, crunched like

the cockroaches and just like the photos that fell out of an envelope sent to my mum years ago. I remember that day clearly. I must have been about 10 years old and we had just returned from a lovely day out together. It was a day when we went on a long bus trip together. One of only a handful of days when our mother and son relationship had any joy in it. As we got home my mum opened the sliding door to the front porch. There was some post that had been delivered whilst we were out. She bent down and picked it up. On the top, there was a brown envelope. She opened this one first and out poured all these ripped family photographs, onto the floor. They were ripped into small pieces but you could still make out the faces of our family in the pieces. Along with the photos came a note from my dad's mum, my grandmother,

"You have ruined our family"

That's how I felt right at that moment. But the note was from my conscience and the photos were my friends.

Chapter Twenty
Don't make me hurt you

After a few days back in the prison hospital, it became apparent that the new guy's noses were a little out of joint because I was taking control of the place. They started to be a bit aggro with me over the smallest of things. But just like in everyday life the little things started to build until one day the small chopped up triad squared up to me and said
"Fighting"
To me. First of all, I just looked at him and thought
"Why"
Then I looked at him again with all his fresh scars and his arm with metal rods sticking out of it and turned and told him to fuck off. He then came round and said fighting again to me. His pal with the smashed up hand was also trying to stir things up. I looked at him and said that I didn't want to hurt him but he wouldn't listen so I said OK fighting. So we went toe to toe and it must have looked comical. I standing at just over 6 foot and this wee waif of a triad held together with stitches and steel rods dancing around each other. I was trying to find somewhere to hit him that wouldn't damage him too much. He was wildly swinging at me with his one nearly good arm but kept on missing. I decided that his head wasn't badly damaged so I punched him the face. He flew back against the wall and slumped to the floor. I said enough but the daft we guy got back to his feet and shouted fighting again. I sighed and punched him in the face again, this time not too hard just enough to knock him back and hopefully get him to stop. But I was beginning to see the ox heart that he had inside that crisscrossed scarred body. The reason that he had probably survived the previous attack. I just started punching him in the face. His body being far too damaged for me to sink my fist into. I suppose I stood there punching him for about 30 seconds before I decided that he had enough and sure enough he backed off. It was a strange feeling afterwards. I had obviously marked my presence as the top guy in the hospital ward and he probably felt really low that he lost. But I quickly wanted him to feel that I held no ill feelings towards him. About ten minutes after the fight and he had licked his wounds and recovered I asked him if he was OK. Over the next few days, our friendship repaired itself as he finally realised that I was a bigger personality than him and there was nothing that he could do.

After a few more visits to the physiotherapist, my leg was a lot better. I was able to get up and downstairs with minimal difficulty. So it was decided that I was to go back into the general population. This was not a move that I was looking forward to. I was now more vulnerable. People had come and gone so the whole social structure would have changed.

Chapter -20
The expulsion meeting

"I need a drink to steady my nerves"
It was 9 am and we were due at the school for 10 o'clock. It wasn't "a" drink; she managed to down a couple before the taxi arrived to take us to the school. So with her nerves settled we drove up and down the hills to get the meeting. The meeting confirms my departure from the school was held in the principal's office. It didn't take long. After presenting their evidence, which I didn't bother to try and explain away, as I could see no point what so ever. And of course, my mum didn't slur anything in my defence. The only time I said anything was when Mr Harding comically stated
"What would happen if we had those cigarettes scientifically studied to see what was inside?"
"You'd probably find tobacco"
I said with a slight sneer.
So they gave me a choice. I could either leave the school voluntarily which meant I could still sit my exams in May or they would call the police and ask them to investigate.
"Investigate what"
I thought to myself. Anyway, that would mean my friends probably getting into trouble so I said I would just leave. I wanted to try and save what was left of my social circle and having the police involved would ruin everything. The police would find nothing on me. But then again how could I prove that it was only tobacco I sold those kids that night?
"I'll leave"
I said
So I left.
I put drunken mum in a taxi outside the school and went for a walk. I wandered the streets for hours. When I had a question to answer, a plan to make, I always walked. And I would walk for hours and hours, not stopping, even when hungry, thirsty or just plain exhausted, I would keep on walking. My dad would be home next week so I had 7 days. 7 days to, to do what and how I couldn't figure it out. So I continued walking.
I walked for about 6 hours that day, from central to the west and then all the way back to the east end of the island. The final walk uphill to my home was torture. I ached all over, internally and externally. As I

fell on the sofa, my mum, now completely drunk and with tears dried and still flowing came over to me,
"What are you going to do, what am I going to tell your dad"
Came her ever so caring questions,
"Get a job"
I replied.
So I did.

Chapter Twenty One

Fight
I was moved back into the general population.
Then....
Fight
Fight
Fight
Fight
Standing in the governor's office I knew that I was at the end. They were going to kill me. I knew it, the guards knew it all the prisoners knew it. It was only a matter of time. Over the last year, I don't know why they hadn't all just got the job over and done with. I then went back to different snippets of conversations I had heard. It was now a year later and my Cantonese was a lot better than the hardly any I spoke when I came in. I tried to remember the words that I heard. Tried to piece together the tones, the syllables. There was something going on. This was clarity; it wasn't me losing it again. Standing there outside the governor's office waiting to hear my fate. His office was full of high-level guards discussing what the outcome of my life would be. I reached a place of calmness. The same Cantonese words kept coming into my head. The small groups, sometimes just pairs of prisoners having quick whispers to each other whilst looking at me.
"Gat Gwai"
"Giordano"
"Hak Say Woi"
"Gwai Gi mo cong yeah"
"Dai lo cong mo da lai, lai ming bat?"
These words I understood but didn't really understand the context. Then there was that time when the si lo said to me about outside friends inside no friends. I was confused about why I hadn't been seriously got yet. Why had it only been little bits and pieces? Every fight I had been in was because of a single incident. They hadn't just one day set someone on me. My thoughts were broken when I was called into the room. The governor shouted his findings to me that I couldn't understand and I was ordered out of the door again. I was marched back to my cell and ordered to pick up my meagre possessions. We marched outside and I was taken towards the cat A building. My heart started to race. No way could they be taking me in there. The house of horrors where the worst of the worst were kept. But yes we went straight to the big double gates. They opened and I

was taken inside. We walked across the open courtyard and came to the main doorway. The guard rang the gate bell and there was a lot of clanking from a multitude of locks and the door swung open. My heart was quite literally in my throat. I had all these preconceived ideas of what behind this gate looked like and everyone was terrifying. A dungeon full of wailing. Rows of cells with cannibals licking their lips at me. Blood smeared across the walls. The wailing the wailing. But it was not like any of that. It was white though, almost medical. It was so clean. The cleanest cell block I had ever been in. I was signed in and led towards my cell. At every corner, I was looking for the execution chamber. The one everyone talked about where they used to hang prisoners and where everyone thought they would start hanging again after 1997. We first went passed the TV room and sure enough, I caught a glimpse of what could have been it, but I couldn't have been sure. I was led up some stairs and out onto a landing. Walked past a number of cells and stood in front of one where the guard opened the barred door. I was ushered into what was the nicest cell I had been in yet. Brightly lit and immaculately clean. The view was directly at the series of massive razor-wire topped fences and beyond them the main wall. It seemed that the longer the sentence the cleaner the cell is. If you are having to spend tens of years in one room with a minimal amount to entertain you, other than doing thousands of push-ups and sit-ups every day you clean your cell. You clean every single part of the cell. In each cell there is a small metal plate on the wall next to the front and right in the middle is the call button. This button is to be used only in an emergency and is supposed to bring the guards running. However, I had previously found out the bell is pressed so often the guards just ignore it unless it is accompanied by lots of loud shouting. Loud shouting was one thing I couldn't do that time when I was having an asthma attack but fortunately, an officer walks past your cell every 30 minutes so I didn't have to wait that long. Anyway, this piece of metal plating can be polished and acts as your only mirror that you ever get the chance of using. The taps you could polish and with a bit of toothpaste, you could even make the ancient sink shine as well. This was your home and one of the only things that you could take pride in. every day you would make sure that your floor was also nice and clean as a dusty floor is more likely to attracted insects and cockroaches and rats love cockroaches. So if you don't want the rats nibbling your toes don't give them a food source. This cell had obviously been loved. Everything was as if it had been done up as a show cell. As you can see sir it comes with all amenities and has been lovingly decorated and looked after by its former occupants who were a serial killer and child rapist. The light was the brightest that I had ever seen and there was as just a bright one outside. It was great, really gave you a big input of energy, as I if you were standing in the sun and if you close your eyes you could even imagine you were getting a nice tan on the beach somewhere. But it was a solitary cell. I hadn't been given any of my books or personal items. I didn't know what was happening really. I thought that I was just being moved into this unit to allow me some peace and quiet. Oh yeah, cause that's what they'd do for me, right!! But there I was left. In the evening my food was brought to me by one of the occupants of the unit. I had seen him before but had never been this close to him. He has killed his whole family I found out later. He was out of his face on something and had an argument with them so he decided to get a meat cleaver and chopped them all to pieces. There was also some talk of him cooking them and raping his little sister's body for a few days until the neighbours were alerted to the rather pungent odder coming from their neighbours next door. I ate my rice and put my pate out onto the landing through the bars. It was collected sometime later. Because of the lighting, I was totally unaware of the time. Staring through so much light to the outside didn't allow you to fully be able to gauge the time. It wasn't until the lights went on one the main prison wall and the watchtowers put their lights on that I knew it was getting late. The radio then came on so I realised that everyone must be in their cells. I sat there listening. From some distance away I could hear different radios playing different music. Category A prisoners are able to get a radio if they earn enough money and are good villains. So this was what I was hearing. I lay back on my bed and listened to the mixture of distant music. The radio then went off but the light didn't. This was new. The light never went off all night. There I lay with the light shining all night long. I had nothing to even try and cover it. I made my bed and tried to do my normal bedtime routine but it was virtually impossible because my brain said that this is not the sleepy time it is too bright you fool, get off your bed, why are you brushing your teeth. It's time to be awake, not asleep. It was a terrible night. There was, as usual, the low murmuring of prisoners talking to each other down the corridors. No-one shared a cell in this block just in case they tried to eat each other, and that's not in reference to anything sexual. And there were some radios that played for hours. I had no idea if they had forgotten to switch off my light, were keeping it on because I was a suicide risk or this was just normal in this cell block with the most dangerous young men that had been caught in this part of the world. The next morning I got up and made my bed when the radio came on and sat there waiting patiently. My breakfast came, rice, fish head, Chinese tea. Then my plate was removed and that was it. I sat there all day until dinner. Rice, some sort of vegetables and Chinese tea. I ate and my plate was removed. I was there for weeks. The same routine every day. I saw no-one, no-one saw me apart from a guard and the family eater. After the first few days, I realised that I was stuck here and had to keep my brain active. I planned a whole exercise routine for myself that would last for a couple of hours. I did a lot of brain exercises where I would remember a book I had read and I would re-write it in my head and even play some of the parts and characters However my senses were highly attuned to a clearly high density and I started to hear, smell, taste, feel so many things. I also imagined that I could reach out beyond my bars and travel anywhere I wanted to in my mind. I was changing; I was no longer a lad from Scotland, a lowly heroin addict who got mixed up with the local triad. I became a triad leader. I had committed so many terrible crimes. I was the Medusa triad. No one could look at me or they would immediately go insane and become under my control. I could cause planes to crash, people to murder others just by merely thinking about it. I would start to shun even the tiny human contact I was having. I would wait for them standing in my cell but with my back to them. I wouldn't turn when they arrived, I would totally ignore them. It was my only way of having power over my environment. I was slowly going mad. They say some people can live a long time in isolation, in solitary and come out quite sane, I wouldn't have been one of those people. I had no idea how long it would take me to go mad as I had lost all knowledge of time, day or night, weekday or weekend. I had even forgotten what month it was. At times I had no idea where I was or who I was. My dreams had somewhat taken over my reality.

Chapter -21
Getting a job

In under, a week I was working in an estate agent in Wan Chai called Connell and Chan. Run by this middle-aged Scottish woman I was employed on the spot. I was a messenger. The pay was good and I got to spend most of my time out and about delivering things like contracts etc. I also was responsible for the post. So off I would go discovering more and more of this fascinating city.

I found myself in some of the most amazing places. One day I was given an envelope to hand deliver to a chef at the Mandarin Oriental in Central. This was one of the poshest hotels around. I was a bit worried for me and Blakey had sometimes sneaked into the ground floor toilets and stole some of the aftershaves!! When I walked through the main door I was worried that someone would recognise me and chase me out. But no, I was safe. So I had to ask where the kitchen was so I could and deliver the letter. I walked up to reception and looking at the letter for the first time started to laugh. This had to be a joke. I looked at the receptionist then back at the letter, and said in a clear voice,

"I have to hand-deliver this to Mr Munch the head chef"

Waiting to be thrown out and utterly surprised to be pointed in the direction of the kitchen, I headed off in the direction I was proffered. Having never been in one of these kitchens before I was blown away. It wasn't a kitchen but a full-sized factory of food. It was massive with people pushing huge carts around with an assortment of wondrous goodies. As it was around 10 am these goodies were for elevenses' I thought to myself. Right in the middle of this food manufacturing empire was the head office of everything fine. A big box room stuck in the middle of everything. I headed towards it, climbed the 3 small steps to the door and knocked politely. I wait and knocked again this time a little louder as there was a lot of background noise. To my dismay, there was no answer, and having nowhere else to go I decided to try the handle. The door opened. I stepped into what looked like the captain's table on an old sailing ship. A big oval wooden table with the finest cutlery, plates and glass wear I had ever seen. This was where they must sit and tasted what the factory beyond produced. Just then a man came in, Mr Munch himself. I handed him his letter and left quickly, just in case I shouldn't have gone into his shrine.

Walking back to the office I bumped into Angus, a Scottish guy that I'd met a couple of times previously. He told me he worked nearby and why don't we go for lunch sometime. So I took his numbers, home and office, and said I'd call him.

Back in the office, everyone was gathered around reading the South China Morning Post. A young Australian guy had just been given a 3-year sentence for killing a guy. He said he had been drugged and woke up to find the guy molesting him. He smashed a bronze horse statue over his head. And he only got 3 years! It shows you what an expensive lawyer can do for you.

Chapter Twenty Two
A Second Chance

Then one day without any forewarning I was unlocked from this torment and taken to the governor's office. On the walk there I found myself growling to myself. I was acting like an animal in a zoo, albeit a tame one. I stood outside the governor's office for about an hour before being taken in. he sat there behind his desk with some other officers standing next to him. He spoke to me in English, although I didn't recognise it at first. It had been so long since I had heard it I just thought it was Chinese. Finally, I realised what he was saying. I was being de categorised from a B cat prisoner to a C cat prisoner so that they could transfer me to the Hei Ling Chau Island prison called Lai Sun. They had no other option as they were unable to put me back into the general population as it would have meant that my life was in danger. They had concrete evidence that I would be killed so they had no other option. I was being transferred tomorrow. I was dismissed and returned to my solitary cell in A block. To my delight and amazement, all my belongings had been returned to my cell. My books, magazines, papers, letters, toothpaste, towel everything. I looked at it all as I was locked in and wept. I realised now that I was going to survive, I had survived. I had been fighting for my life for a whole year now in Pik Uk. I was mentally damaged to who knows what extent. I was losing the power to talk, constantly lost in my own mind. Not knowing reality from fiction. The fiction that I was making up in my own mind, this was extreme paranoia and I was somewhat thinking that paranoia is an extreme method of survival. If you are totally paranoid maybe it helps you to keep away from all possible danger. I didn't think I was being poisoned or that there was a conspiracy, I just couldn't trust anyone, couldn't have my back to anyone. I use to hear them at night taunting me, telling me what they would do to me, kill me, and cut me up into little pieces. It wasn't death that I was frightened of. I didn't want the pain, and it would have been painful. But more than that I didn't want to lose. I had lost my whole life. Everything that I had tried I had lost. But now I wanted to win. I was in the greatest challenge of my life and this time nobody who knew me was watching. Nobody knew what was happening. Before when my parents didn't turn up to events it was their choice, but now it wasn't. What the point of winning anything when your parents quite openly say they have no interest in watching you. They were quite happy that I was out of the house so that they could drink. My mum openly said once that she would never stand at the side of the sports pitch watching me in the cold. They never saw me play table tennis or rugby, two sports I was in school teams for and other local teams as well. They only saw me play cricket once because my dad and his pissed pals organised a match one day and I was made to play. Made the highest runs and took three wickets, two in my first over. But nobody cared. I remember working hard to get our school B team into a cricket final against another south island school A team but then throwing the game as I didn't want to win because there was no point. My parents just thought I was scum, the black sheep of the family. The black sheep that they created they were hiding from themselves. They weren't strong enough to admit their own fault in producing me, maybe that's why they drank so much to hide their pain. But everything is hierarchical. I was not the worst boy in here that was for sure. I had never murdered or raped, had never physically harmed another human being for fun or for a crime. Psychologically I know I hurt people and for that I am remorseful. I had had fights in school. I had had fights out of school. I didn't seek a life of crime. I became a heroin addict and committed a crime for my addiction, my mental disease. I can't say I am blameless, but my parents do. They say that I was born bad, or something made me bad. They never admitted any responsibility to who I am. They couldn't leave the country quick enough when I was arrested. Never paid for any lawyer to help me. Just left me in a Chinese prison to await my fate. Dumped like a piece of garbage. No, I wasn't going to lose this battle, I was going to survive.

Chapter -22
Wan Chai

I headed to the Old China Hand and met with Angus and Jim. After a couple of pints, Jim said
"Party at Pokfulam this Saturday, fancy it?"
"Sure"
I said
"Cool, I'll pick you and Angus up in Central and then we'll all head together".
That Saturday I met up with Angus and we headed up to Thingummy's for a pint before Jim picked us up. Angus had his gorgeous girlfriend Daisy with him. She had long strawberry blonde hair, she was tall, and at least six foot, and had a smile you could just fall into. She was lovely. Whilst they went over to the park for a joint I sat downstairs talking with Mr Lee. It was only 3 pm and he was already pissed. I say I was talking with him but I could never work out what he was saying.
Angus popped his head around the corner,
"Jims here let's go"
I staggered to my feet as I had already sunk 3 pints, and went up the stairs, holding my breath as always when I walked past the toilets.
Jim had gone to South Island School and his yellow jeep had a couple of other guys already in it. Two rockers with long permed hair and a guitar bag slung over their shoulders. I introduced myself and I jumped into the back, Jim put his foot down and we headed west.
Pokfulam is an area with a load of high rise buildings. An estate all to its self with a graveyard on one hill facing it and the sea right in front of it. It was a beautiful location. Everything was there that you needed. A shop selling alcohol is what we needed. Jim slammed on the breaks making us all fall about laughing and we all clambered out to load ourselves up with enough alcohol to sink a platoon. I was last out and Jim had already started to pull away, I had to run and jump into the back with Angus pulling me in. It wasn't long until we had reached the party house. Some body's parents wouldn't be happy as the apartment was already trashed. I headed to the kitchen to find a cup, glass, bowl whatever was available to pour my vodka and coke into when I met this amazing looking girl standing, leaning against

the work surface. She was stunning. I couldn't think where she must come from. It was as if she had the most amazing tan in the world. Her dark skin glowed. It had the silkiest texture and with her mass of very dark brown curly hair falling across her shoulders every time she laughed was completely transfixing. She caught me staring and smiled. Her white teeth nearly blinded me. It didn't take long for us to get to know each other.
"Hi I'm Pru"
The next thing you know we are in the toilets screwing.
She was aboriginal from Australia. She went to South Island School so that was why I hadn't seen her before. We had an amazing night together, but I wouldn't ever see her again. We just weren't in the same circles.
The party started to die down so some of us headed towards Wan Chai. Now Wan Chai wasn't somewhere I had done much socialising in up to this point. It was the seedy part of Hong Kong. Full of strip joints, tattoo shops and triads. We all tried to keep away from the triads. They were notorious. But in general, if you didn't mess with them, they left you alone. The only time you would come into contact with them is if you caused any trouble at one of the local bars as they were all owned, operated and secured by the local gang. There were always bunches of young triads hanging out on corners. They stood out due to their clothing and their interesting habit of having a comb in their hair and a toothpick in their mouths. I had heard a lot of stories about them. But it just reminded me of the gangs in Glasgow; don't know which ones were worse. We ended up dancing in the Pussy Cat club until the early hours.

Chapter Twenty Three
I survived, so far

I was given a chance, this move to another prison. I would go to that prison as a survivor. I knew how my attitude in Pik Uk has caused me so many problems here. In Lai Sun I would go in just like myself. People liked me. I would be careful but I wouldn't be an arsehole anymore. I started to pack up my things. I really should have thrown some stuff out but it's difficult to part with things when things are all you have got. Later that day a bag was brought to my cell for me to put my things in. A large orange jiffy bag just like I had when I was in the navy. I packed it full. It weighed a ton with all my books. That night I lay there on my bed thinking of the days to come and the days that had passed. The confusion had gone. The tricks my mind had been playing on me were now distant. I was no longer lost in a world of despair and mental distress. The last year had been the biggest challenge of my life and I had survived it. Each day had been full of anxiety, threat and the unknown. Every night had been full of nightmares, the yells from the other prisoners of what they would do to me if they could have got their hands on me. Depression was always there in my cockroach-infested cell. I looked forward to its relative physical safety at night but as soon as I was there I felt trapped in my own mind, my own thoughts being the enemy, the enemy that could hurt me, attack me. The night-time routines of washing, exercising and making my bed the only things that could be seen as normal, routine. Thoughts of my own worth would be another constant. The knowledge that I was unloved, uncared for. My family disgusted by what I had become. How would life be with them on release, was it worth being released at all? Should I just go out in a thunderclap of violence, excitement? Should I, could I just kill myself here in this concrete shit hole. But that would have meant giving up, allowing myself to be defeated. I had been defeated all my life up to this point. There was never any excuse why I should be victorious. My family let me know that from an early age. Never attending anything I was involved in. Well, that's not quite true my parents had seen me play cricket once when my dad and his friends one drunken night organised a game and I was asked to make up the numbers. I scored the highest runs and took 3 wickets, 2 in my first over. But no one mentioned it. I just walked off the field as if I was a ghost. My parents never saw me play table tennis which I was very good at. If I had a little more support I could have made it into the national side, but they were just happy for me being out of the house so they could drink. Never even got me a good bat to play with. Oh, how I dreamed of a butterfly bat. They never saw me playing rugby either. My mum said once that you would never find her standing next to a sports pitch as it was too cold. Thanks, mum, each and every time you muttered these things you stole that competitive edge from me. I never finished anything because what was the point, nobody would cheer. The last thing I was involved in competitively was getting my schools b cricket team into the final against another schools a team, I then went on and threw the game, what was the point in winning? But not now, now I had won. I had won the most challenging part of my life so far and probably the most challenging. I had survived the constant threats to my life. Okay so they managed to put me in hospital for a while but I came back. Although I was in a mentally depressed and challenged state I still managed to survive. I survive with my back against the wall with hundred coming at me. Nobody had managed to slip a sharpened chopstick through my ribs and into my heart; neither had they managed to slice me with a piece of metal melted into a toothbrush. I had even managed to fight off 4 of them with socks filled with soap. I don't know how but I had. And now I was to go somewhere new.

Chapter-23
Anecdotes

So many crazy things were starting to happen to me. It's hard to remember the order of them, but most of them sound made up. But Hong Kong is like that. Back in the late 80's early 90's the ex-pat kids almost ran the place. For example one of my friend's dad was a big lawyer so anytime the police considered giving us a hard time for dancing in the street, climbing scaffolding and basically larking about, he would pull out his dads business card and they would leave us alone. We were above the law. A few of us got really drunk one night and ended up climbing through the roof of the bus that took people from the ferry to the peak tram terminal. There we partied for a couple of hours before getting bored and heading off somewhere else. Hong Kong was also a hangout for some big stars. At that time there were none bigger than Kylie Minogue, Jason Donovan and Michel Hutchence.

Once me and my friend Andy were in his car in Lan Kwai Fong and saw Jason Donovan doing an interview walking down the street. Andy decided it would be funny to pretend to knock him down. So we drove around the corner and waited until they came into view again and sped towards them causing him and his interviewer to dive for cover.

Loui from Germany also had an amazing experience one night in Scottie's bar. There were some instruments lying around so Loui went up and started jamming to himself on the drums. Then this guy comes up and picks up one of the guitars and the two of them just jam away with each other. Once the other guy left Loui came back to the table and sat down feeling exhilarated after such an amazing jamming session. Then he was told he was jamming with Michael Hutchence from INXS, he nearly wet himself.

The partying was pretty much every night now. If it wasn't in Lan Kwai Fong it was at someone's house or a beach somewhere. And I mean every night. You just had to go down to Thingummy's at a certain time; say around 5 or 6 pm and someone would inform you of a party somewhere. I was so well known now that I could turn up to any party and would know people there.

My exams were coming up and I hadn't done any study for them at all. I had flunked out of Law because I was supposed to hand a project in but my partying had got in the way of that. My work was starting to suffer too. I'd nearly make it on time but it was obvious I had been out all night. My boss called me and gave me a warning. At lunch that day I met up with some mates and drank too many beers so that when I got back to work I must have stank of booze so I got fired.

Unbelievably I passed all my exams. Every one of them. I got a distinction for a couple of them. Imagine what would have happened if I had actually studied. Never mind I wouldn't have done anything with them anyway. The nightlife was where I was living now. And anyway it was easy to get a job so I started working at an office where I and a bunch of other foreigners just sat there all day doing nothing. I think we were supposed to be selling advertising, I think but I can't be sure.

Chapter Twenty Four
Moving Home

I woke in the morning before the radio went off and was fully dressed and packed for when it went off. I was taken out of my cell before anyone else and taken to the dining hall. The only others there were remands on their way to court. After breakfast, we were taken to the reception where I sat and waited. The others were given their court clothes to change into. Immediately you could tell the ones loved for and the ones with no one. The loved ones had new clothes to put on with designer brands Giordano, Benetton, shell suits, new trainers. The unloved and un-cared for had only the clothes that they had been arrested in. a totally unfair system. We judge someone within the first few seconds so the ones with the new clothes had a percentage point on the ones who looked and smelt terrible. And if the unloved had been unfortunate enough to have been arrested during the summer in their t-shirts, shorts and flip flops they were going to freeze now during the winter as that was all they had to wear, all day. I looked at them all and pondered about who they are and where they were going. At least I was partly through my sentence. I had hope, I knew when I was going to be released, and they were right at the beginning. They would still be being given opportunities to shorten their sentence. To become a prison grass and get a reduced tariff. But everyone knew what happened to grasses in here. You have no chance, and then when they are released if they survive their sentence there would be somebody waiting for them outside too, probably for the rest of their lives. Take the sentence, can't do the time etc. what were they going to get 5 years, 10, 15, 20? Who knew? They could get let off, be found not guilty that was always the dream, for the system to fail and let you go by mistake. The prison is full of innocent prisoners, it depends on how they feel. It depends on their lawyers. I didn't have one, didn't deserve one paid for by my parents. They got out of the country as quick as they could. Hide themselves from their disappointment on how their son had turned out. Of course, I should have turned out just fine. Who needs their parents to bring them up support them love them? My parents used alcohol every day to release them from this burden and how dare I use substances as well to unburden myself. Leave me to my own problems; you'll get what you deserve. I then thought of my own release again. What would be the point of going back to them? They didn't like me, want me. The never wanted me to win, to be the best. But now as I was getting my ankles and wrist shackled to my waist and taken to the high-security van I knew I had won. I had beaten the system that had tried to beat me. I was alive and kicking and ready for my next adventure. That was it I was going on an adventure. I wasn't going to anything as bad as what I had just gone through. I was on the up. I was going to somewhere better and for the first time in my life, I had won!

As we left the prison, through the enormous gates the sun was just starting to rise. I stared out of the heavily scratched and graffiti peephole onto the world that was just awakening to another cold winter's morning. I spied people getting ready for the day ahead, shops opening, cars heading toward the city. I felt pretty cosy in my tiny van cell, yes it was a little bit cramped and cold but at least it didn't stink as bad as it did during the summer. My mind drifted again to the soles that had been transported in this very cell. Back and forth to court, not knowing what was going to happen. Some had killed some had raped. Some would be remorseful, a moment of madness that had led them to be public enemy number one. The ones coming back from court with a full life sentence. The boys that had hung themselves, there had been many, sitting here planning their own death. It was suffocating, stinking, retched. It was physical you could cut it with the proverbial knife. But here I was with hope in my heart. A new beginning. This time it would be different. I was no longer a no hope junky withdrawing from heroin, withdrawing from nicotine. In the worst pain of my life. I had also learnt a lot about Chinese. Not that I had spoken much, but I had been listening and now it was time for me to speak. I wanted to be happy go lucky guy again. Someone full of humour. Someone that could have friends, someone you could trust. I wanted to finish my time with no more incidents, keep my head down, and go through the days, months, and seasons. Get to the end and leave. The van continued through the dawn until I started seeing landmarks I recognised. We were driving through areas that I used to hang out. We finally ended up in the area just east of Central district, Admiralty where the Supreme Court was. We drove into the underground car park and through the low gates that led into the prisoner drop off area. We were all taken off the van, still with our ankles and hands shackled to our waists. We were taken through the search process and then to the cells. I had never been in these cells before. They were the most dungeon-like cells I had ever been in. each cell was huge. I was put into one by myself. Each cell could have held 50 prisoners but because of who I was I was always kept apart. Here I would stay until the end of the day. We were given sugar sandwiches, something I always looked forward to when visiting court cells and tea for lunch and dinner. The cells were very dimly lit. Very dark and foreboding. You could feel the misery and depression in these cells. No ordinary prisoner ever stayed in here. These cells and courts were for only the very bad. Criminals looking at a minimum of 7 years come to the Supreme Court. Although that wasn't always the sentence you would get. Depending on how much your lawyer cost you could always get a lighter sentence. But for the most this was where you would expect decades given to you, so not a very happy go lucky place. I didn't have to wait until the last case finished, I was taken mid-afternoon out of my cell, through the search area and then put onto a prison bus. The bus already had 4 others on it. We were then driven towards the harbour. To my delight, we were driven straight into HMS Tamar, the British naval base until 1997. I had stood outside these gates one day years before and seen Princes Diana drive out in a big black Daimler, on her own, going to some function. She looked like a Princes with a huge ivory coloured dress and tiara. I was waiting for my bus with a small group of maybe 5 people and as we waved she waved back at us. Now I was there for slightly different reasons. We drove up to the water's edge and then were called out of the bus one by one. I was given my huge orange jiffy bag and was made to carry it down some very dodgy steps to an awaiting boat. On the boat, the bag was taken from me and I was taken down into the hold. I at once felt terrified. The hold was dark and stank of puke, piss and shit. I was forced down onto a wooden bench and my leg shackles were then padlocked onto a mass of chains that were on the floor. There must have been about ten wooden benches all with other prisoners sitting and shackled. They all looked exactly how I felt, or maybe even worse if this was their first time on a boat. The door of the hold was shut and it became pitch black. There were some screams for some of the others, whimpering from the rest. The boat was already bobbing up and down with the swell of the harbour. I hadn't noticed before but in the dark, it seemed to be increased. Within a minute the first guy threw up. I found that you could stand up and make your way to a white bucket to piss in or throw up in. but not needing either I kept sitting. It was difficult as with every further vomit or fresh piss the holds stench became more and more vulgar. Then I could feel then engines increase and we started moving. It was very disorientating with no point of reference. More and more prisoners started vomiting. But now no-one even bothered with the buckets so it started swilling around our feet. Before I got any on me I managed to get my feet off the ground which was very difficult with such heavy foot jewellery. I got myself into somewhat of a comfortable position and did my best to meditate. I closed my eyes and just went with the movement. I visualised the route that the boat was taking, past all the ships at harbour. The view of the science centre over in Tsim Sha Tsui with the clock tower. Then came Ocean Terminal with the Star Ferry below it. On the island, the view would have been Blake pier where I first slept when my dad kicked me out and above that the skyscrapers of the financial district of central. We sailed past all the anchored great ships of the USN 7th fleet. With their helicopter ships, aircraft carriers and destroyers. This was all in my mind and it was the only thing to stop joining the rest of the vomit squad. Now the boat diesel fumes were adding to the suffocating environment. I'm sure that I wasn't the only one who thought that we could all quite easily suffocate down here, and what would happen if there was an accident. We would certainly all drown; drown in an ocean of vomit and piss. If you let your mind go you would have terrified yourself. I daren't even think now of the slaves that were transported across the Atlantic. For weeks they had to endure worse conditions than this. Conditions that I can imagine more now since I was in this hell hole. After a time, maybe an hour and a half maybe two, I couldn't tell the engines started to die down and that familiar pulling up to a jetty movement stirred me from my daydreaming. The hold door opened and there were almost cheers for the joy that we had survived. The stink that they must have had to take a minute to recover from it. Anyway someone eventually came down and untied us from the padlocks. We were taken up the stairs one by one and into the light which pierced the back of my eyes like a pin pushed right through my pupils. I found myself staring at an old wooded jetty with a couple of small buildings next to. A couple of open-sided prison trucks were at the end of it and I climbed on board one for the drive to the prison. It was quite lovely. Nothing to point out it was a prison island apart from a sign on the jetty telling you it was a prison and if you did a b or c you would be offered a bed here for free for a couple of years. But apart from that, it looked just like a gorgeous island. With cliffs, trees beaches and one track leading up through the forest. After the last vomit and piss covered prisoner climbed on board, we were driven up the long track to the prison. It was when we reached the top of the hill that I realised that this wasn't just one prison but 3. One prison for youngsters like me, one for old guys and the other was the drug addiction treatment centre where if you are lucky the court send you for 6 months to get rid of your evil addiction. Already I knew that it would work. 12 months minimum is what I had worked out, that's what you need to do to get off drugs, well to start to get off drugs anyway. I was dropped at Lai Sun correctional institution with a few of my other shipmates who had survived the voyage and we were taken to the main gate. This gate was an open barred one, no huge metal gates that hid your view from the outside. We walked in and the gates were locked behind us. We walked down a flight of steps and right into the prison compound. The whole prison could nearly have been fitted into the Pik Uk football pitch. Gone were the big walls and in their place was just a tall fence. There were no guns towers and gone were the huge searchlights. It was a friendlier place altogether. We were taken to the reception office and made to sit down on a bench were right next to me was Mathew James. The Nigerian guy that I had met almost a year ago in Pik Uk. He recognised me straight away and said hello how are you. I immediately knew that this was going to be different. The first person I meet is an old friend who was friendly towards me. Then the reception officer came out. A big happy chap called Mr Woo. He welcomed me with a big friendly smile. He said he had heard all about me but they were willing to give me a chance here. He told me the prison set up. It was split into two groups a group and b group. I was to be in a group and would be allocated a cell with 11 other prisoners on the ground floor. Most of my cellmates were the store guys and the ground keepers, so all long term low-risk prisoners. My belongings were put into the lock-up along with the majority of my books as Mr Woo said that I would have limited space as there would be 12 of us in the cell. Space was going to be an issue and I didn't know how I was going to cope with having to share my space with so many others.

Chapter -24
Meeting Heroin

I hurried from the flat in Happy Valley down to the MTR. When I got into the Inn Place Sharon was the very first person I bumped into. She was standing right at the bottom of the stairs. I could tell immediately that she was pissed off with me.
"I am so sorry"
I said.
"You missed my birthday, how could you?"
She replied.
And then stormed off. I was gutted, I felt so bad, she was my best friend in the world, she meant everything to me and I had put a wedge between us. I wandered off to the bar and got my pint glass. It was there I bumped into Pablo.
"What's up, mate?"
He said as Ricky poured me a pint. I told him what had happened. And he said
"I know mate she told me."
I was so upset I was nearly in tears.
He said
"Listen I've got something that will make it better, come on."
So I followed him through the fire escape and up to the alley at the back. We burst through the fire door and were in the back alley. As we walked down the alley we passed a few couples engaged in teenage activities, kissing, fondling blow jobs etc. until we reached a quiet spot. He pulled out his wallet, opened it and produced a small folded up piece of paper in a rectangle, it was very neat. He said
"Try some of this it will make everything feel better. Get a banknote and roll it up."
As I went into my pocket and fished out some cash he opened up the packet and showed it to me.
"What is it?"
I asked,
"Heroin"
He said,
"Number 4. Snort some up your nose."
I had no idea what heroin was but I did what he said. I put my rolled-up $10 note to my nose lowered my face down to the packet until the note was just about touching the powder and snorted. The white

powder jumped off the packet and raced up the money tube deep into my nose. It hit the back of my throat and I gagged. It was instant, I managed to control my gag and then felt the rush, wow, trying not to be sick and then this huge rush of euphoria washed all over me. It filled every part of my body in an instant. I kept gagging as some more dripped down my throat, my eyes were watering, but I felt fucking brilliant. It was getting stronger and stronger, I felt completely wasted, happy, high. All stress and sorrow had left me. I felt amazing. Don't know how I got back in the club, my face was zinging, waves of tingling all over my body. I found myself in front of Sharon. She asked me if I was okay, my eyes were bloodshot from the gagging I told her I felt absolutely amazing and that I had just taken heroin. She went ballistic, screaming at me about how stupid I was, I stopped hearing her, and I went dancing. And that's the last I can remember of that night.

Chapter Twenty Five
New Beginnings

I was taken to my cell with a couple of books and my washing things. The cell had six beds on each side. About 6 inches apart and with about 12 inches down the middle between them. There was one toilet in the corner next to that was the wash sink. There was a stack of lockers where you could keep your belongings, now I knew why space was limited. One of the store guys brought me over my bedding and I sat there waiting for the others to get back to the cell. 3 of them came back first and swarmed around me. There were two Hong Kong guys and a Vietnamese guy that I had come across before called ah Tai. He was alright a bit more mature than your usual Vietnamese guy. That's why he has here in this cell. About 30 minutes later the rest came back, the 5 store guys and 3 ground keepers. They were all Hong Kong guys. Most were doing a long sentence and had spent time in Pik Uk. They had then been moved here as they were low risk. Some of the guys knew me, maybe had even been in Pik Uk when I was there. I felt comfortable straight away. It was a bit daunting sharing a cell with so many but I had wanted this change, I had needed it. My bed was the one next to the doorway. Every new guy had to sleep there; it was also the one closest to the toilet. The toilet didn't smell. These guys were long-timers, they kept the cell spotless, but what it meant was that you were closest to the toilet when it was in use. You also had the least privacy and your bed was the first in the cell so usually got knocked and dirty. That first night I slept pretty well. It had been an exhausting day but I was free from maximum security. The cell had a really calm feel about it. Everyone seemed to get on well together. That evening different guys sat on others beds. Some were writing some reading. Other little groups were doing exercises. I organised my things and put them in my locker. It felt exciting having a locker. Space was tiny so I would have hours of enjoyment making the most of the tiny space. There were actually about 20 lockers so more than we needed and I did notice that some of the guys had two lockers or more. So that was my target. Get to the point where I get allowed to have an extra locker.

One of the Hong Kong guys was made of solid muscle. He would exercise by holding onto the cell bars above his head and slowly lift his legs up in front of him. He asked me if I wanted a shot. I got up, grabbed the bars and with a lot of grunting and straining managed to get them up once before I had to let go with my burning hands. I then followed him through some more exercises, push-ups, squats, sit-ups etc. We worked out for about an hour then we did some **Kung Fu**. This was great. He slowly showed me some hand movements. I felt great. I felt accepted. A year in here and I would be in top condition and doing Kung Fu every day would be amazing.

Chapter -25
Abandoned

I thought nothing more of it, then a month later my dad went off to Korea to work and my mum and brother went to the UK for 6 weeks for a holiday. They left me in the flat with a pile of cash to keep me going. The only thought I had was beer and party. After the first night of partying the only thought, I had from then on was heroin.

Everyone was invited. Just had to see mum and my brother off at the airport, rush back to 7/11 grab as much beer and ice as I could, grab a cab and get back home. Chuck all the beer and ice into the bath, clear all the furniture out of the front room, get my brothers ghetto blaster and get the tunes pumping. I didn't have to wait long, by 8 pm the flat was full and everyone was pissed. I knew most of the people there but not all. A few old girlfriends had shown up but everyone was being cool. I wasn't snogging anyone in particular at that time. People were dancing, others playing drinking games. The three bedrooms were getting used for sex, a proper teenage party. Mik turned up with a posse. He introduced me to them one by one and finished with,

"Hi, I'm Sam."

She was tall, blonde, slim, hot hot hot. Although there were plenty of hot girls there, she had something about her, I was transfixed with her, and it appeared that the feeling was mutual. We stood there staring at each other for what felt like too long. I shook myself out of it and showed them the bar. For the next hour or so I would turn round and there she was staring at me. However, I was being the host with the most making sure everyone was happy. I was going around chatting to everyone making sure that they were all having a good time. There was going to be 6 weeks of parties so I had to make sure everyone was happy. So, for the most part, I ignored her. Quite late into the night, I got a tap on my shoulder, I turned and faced Sam.

"Can you get me another drink?"

"Sure," I said and went off to the bathroom. I leant over the bath and grabbed two cans, one for her and one for me. When I stood up and turned round to head back to her in the living room I found her standing right behind me. She had followed me into the bathroom, she had locked the door, and then she pinned me up against the wall, stuck her face against mine, stuck her tongue in my mouth, and pushed her whole body against me. She was hot, even feverish, sucking my face, grinding her body against mine, groaning and panting, whispering some quite vulgar but extremely hot things into my ears. She had her hands down my trousers in a flash, had undone the buttons of my 501's. She then dropped to her knees and inhaled my cock deep into her hot mouth. I stood there, not knowing what to do with the two cans of larger that I was holding as they were wet and dripping, I didn't want them to drip on her and put her off her stride, so I managed to nearly dislocate my shoulder and put them on the bathroom window shelf. I thought I had put her off because she got up, but she pushed me back against the wall, and whilst staring intensely at me she pulled, one at a time the straps of her dress of her shoulders allowing her dress to fall to the ground. She had no bra on and her gorgeous tits seemed to be asking me to touch them. But before I could, whilst still staring at me she almost unperceptively pulled her panties down to reveal a beautifully manicured pussy. She then stepped towards me, grabbed me and pushed me down onto the toilet, turned around and with her pert little ass pointed at me grabbed my cock and lowered herself down on to me, guiding me straight and deep into her. She leant back on me and started riding me with the most amazing desire that I had ever witnessed. I reached around and found those amazingly hard tits with amazing nipples. She gasped as I touched them and I could feel her whole body react to the pleasure. She grabbed my right hand away from her tit and placed it heard against her pussy and using her hand she rubbed my hand hard and fast against her. She started to groan louder and louder her body started to shake and she started saying

"I'm going to come I'm going to come, please come with me now, please come with me now"

And at that, we both reach our peak at the same time. She was thrashing about with each wave of orgasm, and whilst still sitting there she grabbed my cock out of her and started massaging me, up and down, I was still coming and it felt amazing. She climbed down to the floor and slowly and carefully took my cock into her mouth again. She used her tongue and her mouth to expertly get me going again and within a few minutes, I was coming again this time deep into her mouth. She looked up at me with hair sticking to her face and smiled, she then whispered,

"Would you like to do some number 4 with me?"

I think she could have asked me to do just about anything right then I would have said yes. She got up, pulled her panties back on, picked her dress up off the floor and lifted it above her head so her body was at full stretch and her beautiful tits filled my world for another moment and then they were gone beneath the loose summer dress that she was wearing. I sorted myself out whilst watching her, she then slipped her hand into her bra where there was a little pocket for un-needed, for her anyway, padding and pulled out a little bundle tied together by some fine string. She unwrapped it by the sink. Wrapped in cloth were a little silver tube and a small silver box. She opened the box to reveal the magic white powder inside. With her fingernail, she took some of the powder out, closed the box and tipped the powder on to the lid. She took the little tube and quickly sniffed the powder up her nose. She pinched her nose threw her head back, held it for a while and then brought her head back forward and let out a little sigh. She opened the box again, nailed out a little more and put it onto the box lid for me. I took the tube and sniffed at the powder, but unfortunately, I didn't plan my breath properly so instead of sniffing the powder up my nose I ended up blowing most of it off the box. She screamed,
"Watch what you're doing for fuck sake!"
She took the tube from me and said
"I'll show you how to do it"
She snorted the remaining powder herself and took some more out for me. She said
"Now take the tube and place it next to one nostril. With your other finger close your other nostril"
I followed her instructions.
"Blow the air out of your lungs, away from the smack then bend down and inhale"
I followed her word for word and expertly took my line. As soon as I did I started to gag again but she did an amazing thing she grabbed my face and started kissing me hard again. It had to be one of the sexiest kisses I had ever had. The ecstasy of that kiss and the sex before mixed up with the power of that white drug was so intoxicating. We floated out of the bathroom back to the party. I felt wonderful, like the king of the party scene, king of the world and everything around me. We spent the rest of the night stuck to each other drinking, talking, taking more smack. By 5 in the morning, there were only a handful of people left. Some were unconscious, others

totally out of their faces on drink and smack. Some were smoking joints. We had run out of drink and the smack was nearly all gone. Those who were still awake decided to head off to Wan Chai to see what we could find. We jumped into Mik's car and went hunting.

Chapter Twenty-Six
Time to meet the neighbours

In the morning when the radio went on the garden guys and store guys got up quickly and left. They would be out all day. The hardest working guys in the prison. But they got paid well for it and would also get extras as well. As I discovered over the next year, we all benefited from it. We always got the best uniforms and anything else they got their hands on was shared out. The prison was split into two halves, Group A, which I was in, and Group B. When Group A marched in the morning, Group B went to early breakfast and vice versa. Every marching morning, each cell would have two of its residents stay behind to clean the cell. This was a position of status and was always hotly contested. By not having to march in the morning you didn't have to polish your shoes or make sure your fingernails and hair were cut and tidy as the officers would check them. Our cell only had a few prisoners after the gardeners and store boys had left so we had a very small number of others that could stay to clean. That first morning I wasn't allowed to stay so had to go out to march. We were lined up outside information. I could feel all the eyes on me although no-one was allowed to look anywhere else apart from in front. This was the first time I was to be made to march properly after having my walking stick taken away from me. I had to show that I could do it. One of the conditions of me being in this prison was to give up my stick as it wasn't allowed. It was tough. The muscles on my leg had wasted away. I hadn't used it like this in a long time. I pushed through. It sometimes felt that I was just throwing a thin stick forward and was worried that it wouldn't take my weight, but it did, just.

After marching, we were taken up to the dining hall. I was given my ON chaan and sat separate again. This was no good. I didn't want to be separate anymore. I would ask to change to the local diet. At the end of breakfast, I was taken down to meet my new Governor. I don't know what I was expecting but he turned out to be a really nice guy. He welcomed me but laid down the law. He said that he had heard all about me and he wasn't going to put up with anything like what I had done before. He said that I was in a unique situation that he understood and he would help me to spend my time there, hopefully

without incident. He asked me if I had anything to add. I took a deep breath and asked if I could go onto the local diet. It was a long shot as at Pik Uk I had asked and was told that it would never happen. Without looking up he said,
"Done, anything else"
I said
"No Sir"
And was marched out of his office. I didn't know how to feel. On the one hand, it was a huge relief, the food was depressing. I had somewhat got used to it, but even after a year half of it was simply inedible. I had no idea what I looked like as I hadn't seen myself in a proper mirror since being inside. I looked terrible when I came into prison but that was because I was a junky and living rough. But now I was clean and washed but I imagine I was skin and bones due to my diet, or lack of it. On the other hand, it was really worrying. I had never been a fan of rice much. We never really ate it at home unless it was plain fried rice. But then I would always add a lovely sweet and sour sauce to it. That was the least of my worries. My memory went back to that first night and first morning a year ago where I was served cold, congealed rice with a fried, and what looked like, mutilated fish head looking up at me. Just thinking about it now turned my stomach. But they did get oranges, which I hated but knew I needed the vitamins so would force myself to eat them. And on Sundays, they would get a meatball in the morning and a chicken wing in the evening. It was the chicken wing I was most excited about. Every Sunday you would smell them cooking from early in the day. The whole prison system must have anticipated the delight of Sunday evening chicken. And it was a wing, not a leg, just a wing, but it was cooked in ginger, garlic and onion. You could smell every separate ingredient, mouth-watering with the thought of putting each herb into your mouth. I would watch the Chinese in Pik Uk eating their wing whilst I was sitting there with my piece of leather meat, rotten, rock hard potatoes and bland over cook slop of cabbage. They would have a perfect routine for devouring the precious pieces of meat that were clinging to the bone, making sure that every last part of soft flesh was meticulously stripped before they would put the bones into their spoon, pour over a little bit of their black Chinese tea and pound it with their chopsticks. They would then put the whole mashed up remnants into their mouths and slowly work out every last drop of nourishment from those hollow bones. Chickens wings were

hot commodities, along with oranges and meatballs they were the biggest item to be gambled in the prison. On Sundays with the officer's eyes turned chicken wings would once again take to the air as they were carefully passed from table to table to pay off some gambling debt. The prisoner receiving them being careful not to have too many stockpiled on their plate for the officers to notice. But then there was also the consideration of lunch. At lunch, I was always given a piece of stale bread with a cheese slice. It really kept me going for a long time but now I would only have the Chinese option. This was the only option that I had actually had before. 3 days a week, you would only know when by the smells coming from the kitchen lunch would be a rice congee. Basically a thick rice soup. It was not just flavourless, it was horrible. The other two days a sweet pungent smell would waft over to the workshops, sweet congee. It was quite difficult to work out what was in this dark green fluid. Sometimes little hard bits that wouldn't give to biting could be found floating in it, but it was sweet. For months it could be the only sweet thing you would have. The times I had had these two lunches was in court cell, waiting for a hearing or transport. And if that wasn't enough I would also be entitled to a sweet bun with raisins at night. For the last 12 months this had been denied me and what I got was an over buttered piece of bread. So over buttered, it could make you, and I often did, gag. But now I would get a sweet bun!! I don't know who came up with the ideas for ON Chaan not getting sweet buns, chicken wings, much fruit etc., but they must have been nasty. It's not as if Hong Kong didn't know what foreign food was! They had more McDonald restaurants per square mile than anywhere else I knew of. Why wasn't I given a selection of burgers, chicken, beef even fish and the occasional happy meal?

I was taken up to my new workshop. I was in the metal workshop. Now, this was a dangerous place but as soon as I stepped in it felt somewhat calm. There were a few faces I recognised from Pik Uk who had been transferred here due to their good behaviour, or bad. The workshops officer seemed a good guy. Tall and gangly with bucked teeth, a bit daft looking actually. There was my African friend, a Hong Kong boy called Levis, who was a bit of a nit and couple of other guys I recognised. I was to be stationed as a workshop cleaner until I had shown my character and maybe allowed onto one of the big machines, drill, lathe, and welder. Lai Sun was different in many ways but one of the biggest was that there was no

education here so you spent the whole day in the workshop, apart from lunch when you were taken back to the dining hall. The first thing I noticed was how well the place was set up. No, I don't mean for working and the rehabilitation of prisoners. Next to the window, near the door, there was situated a wide set of wooden steps that were moveable. As soon as the officer had left and looked at the door these steps had been put into position. Two prisoners took up their position and looked out of the window their sole purpose was to key an eye out for anyone coming so that they could alert everyone else to get into their positions, including the workshop officer who would quickly jump up from his reclined position and look busy. Sleeping bodies would be roused and dragged out from under machinery, shirts would be put back on, gambling games are hidden away and the workshop would become a hive of activity. It really was a sight to behold. The room went from a bedroom, exercise room, gambling room to a busy workshop in literally 2 seconds, it was pretty amazing. Sometimes when an important visitor came, they came so quickly that some of the prisoners actually popped their heads up just as the door was opening and the officer shouted at us all to stop what we were doing.
But as I said it was still a dangerous place. Sharp metal everywhere. Don't want to upset anyone here.
At lunch, we went down to the dining hall and I had to have some rice congee. I was really hungry. Because I was so used to having lunch I had to eat something. It was hot and disgusting but it filled my belly. After the workshop in the afternoon, we went for a shower. There was a huge race to get into the queue first. Well, not for the top guys who just wandered to the front with no-one complaining. I soon found out why. The shower room was rectangular with 20 showers very close to each other. And only 5 of them were hot. These showers were taken by the top guys while we all had to share the cold ones. I had the usual laughter from the Chinese guys. My dick being bigger than all theirs. Yes funny, haha, but stop staring, please. Never felt any threat from unwanted homosexual attention. Maybe it happened in the adult prisons but it never happened in here. After the shower, I discovered that there was another dining hall, dining hall B. Here we had dinner. A huge plate of rice and mixed vegetables in a black bean sauce. All my worries about eating rice were dispelled in the first spoon full. It was delicious. The best thing I had eaten, apart from sugar sandwiches! I finished my plate and was the fullest I had ever

been in my life. I then had my orange. Disgusting but healthy and I washed my fingers with my tea just like the other lads.

Chapter -26
Spring Garden Lane

Everyone else had left it was now just Sam and I. And we needed more heroin.
So Sam took us to Spring Garden Lane which is situated between Causeway Bay and Wan Chai, near the Hopewell Centre. The lane had all Hong Kong had to offer. At the top end, there were a few little restaurants, and across from them, there were a couple of games arcades. This is where we started our search.
"Do you know where to go to Sam?"
"No, never bought it myself, always had someone get it for me"
"So what do we do?"
We both stood there looking around, hoping to see some guy standing with a sign saying,
"Heroin for sale, best in the lane"
But we were two ex-pat kids, standing in a lane, filled with locals going about their business.
We walked further down the lane. The place was filled with all the exotic smells you come to ignore once you've been in Hong Kong for a while. Halfway down there was a concrete building that housed the local toilet facilities. The smell coming from that along with the steady flow of rotten water flowing down its crack and littered steps was enough to tell you never to enter there. There was a thunderous noise coming from the flats above. The cracking and shuffling of ivory playing pieces that informed you that illegal mah-jong games were being played directly above you. Thousands of dollars were being won and lost; lives were being changed forever with the crack of the pieces coming down on the boards. Seeing nothing further down the lane, and thinking that the top seemed the more likely place to score because of the games arcade we wandered back up the lane.
At the top, we hung around for a while hoping that someone would just walk up to us and say,
"A very good morning to you sir, I believe you and your lovely lady friend are in the market for some of the Orients finest opium derivative"
But that wasn't going to happen.
Eventually, after seeing him standing at the same place for quite a long time, I decided to wander up and speak to a rough-looking local. He was standing against a wall, sunglasses on a white t-shirt.

"Excuse me"
I delicately put, trying to conjure up what I should finish the sentence with,
"200 dollars"
He said straight back to me.
"What I said"
"Say Gi 200 dollars, number 4"
I quickly understood that he understood what we were looking for. I quickly gave him the two notes and he said,
"Come arcade, now"
So I quickly followed him across the lane and into the arcade. We walked to the back of the machines; he took a small straw out of his pocket and gave it to me,
"Put your mouth"
I put it into my mouth and walked out.
Done, I winked at Sam, and we were off.
At the top of the lane, we took a right and headed towards a local McDonalds. I went into the toilet first wanting to try it out, but Sam had other ideas and pushed past me into the men's and straight into a cubicle. She wasn't going to wait. I bit the top of the straw, poured some smack out on top of the closed toilet lid and made two lines that we inhaled quickly, one after the other. That was it for me. The next couple of weeks went by in a flash. I spent all the money I had been given to last 2 months in those weeks. And when it had all gone, so did Sam. I only ever saw her once again, and she looked terrible. I met her with her mum in Lan Kwai Fong. We met on the street and went into a bar. Not one minute later she was off. Her mum had sent her to score some smack. After she went her mum leant over to me and asked if I had any.
"I've got a bit I said, not much"
"Can I have some?"
So I gave her what I had, she went to the toilet and came back a minute later. I had actually just scored it and had most of my score left. When she came back out I held out my hand for the score back.
"I finished it, how much do I owe you?"
Fuck, although she gave me the money it meant I had to go all the way back to Wan Chai to score again and I hadn't had any yet.
Fuck! I took her 200 dollars and headed back to Wan Chai.

Chapter Twenty Seven
Mahmood

The next week a Pakistani guy came into the prison. He had been done with a fake passport and had got 10 months. He had been at Pik Uk for a while so he only had a couple of months to go. As soon as I met him I didn't like him. He was a bit of a moaning arsehole. He actually moaned about all the things that pissed us all off but we didn't go around talking about it all the time like he did. Yes the food is shit, yes the uniforms are shit, and yes the cells are shit. Yes, the whole being in prison thing is shit, but you are in prison you fucking idiot. It is all going to be shit and listening to you go on about how shit it is, well it's shit!

He got curry twice a day and I sat back and watched as the Hong Kong guys befriended him and then started to steal his chapattis and curry. They would actually take the whole plate off him. But unlike me, he got up and grassed them in straight to the officers. Everyone was shocked, what the fuck was he doing? Did he not realise what he was doing? One day the word went out that if anyone touched him they would get a police charge. Not just normal prison justice but the police would arrest you and you would get another sentence. Unlike out on the street, a police charge in prison was a definite sentence. How could you be defended against the prison establishment? If they found you not guilty it would look terrible against the prison system and there would come free for all. So anyone who got a police charge always got an additional prison sentence. You would also be transferred to Pik Uk, lose your wages and privileges and probably have another year added onto your sentence. That mattered a lot here in Lai Sun because most of the prisoners either only had less than a year to go or had only been sentenced to under a year as it was. No-one was going to risk getting an extra year for that prick.

He really pushed his luck though. He would grass anyone up for anything. Nobody felt safe around him. There was talk of doing him in but nobody had the balls here. If this was Pik Uk he would have been done in. Guys serving 10 plus years don't really worry about having a poxy 12 months added on to their sentence. And some of the guys don't even have a release date so getting another life sentence really isn't much of a drag. Most of the Hong Kong boys were coming to the end of their sentences and just wanted to go home. Don't get me wrong they would fight and fight they would. But they would only get prison time 3 days extra, 7 days, 14 days and if you were really naughty 28 days. But the extra days weren't the only thing to think about. You would go down in your wages. From gold to silver, silver to bronze, bronze to basic. You could lose your visits and other privileges too like playing football at the ground outside the prison, a huge privilege only for the best boys! But the worst thing was solitary. When you went for a shower you could catch a glimpse of solitary here. Not like Pik Uk at the bottom of one of the cell blocks, cold, damp, dark. Solitary here was in the boxes. I was told about them and never wanted to go. Situated out in the open, no shade from the hot sun stood 6 stone boxes. Nothing inside, you would have your clothes removed and be thrown in. sleep on the floor with everything else living there, mosquitoes, cockroaches, rats. At the back of the box was a trench that ran the full length of the back of the box. Most of the time a trickle of water ran through it from the rain, a little stream if you like. But in the summer months, it would be dry. This was your toilet. Luckily you were on basic rations so if you had a short stay you could go without shitting in it and having the stench being with you for your whole stay.

It sounded like hell, and I was told that it was especially when it was hot. It was so bad that even the prison wouldn't allow anyone to stay in there more than 28 days due to the risk of health. The prison really didn't want to kill you; they just wanted you as close to death as possible so that you wouldn't be any more trouble.

So this was the dilemma. Fights would happen on a regular basis between others but Mahmood was off-limits.

One morning I was cleaning our cell when Mahmood walked past.

He was being released tomorrow. We all knew because he was again going against the unwritten prison rules. You do not talk about your release date. Some believe it is bad luck, but most of us didn't do it because it was just bad news. You do your time for the crimes you have committed. Don't complain about it just do it. Keep your head down and no-one will bother you. Some will never get out, some are spending long sentences and when you go around talking about getting out all the time it only goes to remind others that they are not. This causes others to feel sad, down and lays an invisible depression over the prison.

But he wouldn't listen and continued to talk about it the whole time. I had kept out of his way for a long time. Eventually, he had been moved out of our workshop and into another as there were other prisoners from India in that workshop and he was causing too many problems in ours. So I hadn't seen him for a long time but had heard of what he had been up to. So here he was walking past my cell on the way to the cleaning storeroom. This was on the ground floor next to my cell. It just came over me, and without thinking I was out of my cell and heading towards the storeroom. I stood there at the door and watched him, waiting for him to turn round. When he did he just looked at me, he didn't smile, he knew. I smashed him straight in the face, an uppercut that he didn't see coming. He flew back into a pile of mops and buckets. I leapt at him, grabbed him by his shirt and dragged him out of the storeroom and into the middle of the yard.

If this was just a fight it would have stayed in the room, but this wasn't just about me beating him, this was about justice. If I had just walked away at that point nothing would have happened. He would have been found on the ground. If he had turned me in he knew that both of us would have got extra time, so unless he was totally stupid nothing would be said. I knew this and I wasn't going to let it happen. I took him to a place where everyone would be able to see us right into the middle of the yard. You see there is a rule in the prisons here. Anyone involved in a fight, no matter if they fight back or not, gets hauled in front of the governor and faces the same charges. He knew it and he screamed at me,

"Please stop, I'm going home, I'm sorry"

But I didn't listen I picked him up and started punching him in the face. He fell down, tried to defend himself but I kept going. The alarm went off and the officers charged, they knocked me off him and held me down. He was crying,

"I didn't do anything, he attacked me, and I'm going home tomorrow".

"No, you're not"

I thought to myself.

We were dragged to the governor's office and made to wait for a long time. I wasn't bothered. I had another year to go on my sentence, he wasn't a threat to me, and there would be no prison reprisals.

The governor called us in. we were marched in and made to stand in front of his desk. He went through the usual questioning, I answered nothing. Mahmood couldn't stop talking.

"It was him, not me, I didn't do anything, and I'm going home tomorrow".

The governor listened and then gave us our sentence.

"14 days extra sentence."

"14 days loss of privileges"
"And 14 days loss of wages"
Mahmood started crying louder.
"My family is picking me up"
He cried
"My flight is booked. I'm going home tomorrow".
The governor just waved his hand and we were ushered out.
14 days extra sentence, nothing to me just now, but for Mahmood it was dreadful. I nearly felt sorry for him, nearly but not quite. I had dished out prison law, a dishing that many others wished they could have done but had hands tied. I took the rap; I did what was needed to be done. It never crossed my mind what would happen next, I didn't do it for respect, I didn't do it to make people like me, and I did it because at the time it seemed fair and right. The law in prison is harsh. Those next 14 days for him would be the worst he'd served during his whole sentence. I doubt he will ever forget them, and I doubt I will ever pass his way again.

Chapter -27

Bucca

I was sitting in Thingummy's one night nursing a pint because I had spent all my money on heroin when Lennon came down the stairs. We exchanged pleasantries as normal, but not normal was the next thing he said,

"You like bucca now"

"What"

I said back to him not knowing what we meant.

"You like bucca, say gi, number 4"

"aah, yes, smack"

"Come with me"

We went up the stairs and across the road to the local park. It was dark at night with only low wattage light bulbs throwing shadows like dancing dragons around the small area of peace in the thronging metropolis. There were parks like this all over Hong Kong, places where normal citizens could practice their Tai Chi in the morning, meet up during the day, play chess and read the paper. But at night it was turned over to us, drug addicts, alcoholics, prostitutes, gangsters. It's where the homeless could sleep, somewhat peacefully. A horrible place where I tried not to stay for too long. You could feel the place could get a grip on you so if you stayed too long you wouldn't be able to leave again.

I took out my little stash and he then brought out what looked like 3 or 4 grams. My eyes lit up, I'm sure he noticed.

"How much you pay"

"HK$200"

I told him

He laughed and said

"I take you better place next time you pay HK$100!"

Chapter Twenty Eight
The Boxes

But this was the first time I was to face the boxes. I was taken to solitary to calm down whilst they dealt with moving him to a safer location away from me.
There was no one else in them when I got them. Just 6 empty brick huts. I was told to take off my clothes and pushed inside. The door slammed behind me and left inside an earthenware hut. The roof was low and I'm tall so I struggled to stand up. The floor was just earth, rough to the touch and the place had a smell that was not terrible but thick, and to be honest a little threatening. It was not nice, the only light coming from the front door. No bed, no seat, no nothing not even a tap or toilet. Nothing to drink you had to ask for water and it was up to the officer in charge whether he would bring one. The day wasn't that hot but the bricks and earth just soaked up the sun and it turned into a sauna. Heat pulsing in the place, no breeze, ever! This time I only did an hour or two, it was difficult to tell but it was after lunch I was let out and taken back to the workshop. There was an unusual feeling back in the workshop, an underlying hubbub of something I didn't know. I went to my usual hangout to chill out after the excitement of the morning and one of the guys came up and asked me what I got. I told him and he said,
"Very good"
And he walked away.
This happened a lot; guys would walk up and just say to me,
"Very good"
It was if my whole position had changed without anything having to be done. It just happened, naturally, instinctively. The prison evolved as if organic. If you joined it you moved too. If you fought against it you would be drowned in its undertow. I had fought against for a whole year. It had eaten me. I'm lucky my sanity returned to me, lucky that the prison bosses did what they could for me. They could have just left me to what was coming. Left me to my enemies locked me in solitary and left me there.
At dinner I sat with a bunch of Hong Kong guys, there was a round of well-done's at that table too. It felt good. I had propelled myself into the group. I was no longer on the outskirts looking in. No longer a loner trying to survive and not upset anybody. But just like everything in my life, it wasn't going to be easy to maintain. There wasn't a long

line of Mahmood's that I could turn on every few weeks to keep me in the gang. This may be the most difficult bit in front of me. For when you are in a group you are safe but when you fall out of favour it can get a lot worse.

Chapter -28

New deals

So one night off we went. We took the MTR underground train to the mainland and he quickly took me Chung King Mansions. A massive hell hole. Cheap shops at the bottom selling everything from fake watches to carpets and above cheap hotel rooms. Very cheap rooms full of prostitutes, alcoholics and now I knew drug dealers. We went to one such room and were let in, bought some heroin quickly, took a couple of lines and we were off again. Instead of going back to the island he took me to the local park where we stayed for what felt like hours, taking all our shit, then he headed off saying,

"Be at Thingummy's tomorrow at 7 we go somewhere"

That next night we met at Thingummy's and said that we had to go and take care of some business. I said ok and we headed to the park to take some smack before we set off to an area that I was unfamiliar with. It was over on the mainland, past the areas that I was familiar with near Mong Kok. We walked into a café and Lennon walked straight up to the cash desk with the ubiquitous goldfish bowl on the counter. I was about to take a seat when he reached inside his coat and pulled out a short baseball bat and started whacking the guy behind the counter, the guy screamed and quickly fell to the floor. I just stood there incredulous at what I was seeing. Everyone else seemed to just ignore what was happening. Then it was all over and Lennon and I walked out the café. Lennon turned to me and said,

"The guy borrow money and not payback".

And that was that. He took me to a local park where we did some more drugs and nothing was said about what happened. So many questions came into my mind but there was an air about Lennon tonight, an air that said,

"Don't talk about what happened".

So I didn't. It was one of the first times we had ever sat quietly together in all the times we had been together. I didn't feel in danger, I was just thinking to myself that I didn't really know this guy. I *guessed that he just had to do business. He did it, and that was that. If it was for him or ordered by someone else, he was good at his job.*

But on the other hand, sometimes he was just crazy.

We were going to a party one night and had taken a taxi from Central to Pokfulam. As we arrived Lennon directed the taxi to the bottom of a block of flats, but not in front of them, round the corner in an alley. Just as the taxi pulled to a stop Lennon pulled out a chopper and held it to the driver's neck.

In Chinese, he said quietly,

"Give me all the money, or I chop"

The driver passed a pile of cash and we got out of the car and slowly walked away.

Once again nothing was said about it, we just went up to the party and enjoyed ourselves. I was so full of heroin those days that nothing was a reality for me anymore.

Chapter Twenty Nine
A Split head and an old friend

There were more sports at this prison. An outside volleyball court that I never bothered with and a stone table tennis table that I did. It was outside and the bats were rubbish but on Sundays when we had free time I managed to get a few games. Of course, there is a strict hierarchy so I never got a game before the fight with Mahmood. But now I was invited to play. I made sure that I didn't make anyone lose face, as that can be the worst thing you can do to a Chinese guy. So I played well but not well enough to win. After a couple of weeks, we were told that the prison was going to introduce some table tennis training and that you could put your name down. As long as you were behaving once a week we were taken into the dining hall where 3 tables were set up. One good one and two crap ones. There were only ten of us so we all got a chance to play. We had a few competitions but I still held back because I didn't want any arguments. One day we were playing and I was on the big table. I was playing one of the guys I got on quite well with so we were throwing our bats about and getting right into it. I went for a short drop on the far side of the table, slipped and whacked my head off the corner. I immediately felt the blood flowing down my face. The other guy pointed it out straight away and as quickly as I could get an officer. If you have any wounds or marks on your body you are immediately put on report for fighting even if nobody saw it and you are by yourself. So we had to explain what happened. Fortunately, there was some blood on the floor next to the table. My head was bleeding quite badly so I was taken straight to the first aid room which was actually the reception office. The officer there took a look and said that I needed stitches so would have to go to the hospital. The hospital is located outside the prison. It serves all three of the prisons on the island, the old-timers, us and the drug addiction and treatment centre. So I was handcuffed and taken to the main gate. It was only a short walk up the hill to the hospital but it was exciting being out of the prison. When we got there the cuffs were taken off and I was made to stand in the waiting room. Waiting to be seen with a head wound still did not warrant being allowed to sit down. As I was standing there I saw that there were some other guys from the drug centre. They looked like shit, just over their withdrawals and with their terrible first prison haircuts. Uniforms a mess and faces full of spots. As like anywhere we go we are never allowed to talk. Anyone caught talking to someone from another prison would be on report quicker than the blood dripping down my face. But one we guy to my left decided to have a go. I had been in prison for quite a while now so was well known so what he said at first didn't come as a surprise.

"Gwai Gi, Gwai Gi"

I ignored him. But he kept going.

"Gwai Gi, Gwai Gi"

"Sshh"

I said back to him.

"Gwai Gi, it's Lennon"

I almost came off my feet as I swung round to look at him. I couldn't believe my eyes. It took me a few seconds to recognise him because he looked terrible. But true enough there he was smiling right back at me. Lennon.

Chapter -29

Best view in the world

Before I had met up with Lennon again I had been sleeping on Blake Pier. It was at the edge of the harbour below Central district. Behind the restaurant at the end of the pier were a few benches. I choose one looking out onto the harbour. I was there because my dad kicked me out. My parents were having a shouting match with my brother and me sitting having to watch and listen. This had gone on for years, so wasn't anything new. It was getting more and more heated until my dad moved towards my mum. In that second I assessed the situation. I wasn't a young boy anymore; I had turned into a man, an angry one with that. I jumped up and stood right in front of him.

"Get back, you're not going to touch her"

Time froze. We stared at each other, but now I was looking down at him. There was fire in each of our eyes, but mine had pure determination in them. His red and watery from his alcohol abuse. I waited for him to attack me. Wondered how I was going to respond. If he hit me would I hit him, or just take the beating for my mum. So I stood there, looking straight at him. Then I saw a flicker in his eyes. The man had gone. At that moment things had changed, I saw it in his eyes. He had been the man his whole life, but now I was the man. I saw it in his eyes. I saw my father mentally collapse through his eyes. He slowly turned around, sending ripples through the energy that had just filled the3 room. Like oil tanker turning and churning up the sea around it. He headed towards his room and shut the door without a word. The next morning he left to go to South Korea. When he got back he threw me out. He never said why. It was during that work trip that I had got into heroin. I had tried it once before, but that time sealed my fate. It was the very first day I was left alone in our apartment that sealed it.

Chapter Thirty
Old times

I was called to see the doctor and knew exactly what I had to do. I feigned dizziness and said I thought I was going to be sick. He told me to sit down and pulled out his needle and thread. He started sewing my head back together, only two stitches but they did sting a bit. He then asked me again how I was feeling and I told him exactly the same,
"Dizzy doctor; think I'm going to be sick"
"Well, we'll have to admit you to the ward then for observation".
Yes, I thought.
I was taken to the ward and allocated a bed.
Twenty minutes later the ward door opened and Lennon walked in. I went up to him and we embraced. We held on to each other for a long time. Then I pushed him out to arm's length and looked at him,
"You look terrible"
I said
"Too much bucca"
"What happened to you?"
"I stole two CD from shop"
This from a man who had got me involved in some high-level stuff before, the reason why I was in this place. He got done stealing two CDs!
"One minute," he said. Another guy had walked into the cell. They went to the other end of the ward were the open toilets were. They had a heated prison argument. The ones when no-one could really tell what was going on as there was no hand waving or anger on their faces, and they were speaking very quietly. The trick was to not draw attention to the conversation by over curious officers. If they did happen to look over they would only see two prisoners chatting. But I could feel the energy coming from them. And straight away I could see that Lennon was the one in control. After a minute or two, the second guy bowed his head, took a step away from Lennon and just stood there with his head bowed. Lennon took a quick look around before he punched the guy really hard in the guts. All this without a noise. The guy took it heroically. And then he calmed himself and walked away to a bed at the end of the ward where he lay down with his back facing away from us.

"He asked me why I talk to Gwai gi, so he had to take punishment". The guy had made Lennon lose face by asking this and it would seem that Lennon was still a man to be reckoned with even in here, even in the drug treatment centre, even looking like shit, he was still a triad and an important one.

Almost immediately I felt the effect of his presence. All the other guys in the ward would get us whatever we needed. Lennon would just say get me some water and someone would run and get it. We got the two best beds and could change the channel on the TV to water ever we wanted. The feeling of power didn't overwhelm me, it allowed me to relax. I had forgotten the feeling of calmness. I could feel the muscles on my head relax, they almost cramped straight away from being in such a strange position after all this time, relaxed. In a very strange way, I felt safe. Safe in this prison hospital with someone who knew me, who actually cared for me. We had hugged when the cell door had first closed, that was the first hug I had in over a year and a half. It was a manly hug of course! But the feeling of being that close to someone from my life, it wasn't real. And as soon as realised that this time was limited the sadness came again. It was an almost instant reaction. But it wants the huge reaction that it could have been, it wasn't followed by depression, it was followed by a realisation that I had this short time and I was going to enjoy it. As I was contemplating this there was a noise from outside a window in the corner of the ward. Lennon and I went over. The ward was on the first floor and when we looked out of the window we saw were they washed the dishes for the drug centres kitchen. And right below me, directly in my field of vision was someone I knew. Wonghen, unbelievable, in the space of a couple of hours after months of solitude, fear, desperation I have two people who I knew within 10 yards of each other. A huge smile broke over his face but immediately disappeared whilst he looked around to see if any officers were around. Without a seconds pause, he reached into his pocket, took a packet of cigarettes out, got a rag and wrapped them and threw them up to us. I was caught totally off guard but managed to grab the rag and pull it through the bars on the window. He then looked away and got on with his job. I wanted to thank him but prison protocol told me to disappear as quickly as possible. Lennon and I went to the bathroom and open the 10 pack and shared a cig together squatting over one of the holes in the ground. I tried to be cool but I instantly felt dizzy and sick. I stayed

there trying to quietly take some deep breaths, but I thought what am I doing, this is a friend. So I told him that I hadn't smoked for so long, he laughed and I went to lie down for a while on my bed. I lay there and smiled with sadness. I was lying there on a comfortable hospital bed with a mattress and white sheets, a nice pillow. I felt at ease. I wasn't sleeping with one eye and ear open, ready for an attack at any moment. I slept the sleep of a free man whilst still being locked up. During that sleep, the last couple of years of fear and loss seemed to leave me. For the first time, I felt fully relaxed, confident and at peace. When I woke it was dinner time so Lennon and I got our food, before everyone else, and sat and ate together. This was another prison first for me, the ability to chat whilst eating. Instead of wolfing down my food, watching out for others intent of stealing it, I sat back and slowly ate. Enjoying each mouthful of an otherwise unsatisfactory meal. The environment made the food and the company feel like we were eating in a 5-star establishment. I could almost imagine us sitting there in suits and ties, discussing the latest updates on our investments rather than what had happened to the gang after I had got arrested. He told me of how he had turned and run as soon as he saw the van pull up on Pedder Street. He said how sorry he was that he didn't react quickly to save me but that I had to understand the rules. He was genuinely sad about it but I told him that it was okay. It was the rules; we all knew what we had to do. He thanked me for not saying anything. I asked him how he knew that I hadn't said anything. He looked at me, that look that he had given me a few times before. The way his face changed, to the one that caught my breath previously. From the friendly local guy I had met in the pub to the ferocious triad who I had seen taking revenge on those who owed money and other things to the gang. He looked at me for what felt like an hour but was only seconds,
"I know".

I looked down, for a moment I had questioned a triad, I had broken one of the rules. I had questioned him and if I had done that in front of anyone else it would have meant that this lowly foreigner had made this important gang member lose face. But then his face softened. We were in a different situation. We were friends, even though in reality he had probably been sent out to find someone like me for the gang to use. There was a certain level of trust. The trust you can only get in these interesting circumstances. The trust between criminals whose trust for each other is based on not talking to the police. Not making deals to improve your situation by sacrificing others. Those deals didn't end well for people here. I have witnessed numerous reprisals in prison. They come quietly and quickly. The level of violence dependent on the "crime" and the big brother's word. Lennon was my big brother. He was a foot soldier by name, but a big brother to those he controlled, and he controlled me. Well, he used. We sat across from each other with a different level of respect. His respect for me he told me was that I didn't speak when arrested, and afterwards, when offered, I didn't speak. Also, I had been inside for quite some time. And with total surprise, my name was known in the system. He said he had heard about me and was proud of me. He said that the talk was of this crazy Gwai Gi who wouldn't stand down, was always fighting. He said that there were stories about me, some obviously not true but others that were. He told me some of the outrageous ones and I nearly fell off my chair. But he also told me of the other ones and the importance of them in keeping me safe in prison. He said that others respected me for fighting with some people. He said that the big brother in Pik Uk had put out the word not to touch me without his permission. That I had shown "good face" in dealing with fighting bit never saying anything to the officers. After my stay in the hospital, which seemingly everyone knew about, there was an unwritten rule that I had to be left alone. This was completely lost on me. I didn't understand the language enough to fully comprehend that many people had tried to tell me. Those days, weeks and months after I got back to prison were full of pain to me. The time in the prison hospital had been pretty calm but it was when I was put back into the halls that my psychological problems took over. I thought that everyone was out to get me so I decided that I wasn't going to take it anymore. I was aggressive from morning to night, trying to see off attacks that I now know in reality weren't there. I was being protected but didn't know it. I had conjured up in mind that they would kill me at any opportunity. Where in I had lost my mind and was seeing things that just weren't there. I had completely lost it. For a moment I felt ashamed of my behaviour. I felt sad that it was actually me that was the cause of all my problems. I don't know how I came out of it, I'm glad I did, but I imagined for an instant that I hadn't. I could have got insane and stayed that way. I could have been shipped off to the mental prison and had the dreaded oil and water injections that would have left me lying there on the floor like a zombie. Sectioned forever.

Over the next few days, Lennon and I followed the same routine. We exercised together, ate together, talked, joked and laughed together. When we were out of smokes we would go to the window when the kitchen guys were there and Wonghen would send up some smokes.

Each day we had to see the doctor. There was only a certain length of time that I could fain concussion, so each day I said I felt a bit better but not quite ready to go back yet. I don't know how much the doctor realised I was kidding him. Maybe he just didn't care or maybe he was being kind to me. We didn't have much interaction with the guards. We were left alone to our own devices all day apart from feeding time. Each day new prisoners would be brought in and some would be released. Most just kept their heads down, well I suppose they were sick and kept to themselves. Lennon and I ran the place he was the Big Brother and I was his foot soldier and everyone accepted it. The alternatives were probably not worth it.

Chapter -30
Destiny

When I did sleep that night I dreamed.
This was it; I had fulfilled something in my life. Succeeded in something when I had never succeeded before. This was my destiny. Ok so it wasn't exactly how I had perceived it, but it was damn close. Although I had never thought that I would have ended up in prison, I thought I would have been dead long before being arrested.
I had always known I was different. By the time I was 10 I had found some books in the local library and had worked out that I was either a sociopath or a psychopath. I expected that I would kill someone before my 18th birthday, as that was what the book said. It also said that I should be setting fires and torturing animals. Well, I did make a few fires, but not inside. In the woods and fields around my local town. But I never harmed an animal. Although when I found dead ones I would like to take them apart to see how they worked. So for me, that was close enough for my diagnosis.
So when, a few months before my final arrest, I found myself in the Western end of Hong Kong Island with a gun, I didn't think twice about it. It was my destiny.
It was dark. Lennon had taken me here. We had taken a taxi to a few blocks away from our destination and walked the rest. This was to be the first thing I did for the gang. It was really a test. A test to see if I would do exactly as they asked. As they already knew though, as long as they kept giving me heroin I would do anything for them.
Round the corner from where I was to do what I had been told, we ducked down a thin alleyway, the dripping and whirring from the overhead air-conditioning units blocking out the street noise. Here Lennon gave me the gun. It was heavy, cold, and hard. I slipped it in my front right pocket. He also gave me a photo. It was a passport-sized photo of a middle-aged Chinese guy. On the back was written his name and address. Lennon looked at me,
"He come home every night ten o'clock in taxi. When he gets to door, go shoot him, then go harbour throw gun and come to Tuen Mun. Call me from 7/11, ok?"
"Ok"
I said.
And he left.

I slowly came out the alley. I had decided to become like a ninja. This was to be my first killing. I hugged the shadows; I believed I was a famous assassin sent to rid the world of scum. This guy owed money for a gambling debt, so not quite scum, but I made myself believe I was doing the right thing. I was totally out of my face on heroin as always and able to take myself to my own psychotic world anytime I liked. The line between reality and delusion was totally under my control. Well, that's what I thought.

I found the address. One of the hundreds of apartment buildings that filled this part of Hong Kong. The only difference being their number. All the same outside colour, with the small religious alters sitting outside.

I had been told that he came home every night at 2200. I looked at my watch, it said 2100. I had an hour to kill. So like any good little junky, I went and found a place out of view to line up some smack. After I had taken a good thick line I wandered back to the apartment block. Still hugging the shadows. The gun was really heavy in my pocket and banged against my leg every time I took a step. It was a revolver with a short barrel. We had fired an assortment of weapons a week ago over on Lantau Island. Lennon had a great collection of automatics and revolvers. We had climbed up a steep hill and sat there taking shots at rocks about a hundred yards from us. It was a strange day. We had actually got drunk on 3 snake wine in the morning which was unusual for us then had taken the boat from Central. Lennon carrying a big hold-all. As usual, he hadn't told me what we were doing until we arrived.

That night as I hid in the shadows waiting for my business to turn up you could hear the whole of Hong Kong in the background. Hong Kong has a sound that never really fades until around 3 to 4 in the morning. Then there is an hour or so of silence before it all starts again. I wanted a cigarette but didn't know if it was a good idea. But I ducked down behind some cars and sat in the gutter and cupped the tip of it so that the orange glow wouldn't give me away. I finished the cigarette and then found myself setting up another line of smack. Took that then had another cigarette. At 2145, I stood up. Cars had kept coming up the narrow road but none had stopped. Every time I heard one I would jump to my feet but kept my body bent over so that my head wouldn't pop up over the cars I was hidden behind. I would look through the windows to see if it was my business, but it wasn't. At 2200 I started to get a bit nervous for the first time. In all this time

I hadn't touched the gun much in my pocket, but now I did. I gently stroked it, felt the hard metal, the weight of it. I stood there, waiting. I could now hear every noise that came close. All my senses were heightened. I was almost excited that my time had finally come, that all those years of pain and depression as a child had been leading up to this point. But nobody came. By 2300 I thought I had waited long enough. It wouldn't happen, not tonight. I headed back towards the nearest MTR station which was quite a walk away. I started to feel a bit paranoid, here in this busy underground train station with guards and the odd policeman. I got on the train and found a seat by myself. Should I have thrown the gun away? Should I run away? I didn't know what to do. I was sometimes scared sometimes ok on that journey through the night. I occasionally put my hand in my pocket and felt the gun sitting there. A monster of extreme power sleeping in my pocket. How did it stay so cold in its dormant state? I walked to the 7/11 and called Lennon. He told me to come straight up as they were all waiting for me. Walking up the stairs in the apartment block I started to feel a sense of doom. Maybe they would kill me because I had failed to do it. Maybe it was all just a trick to get me to the flat, my fingerprints now all over the gun. When I got into to the flat Lennon didn't seem that bothered. I thought I had let him down. I was wondering if he thought that I had seen the guy but hadn't gone through with it. There were a few other guys in the flat and he was talking to them and they all started to laugh.

"Give me gun"

He said

So I reached into my pocket and pulled the gun out. I passed it to him carefully and he lifted it up, pushed out the revolver part and waved it in front of his friends.

"Empty la".

Chapter Thirty-One
Face, don't lose it

On the fourth day, another prisoner came into the hospital. We heard him before we saw him. Screaming and shouting. We went to the cell door and peered through the bars. Usually, the guards would shout us to get back inside but they were so busy with this one guy that we able to watch. He was being dragged by three guards, trying to kick and bite everyone. As he disappeared into the doctor's office Lennon and I looked at each other and said at the same time
"Chee seen" (crazy).

It went quiet, pretty quickly, then the doctor's door was opened and the guy, now very unconscious was dragged out. To our disbelief, the guard came to our cell door and opened it. What were they doing putting that crazy guy in with us? He should have been dragged straight to Siu Lam crazy hospital. He was thrown down on a bed and the guards quickly left and locked the door. We went over and looked at sleeping beauty, slowly drooling and snoring like a violent baby. We both knew he was trouble and then sat in the cell for hours waiting for the monster to stir and wake.

And he did, many hours later. He was disorientated and looked frightened, so we went to him to help him. We got him to sit back down on his bed. And he went back to sleep. That night he woke just before dinner came. As we were waiting he just sat there looking at us. He seemed to be muttering to himself. When the kitchen guy had left we all started to eat. That's when he said to anyone who was listening.

"What the fuck is the foreigner eating, where is his foreign food, I want his foreign food"

He spat this out. Lennon hit back with
"Sou soi" (stop water, Shut Up).
Then it started, the guy looked straight at him and in a continuous flow

"Fuck you foreigner lover, are you fucking his arsehole, you aren't Chinese, you have no face, fuck your mother".

Lennon was up before anyone could blink, and almost silent like the strike of a cobra, smashed the guy so hard in the face he immediately collapsed, the only noise was the guy's rice plate falling as it hit the ground. The two other guys next to him quickly grabbed his plate as they picked him off the ground and propped him up with his back to the cell door. The guard came to the door and shouted asking what was happening, and in good old prison-style everyone said

"Mo yeah" (nothing).

The rest of dinner was done in silence, everyone staring at each other, the crazy guy slowly coming round, groggy and confused. When the dinner plates were taken away, Lennon grabbed the new guy and took him to the toilets. There was a long discussion, everyone trying not to pay attention but 4 pairs of ears could be imagined turning in unison, straining to hear what was going on. After a few minutes, Lennon called me over. I was tense, it was a strange feeling. I had totally unwound over the last few days. I had been a coiled spring ready to pounce at any moment over the last year or so and the journey back to tightening that spring was not easy. The feelings in my stomach, the waves of old fear rippling up and down my skin, made worse with a full belly of rice. I went over.

"Punch him in stomach," Lennon said.

I hesitated, but not for long as to do so would have meant Lennon losing face if I didn't carry out his command immediately. So I punched him, hard. The puke came out his nose before his mouth as he bent over and crumpled to the ground. He kept heaving and I felt sorry for him, not for the pain but that he had lost his dinner and would be hungry, but that thought was fleeting. Lennon and I left him and went for a cigarette in one of the other toilets. Nothing was said, it was eerily silent and it stayed like that the whole night. I lay in my bed with senses heightened, waiting to hear the smallest movement, expecting an attack to come at any time. Trying to think of all the likely weapons that could be used with the materials at hand in the ward. But nothing happened.

As soon as the radio announcement came in the morning he was gone. Not a word was spoken that morning. Everything was very quiet, unsettlingly quiet. Then Lennon took me for a smoke. Squatting there in the cubicle Lennon said:

"He make you lose face, you are my friend, I told him, he agreed for you to get face back by punching him".

And that was it. At 2 pm after a green congee lunch, I was called to the doctor.

"You go back now".

And that was it. I was sent back to the ward to wait for a guard escort back to the prison.

I got Lennon to write me a letter that I would stick in my songbook.

Stewart,

You know I am really happy that I can see you again. But to see you in here I feel very bad. You are my good friend. I don't want you to take bucca again. I remember the time when we go to my boat party. You teach me so much English. Now I can talk easily with anybody. After we always go to Thingummy's and take bucca. You know when we take bucca we lose so many things and friends. We always walking in the streets. Always see the big boobs girls and say "Hello". But when we don't care we said "Fuck". I hope we can stop taking bucca. Can get our bodies strong. And meet girls and make-Love. We used to go to Thingummy's and the park to take bucca, very good high, But after we always throw-up so many times. I remember I go to your home to a party. I meet so many friends and smoke hash. But maybe I am very strong so the hash can't give me good high! I was very surprised to see you in hospital. But I hope never to see you in prison again.

BYE = BYE 23-7-92

in Hei Ling Chau hospital

Your good Friend Forever

Chapter -31
The walled city

"You wanna try brown?"

I didn't know what "brown" was but I nodded anyway. I had learnt just to nod when Lennon asked me anything. If I ever asked him a question back he would get pissed and say

"Why you ask, you don' trust me?"

We left the Mong Kok flat and headed in a direction I had never gone before. The streets narrowed, they were darker than those off the main roads. The noise of mah-jong tiles filing the thick night air. The stench of raw sewage grew stronger as we passed over the rubble of a partially collapsed wall. Immediately on the other side, the streets became almost nonexistent, tight passageways with walls leading ever upwards but never coming together. Masses of power cables like huge crows nests obscured some of the vertical views. It wasn't raining but the water seemed to drip from everywhere making the walls and ground slippery with moss and slime. And everywhere came the nattering of Cantonese, the clearing of throats and the cry of babies. It felt like I had entered a time vortex and had been thrown back a hundred years. Every doorway had eyes staring at us as we hurried past. Untrusting eyes. Every so often there were two or three youths at intersections, hand signals were given and the way was cleared for us to continue our journey into this unnatural cavern. We started to climb up some stairs that led into nothing but darkness. There was sweet and pungent stink coming from deeper into the building we were now swallowed into. Like someone cooking a big vat of something edible and inedible at the same time. We came up to a heavily embossed wooden door. The carvings were ancient with dragons flying over mountains, their tails wrapping around each other in a fight, or lovers embrace. With a quiet knock, it was opened and we were quickly shown into a low lit reception area. Lennon and the receptionist shared a few words and we were led down a series of passageways, deeper and deeper, I felt the first pangs of fear creep into me, trying to remember the way back out if there was trouble. There were doors running the length of the passage with moans and groans sounding like they were from a multitude of asylum patients, deluded and protesting. There were men sitting on the passageways, some old with long whiskers. Some dressed only in bits of fabric just

sitting there staring into their past, maybe? They could have been ghosts, the ghosts of Confucius monks. We were led into a room with half a dozen wooden beds, no mattresses just the wood panelling.
"Now we dream"
Lennon said smiling to me.
I sat down on one of the beds and watched Lennon prepare for his dreams. He took his shoes and socks off and then his shirt. He drank some teas that had been put on the floor next to his bed and then he nodded to the old man. From a place I couldn't ascertain the old man produced a pipe and handed it to Lennon, Lennon nodded and the old man took out a cloth sack that he had tied around his neck, a necklace of dreams. He undid the string holding it together and broke off a piece of brown and put it into Lennon's pipe. He struck a long match and held it to the pipe as Lennon inhaled. Taking great lung full's of the smoke deep inside. As he started to exhale he began to lie back on the hard bed. The smoke circled above his head like the two dragons on the front door, but this time the smoke was embracing Lennon. The old man put the pipe down next to Lennon's cup of tea and turned to face me. I did as Lennon did and sat on the bed and took hold of the pipe I was offered, now seeing it coming out of the long folds of the old man's shirt. I saw the brown as well, and now I could smell it up close, sweet and welcoming,
"So this is opium"
I thought to myself as I took the first lung full of white smoke as deep as I could. The smoke felt like it was expanding in my lungs, bigger than I could hold, but hold it I did. I didn't want to lose face by coughing it out. Instantly my head started to get warm, I let the smoke out and watched it swirl around me, but instead of putting the pipe down I took another long hit, now it felt like my brain was sweating, not an uncomfortable feeling but a feeling of complete wellness. A feeling of protection and love. I lay down on the bed, what was once a hard bed but was now the most comfortable bed in the world, watched my exhaled dragons dancing together between the wooden rafters on the ceiling, that ceiling darkened by decades of opium smoke, and allowed the opium high take over me, lying here in the depths of the walled city and wrap me in cotton wool and carry me off to my dreams.

Chapter Thirty-Two
Goodbye old friend

The guard came to the door
"Gau ling chat lok ling "(90760)
And I left the ward. I knew I would never see him again. That night back in my cell I lay on the hard bed and thought of everything we had been through. And thought of the chances of meeting him like I just did. It was more than just coincidence, wasn't it? A chance to talk and say goodbye properly. A chance to put a full stop to that part of my life. Nearly exactly halfway (although I didn't know it) through my prison sentence. The meeting was my hump day. The struggle to get there, to the midpoint of my despair. Now the slow glide down the other side. Down towards the future, down towards my release, down to having my life back. It was going to be easier from now on. I had changed, everything had changed, I was for the first time moving forward, and nothing would get in the way now. I was counting down the days; I felt at peace, I felt almost happy, not joyous, but content. I had broken the back of my sentence and despondency. I could never blame Lennon for what happened to me. He probably helped me in some ways. When I was first living on the streets I had no other option than to beg. I remember one night being so desperate for heroin I was begging in Wan Chai. This guy went past me and I saw that he had HK$10 in his top shirt pocket. I grabbed for it, and he punched me in the face. Straight away I shrank into the shadows. What had I become? A common thief, a nobody, scum, a junky. That was one of my lowest points. Lennon took me out of that. Okay, it was to get me to do things for him, but at that time he was my only family. I did what he asked without question. I had reached so low that I felt that I was expendable. It didn't matter what happened to me, I was nothing. I lost my complete social responsibility. From a guy who would do anything to protect people, I saw myself as now the complete opposite. This was who I was now, my transformation was complete. I would do anything for drugs, I would do anything for my new family. I had a complete psychological breakdown and expected to be killed at any moment, I just didn't care anymore.

But now. After my months and experiences of being in prison. And after seeing this once powerful triad looking like shit because he got caught stealing two CD's, I saw that I was wrong. I had spent the last couple of years not just thinking but analyzing everything that had happened to me. Okay, so I wasn't able to act the way that my analysis suggested I should act whilst in here. I had to survive this hell before I could carry out my metamorphosis. I knew deep down that I was a good person. I had succumbed to my environment. I never had a good education on how to be in society. I had winged most of my life's experiences and fucked them all up. But I knew that I was, when it came down to it, a good person. If I hadn't come to that conclusion I believe that I would have lost in completely in here and would have actually killed someone and become this prison crazy person. I had considered it many times. I had urges to just completely let go and become the monster I believed I was all those years ago. But I didn't do it because I'm not a monster. I don't have a psychological disorder such as a psychopath or a sociopath. I don't know what I have, but I know that I'm different. I've always known it. But even after all my self-study I still can't figure it out, what I am. Who I am. I see everything that happens, I sense everything that happens. I retain it and study it so that if I find myself in the same situation again I can go back to my filing system of situations and try to find a way to respond accordingly. I don't have the innate ability that most people have to deal with certain social situations I have to try and intellectualize what's going on and try to find the script to act the way I believe that situation requires me to. I get feelings about people as well. I don't know what it is but I haven't been wrong yet. When I meet someone and I can't link in with them it is as if I know they are not being genuine with me. I try and stay away from them in the future, a lot of the time I struggle to remember their names or even faces. It can come across as really rude, but I truly can't remember. It is as if my brain is telling me not to engage with this person. And then later they do something that proves that I was right. It's all very confusing. Every second of the day my brain is trying to work all this stuff out. So Lennon came into my life at a certain time. And now after seeing him again I actually feel better about myself. I feel that I'm going to make it when I get out and guilt isn't going to destroy me. It's going to work, I don't know how, but I believe that it will.

Chapter -32
Dreaming

I cried in my dreams, I sure I did. I could feel it. I loved being high but I knew I was dying. I was destined to die young. There was no point kidding myself. But somewhere deep inside me made me want to try to live. A gram of self-belief kept my life force flickering. No matter what I threw, of was thrown, the flame continued to splutter in existence.

I felt free to hate myself, it felt safe to criticize who I was, was becoming. At one point I dreamed that I was on trial. Invisible judges and lawyers were discussing my right to life. Based on my personal flaws, not anything that I had done. My thoughts feelings and emotions were under scrutiny. Should I be allowed to continue to hurt those around me? Did I have anything to put forward in mitigation, I did not. I felt like I was scrooge from the Dickens story and they were my past, present and future.

I woke once to find my host making a fire in the corner of the room where a pot sat upon some bricks. He noticed me looking at him and came over with a mug of sweet milky tea. Once I had drained it he picked up the pipe and passed it to me. The cloud came and the dragons took me away.

I have no recognition of how long I was there or how many times my host served me. When I finally woke up I fund I was sobbing. I was sweaty, hot and dirty; I stank of stale sweat and found that I was alone in the room. Lennon had gone. I struggled to sit upon the bed, my body cracked and creaked. Waves of nausea flowed through every nerve ending. I was dizzy and I dry retched a couple of times. I reached into my pocket and found a wrap of number 4 and quickly made a long line to set me up for my departure from this place. I got dressed as quickly as I could after the healing powers of the drug I had just sorted melted away the tiredness of its big brother drug that I had been taking for I had no idea how long, It was more than one day, I was sure about that, but was it two or even three? I had no idea I just knew that I had to get out of this prison. I stopped at that thought, it took me back to the dream I had before. For a second I almost beloved I was in prison I was that confused. But when I turned the door handle the door opened so I was free, physically but no longer mentally. That had changed in those hours I had been there. There had been a shift in my consciousness. I was no longer someone of years left to live I was now someone who maybe had months left. I didn't know how I was going to die; just something inside me told me that it was inevitable. Turning into the corridor and through the main door at the reception where the old man was sitting but did not look at me, I realized that I was going to die and I didn't care. I was interested how I was going to die. Would it be in a blaze of glory or found rotting in an alleyway, dead from drugs or by the hand of another? An hour later I found myself on the star ferry after a quick trip to Chung King Mansions. As I looked out across the harbour my mind was numb. Realising that you are going to die, preparing for it, was a surreal experience. But then, whilst standing there with the wind in my hair, I finally realized it didn't matter. Because when you die it is all over. No memories no thoughts of why didn't I do better, just nothingness. Like falling into the smoke of opium but without the dreams. There was nothing to worry about, but that was the biggest worry of all.

Chapter Thirty-Three
At last, something to do

The next few weeks just seemed to tick by. Some old friends were released and new prisoners joined us. The workshop was a little different. Most of the guys tried to sleep most of the day. Stuffing themselves under lathes, workbenches and under the stairs. Anywhere that they could sleep and not be seen. I didn't. I didst want to get like that. I chatted to people, played games, like chess with the board we had fashioned out of bits and pieces do some exercises, anything to count down the clock until lunchtime or the end of the day. But one of these quiet days the workshop master called me over and said that they had an order to make ashtrays for the top of litter bins and would I like to make them. Following prisoner protocol, I said I would think about it. So he went away and started to fashion a tool to make the curved ashtrays. Later I went into the welding room, where the Hong Kong boys hung out and went up to the top guy of the workshop. I told him what the master had offered me. He laughed and said go ahead. He had asked everyone else and no-one else could be bothered doing it but you Gwai Gi can go ahead with no problems. So the next day I went to the master and said I would help. It was the best thing I had done in ages. I had to pick up a piece of already cut metal that was rectangular shaped. Attach one end of it into the tool he had made which had three big nuts at one end, a slot for sliding the metal in to, a large roller and a handle to turn it. Once the metal was firmly screwed in place I would grab the handle and push the roller around the metal making it go into a half-circle shape. I would then unscrew it and start all over again. In a short time, I had my technique down and could do one every ten seconds. It didn't just fill my time it was a workout. I did it all day every day, the pile of ash strays getting bigger and bigger beside me. It was hot work. The temperature in the workshop was in the 90's most of the time and most have hit 100 easily. The sweat poured off me every day. I started to look forward to going to work. And it also kept my mind off something else. Something that was going to be a constant friend for the next 9 months, toothache.

Chapter -33
Waiting to die

The next few weeks I staggered towards death. Coming so close so many times. I didn't even know it. To know something you must think about it, and I wasn't thinking about anything.

When I was in the flat with Lennon in Mong Kok I just stood there listening to him. Whilst we stood there he was always tipping number 4 out onto the worktop, making lines whilst he spoke about what our next job was going to be. As I bent over to snort the lines up my nose I watched him gesticulating and giving me instructions that I had to repeat to him precisely as he had said them to me. I had even become adept at using the pigeon English he used, that I had taught him.

"You got that?"

"Yeah yeah"

Every job with Lennon was well planned out with a beginning middle and end. The instructions included how we got there, exactly what I was supposed to do, and how we were supposed to exit, split up and make our way to wherever we had to get to. It always finished with,

"You get stopped by police; you keep your mouth shut"

"Police triad, prison triad, everyone triad, you talk you die"

This was an order, not a request. A few months before we had been lying on our favourite slope on Lantau Island where he had told me all the prisons here in Hong Kong and there was no way I would ever want to go there, I would rather die than go there, and it was hell on earth.

Chapter Thirty-Four
Toothache

The first I noticed was a sharp pain in a bottom tooth. This wasn't new to me. My teeth had always been bad due to lack of care originally and in the last while down to my heroin use. Heroin kills your teeth, not many junkies with a winning smile. I had a couple of teeth taken out in prison already. As soon as I felt pain I would ask to see the dentist. And once a month, in Pik Uk, he would come and rip the tooth out. No niceties in prison, no work to try and save said tooth, of no, out it came with nothing to ease the pain. But as I said that was Pik Uk, this was an island prison and the dentist came once every six months. A few days later I woke up with intense pain, my face was swollen and I could barely eat anything. Any time pressure was put on the tooth it screamed at me with displeasure. When I got to the workshop I was able to see myself in a mirror we had made out of polished metal. My jaw was so swollen and red and when I looked inside my mouth there was this orange lump that glowed with an off-yellow head. I found a piece of metal shavings, cleaned it the best I could and whilst bending my head and holding open my gum I managed to guide the shard to the boil in my mouth. As soon as I touched it I nearly collapsed dropping the metal on the floor of the toilet where the mirror was. I picked it up, gave it a wash and took a really deep breath. I knew that this was the only way to relieve the pressure and I had to do it. To I started again but this time just rammed the shard into the boil. It immediately burst with fire and a bullet full of pain. I could taste the poison in my mouth, but the pain quickly went away. I looked inside and saw blood and puss, I managed at my strange angle to get my fingers in and squeeze the boil. It was agony put pleasing to see more of the puss drain out. When the doctor guard came to the workshop to ask if anyone wanted to see the doctor I gave him my number. An hour later I was called to see the doctor. I told him what had happened and asked to be on the list to see the dentist and get some pain killers. He said the dentist comes in three months and that he cannot give me pain killers as it is a dental issue, and sent me away.

So the daily ritual, that became a twice-daily ritual commenced. As soon as I got to the workshop every morning I would burst the boil and just before we left the workshop I would burst the boil. When

that didn't give me enough respite I started bursting it in the morning
I the cell and last thing at night as well. Sometimes I would be trying
to burst it a dozen times a day to deal with the almost incessant
pain.

The days weeks and months past so slowly now. I was still doing my
work in the workshop, but I stopped any other activities. I didn't
manage to do any exercise in this time. I was reading less and was
becoming more and more withdrawn. The pain took over every
aspect of my days. I couldn't eat properly. I just ate enough to
survive. One day I got so sick I just made it to the toilet at an allotted
toilet break. My bowels exploded in the toilet with the worst stink
ever. And it was a stink that wouldn't go away that whole day. It was
a Sunday and we were in dining hall A. it was hot so not much water
around. I was sitting in the dining hall one lunchtime and my stomach
started to let me know something wasn't correct. The pain that hits
you before your bowels explode is a pain that is known by everyone.
You know that you have limited time to go to the toilet or soil
yourself in the most dramatic of ways. The pressure keeps building
but you know you can't release the tiniest of gas because that would
only open up the gates of internal hell. I was less than 3 metres from
sanctuary. The toilets in the dining hall were right behind me, but I
couldn't go. Nobody could go until the allotted time. And that time
was when everyone had finished lunch and everything had been
cleared away. And then and only then would the officers, smiling at
their own power, as they watched a number of prisoners desperate
for the toilet, sitting on the edge of their seats with that desperate
look in their eye, give the signal. At that signal, anyone who wanted
the toilet would spring from their chairs and launch themselves
towards the rectangular box in the corner of the hall. There were only
3 toilets inside for hundreds of prisoners so you had to be quick. And
today, I was quick. With the merest wave of the officer's hand, I was
up and away, taking off from my seat like a missile. My trousers were
undone already by the time I flew almost horizontally through the
door. I landed beautifully with my arse pointing at the stained and
broken porcelain and just let go. It was like giving birth to an angry
child. The noise rattled the solid bars in the windows and if the smell
had been ever so slightly stronger, those bars may have melted.
There was an audible gasp from everyone within ten feet, then moans
from twenty feet, and then everyone seemed to explain some great
expulsion of grief as my innards danced in their nostrils. But I didn't

care I was in heaven. And it kept coming. I was exhausted by the end. I walked back to my seat to meet with hundreds of eyes looking back of me, their shirts hoisted up over their mouths and noses. I barely sat down when we were told to get up and move outside because today was the one day a week where we were allowed to have a full half-day outside. But nobody wanted to because the toilets ran down an open gully right next to the area where we could hang out. Everyone knew there was little water. So my expulsion was there, slowly, by the use of gravity only, making its way to whether these things went too. The whole area was a nauseous nightmare. That was day one and this went on for a week. I don't know what was wrong with me. I couldn't sleep I couldn't eat, I had a fever. I tried to see the doctor but he didn't believe there was anything wrong with me so just sent me back to the workshop. There I lay for the next week, under the stairs where some kind fellow prisoners gave up their space because they knew I was ill. So with the toothache and the fever, I squirmed and moaned until it passed.

Chapter-34

On the move

Sometimes I just couldn't find Lennon, he had disappeared. I would go to one of the apartments he used, but there would be nobody there. I went to Aberdeen on the south of the island where his family lived but I couldn't find him.
These days I found myself back t sleeping on Blake pier. It was getting colder now as we moved towards Christmas. At one point I had no money and resorted to robbing a couple of taxis just so I could get money. I hated doing it, but I needed heroin. But most of the time I just begged. I would get up and head over to Nathan road. There was an alley running parallel to it and I would go in there and change out of my regular clothes and put on really filthy ones. I would rub muck on my face and take out an old fruit box. I would head over to an intersection that was always busy and sit down there. I took out my new testament and just sat there begging. Coming up to Christmas and everyone was in the festive spirit. Some day s I would make about a thousand dollars, but then some days it would closer to 5000. It was amazing; I could make more money begging than working. But then there weren't many white guys begging in the street so kind of stood out. After a few hours. I would head back to the alley and get changed again and head straight to Chung King Mansions where I would buy usually 5 grams. I would go to Tsim Tsa Tsui Park to take the first gram. I liked doing it in the park now instead of hiding away in horrible little places. The park was open and pretty and I didn't care if anyone saw me, I just didn't care anymore. Io would then get the start ferry back to the island and head to the toilets where I would get washed up and then head off to Thingummy's via my bed next to the harbour where I stashed all my begging stuff. All my belongings were there. Nobody had touched anything whilst I was there so I felt pretty safe there now, especially as I was so much higher now than I had ever been. I would take a gram in one go now. It was so much easier than having to take a line every hour or so. I would take a whole gram and that would last me 4 hours. It wasn't about getting high anymore it was about feeling normal. When I got to Thingummy's it wasn't really for the company anymore. My friends were staying away from me and I never went to Inn Place anymore. It was really just out of habit I went in. I found myself talking to strangers more than people who I knew. I wouldn't

stay long I would be off up to Lan Kwai Fong to see if I saw any of my drug-taking friends and if not it would be off to Wan Chai where I would go down into one of the pubs there for a couple of drinks. In I walked most of the time; always watching for police who I'm sure must have been after me now. But I walked because I was restless. I didn't trust anyone so I kept on the move. I would find new places to stop and take in the view over the harbour whilst taking some heroin. I would sometimes just sit on Blake Pier for hours watching the boats go backwards and forwards. I had absolutely no direction in life now, no plans apart from waiting to hear from Lennon when he had a job for me to do. I didn't know then that I would only have one more job to do, and this one would go wrong. The last job always does.

Chapter Thirty-Five
WEE II FIGHT

Whilst I was ill I was unable to do my cell duties so it went back to the normally shared responsibility. We had a couple of IIs move into our cell, and we all seemed to get along with them. When I was back to full health, apart from my toothache, I told them that I would be taking back my duties every day so I didn't have to march but they did. One of them was ok with it but the other one wasn't. He went mental at me swearing and threatening me in the cell that first morning. He launched himself at me but others held him back. Just them the marching stopped and we were told to get ready for breakfast. He made it obvious that he was gunning for me. So after months of peace, I now had to be ready. He wouldn't want to lose face so he would have to attack me. He was a barrel of a guy; the issue was that this barrel stood only four foot high. It took me back to the time in the prison hospital when the guy who was covered in chop scars had wanted to fight me. It would be one-sided, and I didn't fancy pummelling the guy because of that. I only ever liked fighting with guys the same size as me or bigger, it just seemed fair. So the thought of this guys didn't worry me about my own safety, I just didn't want to hurt him too much. So when we left for the dining room I made sure that I would be sitting somewhere I could keep and I on him. I got my breakfast and sat at my table. I found where he was sitting and saw that he was looking directly at me. I knew it would happen here. I could feel it but knew it wouldn't happen until after we had eaten because neither of us would be stupid enough to miss out on filling our breakfast because after a fight you would be lucky to get anything more to eat that day. So we both ate our food staring at each other. As at the end of all meals each table was to get up in a certain order to take their dishes back to the kitchen. I was watching him as it got closer to his table. He started muttering stuff under his breath, calling me a fucker etc. etc. as soon as his table was told to get up he made the move. At once I was at my feet, he launched his plate at me, and at once I began to smile. This was going to go my way. Imagine throwing a plastic plate at someone, it was laughable. So I went towards him and kicked him sideways in the stomach. He had a large round stomach so I didn't miss but he just bounced up again. Everyone cleared out of our way and the alarm bell went off, but I didn't flinch. As soon as he was on his feet again he came for me put with one punch with my right hand at the end of my long arm I smashed him in the face. He then came again, a bit slower this time and I manger to place my left hand on his head and stop him whilst punching him time and again in the face with my right hand. He started to bleed straight away. I couldn't stop myself; it was just automatic, punch after punch. And then the guards were on us but I was still punching him. The guard on me got both my arms behind my back but I managed to slip one arm out and hit him with a resounding thump with an uppercut directly under his chin. It was the last thing that happened. I was dragged to one corner and he was dragged to another. We were both thrown to the ground and the guards did what they loved to do. After the guards had exercised their rights we were dragged to see the governor. I didn't care, time added on, who cares. I was at peace with myself. The fight was a one-off not what I had experienced before, or had thought I was experiencing. It wasn't some conspiracy to kill the foreigner. Nobody was out to get me. We were two young guys who had a fight and that was it. Nothing to worry about. I think the governor got that as well because all we got was 5 days added time and 5 days loss of wages and 5 days in solitary. I was then taken to solitary or. They were full so I ended up in one with two other guys. These boxes are made for one prisoner so to have three of us in there was pretty uncomfortable. All three of us did our best to keep cool. But it wasn't easy. The dirt floor was the only thing we could lie on and there wasn't a breath of air coming through the door. The heat was excruciating. Breathing was difficult. I spent most of the time with my mouth near the bottom of the door, trying to suck in any wisps of cool air that blew past. But you end up sucking in a lot of dust so end up with a dryer mouth than before. You sweat so much that your body gets covered with dirt, sticking to you like a second skin causing you to feel even hotter. I tried to meditate at the worst moments. Waiting for water that was only passed round at irregular intervals. It really depended on the guard who was on duty. This time it was one of the shit guards. All he did was sit on his stool and order the prisoner who worked in solitary to polish his shoes, get him a paper, and bring him some water. He would drink from the cup and then hand it back to his slave. He wouldn't let any of us talk, wouldn't allow any communication. You should get out once a day to stretch your legs. And he did let some out, but he never let our box any freedom. The toilet at the back was a stinking trough due to the intense heat and little water running down it. You tried not to use it but eventually, you had to apologize to your box mates and go and squat over the opening, hoping that you weren't going to stink the place out. We were so dehydrated that the stench of your own urine was enough to make you wretch.

Chapter -35
Is it New Year already?

I got up that morning and decided to try and find Lennon. I found my morning bit of smack, set it up and inhaled it, feeling its rejuvenating powers almost instantly. I was starting to get a buzz from the whole process now even before the drug hit my system. I got my begging bag together just in case I couldn't find him and had to raise money some other way. I wandered down to the star ferry and jumped over the barrier. I didn't care if anyone saw me anymore. They must have, and my fellow passengers usually let out some sort of expletive when they saw me doing it, I stared back at them and told them to fuck off in my best accent I could muster at that time in the morning. It was only about 8 am but this was the best time to travel. Everywhere was busy so I could disappear in the crowds. I went to the bow of the ferry and sat there staring over the harbour checking what kind of ships were at anchor. There were a couple of big cruise liners at the docks. Christmas time brought lots of them in for the rich on board to come and waste their money in cheap Hong Kong. Funny how they cruised around in their luxury apartments on the sea and came to buy fake Rolex watches on Nathan road. At Tsim Tsa Tsui I got off the ferry and head towards Mong Kok. I went in into the park on my way to take another line; it was my last line so I started to feel a bit apprehensive. I didn't have a clue where Lennon was so I decided to start at the Mong Kok flat first and then work my way back towards Chung King Mansions as that would have been the last place he would be. And if he wasn't there I would set up my begging stall and would make enough money within ten minutes to be able to duck inside the mansions and get the hit that by that time I would desperately need. The Mong Kok apartment was empty, no-one anywhere. Same with the flat on Argyle Street. I checked all the local dai pai dong and 7/11 on the way back. Nothing. I recognised a couple of the boys standing at a corner with the combs in their hair. We said hello abut they couldn't give me any info either. Maybe they knew but dint want to tell. That was fair enough. So it was back to Chung King. I didn't have to go all the way in as the wee guy I had spoken to before was in his shop and he told me that he hadn't seen Lennon. So I went into the lane at the back, muddied my face up. Dug my disgusting jacket out of my bag, put it on, grabbed my new testament and went out onto Nathan road to beg next to the traffic lights. My favourite spot. I sat down and put up my sign and within minutes I had a crowd around me dropping money into my box. I decided to read 5 pages of my book before I got up and went to spend my earnings. I ran into Chung King and as it was Christmas I bought myself a triple bag of delight. I set myself up 3 lines all about the length of a pen each and wolfed them down. For the rest of the day, I went from bed to road multiple times. Each time getting higher and higher but the money was coming in so fast that I wasn't spending it all. It was accumulating in bundles. As soon as my box was full I would empty it just leaving a few hundred bucks in it to show people that others had given me money and then stuffed the rest in my pockets. I had enough money to last me days now so I wasn't caring so much about seeing Lennon again. And to be honest I was starting to get weary of all the cloak and dagger stuff. I didn't fancy doing any more hold-ups or any other jobs he had planned. I was also getting sick of him disappearing all the time, leaving me high and dry with nowhere to go. In a weeks' time, I was going to be 18 years old. I was sat down near the star ferry terminal doing the last bit of begging before I went back over to the island. I had decided to get myself cleaned up to go out that night. I had completely forgotten it was New Year so I would head up to Lan Kwai Fong for the bells. So I needed as much cash as possible to spend on what I needed to spend money on. I had taken at least 3 grams of smack that day and was feeling very dreamy, emotion-free, free of everything really. It was as if I had reached a point of clarity because I had taken so much, much like when they say you can drink yourself sober. As I sat there in the dirt I had clarity, I didn't want this anymore, and I knew that this was going the wrong way. I was slowly dying. I would either die on the street by myself, in a fight or whilst committing a crime. I went back to earlier in my mind when I had the realisation that I was going to be 18 soon, within the week. I didn't want to be doing this when I was 18. Right there and then I wanted freedom. Freedom from the streets, freedom from heroin freedom from the death that was stalking me. I needed to leave Hong Kong before it killed me. I was already firmly in its embrace but I still had the strength to escape. I could get away, but where would I go? The only place I could think of was back to the UK. What I would do there I had no idea but I knew that I had to get away from here if I wanted to survive. It was getting dark by the time I had managed to shake myself conscious enough to gather my thing together and get the ferry back to the island. I still ha this huge funk hanging over me, thinking about my coming death or freedom. I went back to my bench and lay down again. I didn't know how I was going to do it but I wanted out, I wanted to escape and I wanted to do it before the 5th of January. I had this feeling that if I didn't I would die or something worse would happen to me. I had this feeling of impending doom. The heaviest that I had experienced in a very long time. I hadn't felt anything like this for almost a year, I think. I had been in a drug-induced haze for so long I had forgotten about feelings.

I thought,

"Screw this"

And I got my wee bag of magic out of my pocket, did a nice big chunky line of fairy dust and grabbed my wash bag. I headed up to the local public toilets, stripped to my pants and gave myself a sink shower to the amusement to the constant stream of Chinese men who came to do their business. It was a hoot for them to see a foreign devil in his pants in the stinking toilets. But when that first mug of cold water went over my head I felt rejuvenated. I shaved, shampooed, polished and preened myself. I headed back to my bench, marvelling with a new sense of belonging and direction. I pulled out the best clothes that I had and got myself suited and booted and headed up towards Thingummy's. The last time I headed there at this time of year the evening was full of magic. That was the night that I kissed Anne Marie for the first time. I wasn't looking for that kind of thing tonight I was looking to be with people. I had been shunning people for so long that now I hungered for the company. They had also been shunning me, and quite right too. Crossing the road when they saw me coming. Hiding inside streets or shops until I had walked passed. How disgusting I was to them all. But they were right I was disgusting, but they only knew part of it. They just knew that I was a disgusting low life junky; they had no idea about the crimes that I had been committing with the gang. But those days were over, I had decided that this New Year it was all going to change. No more would I just jump at any commands Lennon gave me. I wouldn't be dragged around Hong Kong to better poor bastards who had fallen behind in gambling debts. I would not rob anymore *either. I felt sick when I thought of what I had done. The taxis, shops and business that Lennon and I had gone to and robbed. Some for business to get money and some for fun like the taxis. I would get myself cleaned up and celebrate my 18th birthday. I would be a normal human again and be the success I always thought I would be.*

Chapter Thirty-Six
The worst solitary experience

After spending 5 days in solitary I was taken back to my cell. There had been a few changes since I had been away. The most obvious was that a crazy II had been moved in. I had known this guy for a year or so and he was nuts. It seemed that he had been getting into a string of fights In other cells and the governor thought that moving him in with us would calm him down a bit. But that wouldn't be what happened.
The next morning he came to me and said he was cleaning the cell. I said no, he could do it tomorrow as I always did it every second day. He started the usual fuck your mothers and that he was the big brother, not me. We stood there shouting at each other until an officer came in. now this officer was a creep, he started to shout at me and I reacted and shouted back. Well, that was it the baton came out and hit me on the side of the head. He yanked me up and told me to go to the office where he screamed at me for about 10 minutes. I don't know why but it really affected me, I actually felt like crying. This overwhelming feeling of sadness just came over me, I managed to hold it back but I really just wanted to break down and cry like a baby. I had spent nearly two years acting as a hard man but now I just wanted to cry like a baby. He sent me back to the cell to get my shirt as I hadn't got dressed yet 91703 was still there and started cursing me again but this time two of his dogs II mates joined in one from Szechuan and one from Fulam. We were all dragged to the reception office where we were given a right bollocking and told to stop our arguing. This didn't look good, these II didn't mess about. They were like wild animals when they got together; I knew there would be trouble. I asked to be moved to the next cell but it was refused. I was told that if there were any problems tonight to tell them tomorrow. What if I was still breathing you wanted me to grass on another prisoner so that my breathing would be extinguished for me. We were sent away to our workshops but I sensed real danger. They were staring at me as they were being taken away. I was stressed for the rest of that day. In the workshop, I thought about what kind of weapon I could arm myself with. How could I sleep that night knowing that any point they could jump on my bed and kill me. If I didn't die I would be badly hurt. I had seen the damaged that can be done by these kinds of guys. They would rip the skin off my bones,

try and dig my eyes out, and I would be lucky if I escaped with my life, I really would be. To be locked in a cell with them whilst they are stabbing me with no way to escape, an officer may get called but by the time he got the keys and other officers as back up, I would be lucky to still be part of this world. For the first time in a very long time, I was terrified for my life. But I didn't know what to do. If I went to speak to someone I would have been labelled a grass, and be on the defensive for the rest of my sentences which had a minimum of 6 months to go. But if I didn't I thought I was as good as dead. So basically this was it, there was nothing I could do. The only thing was to go out fighting. But I don't know why but I felt week. It was as if I had used up all my mental strength the last year and a half. I had nothing left to give. I was weak and they knew it. During dinner I was half waiting for an attack, maybe I should do something now so that it could have been dealt with quickly, but I didn't. But at the end of dinner may be a reprieve, we were told that all the II's on our floor were getting moved to another floor. I was immediately filled with joy and dread. It's like Christmas morning opening one of your presents to find a puppy then realising it has suffocated in the box. They would think it was to do with me. As we were told I scanned the room to find the two of them whispering and staring at me. It was going to happen during the time we were going back to our cells, I could just feel it. They didn't move the II's early enough so they were still getting moved when we arrived at the cell. Keeping my eye on them at all times, and seeing that they were doing the same thing I had to enter our cell. It felt like being forced into the execution chamber. The air was solid with trepidation. Almost everyone was expecting something. Alliances would be tested. Is it better to help the Gwai Gi or leave him to his fate? We were in the cell for about ten minutes. There was a lot of commotion because we had a number of II's in the cell getting moved out. I didn't have problems with all the others. In one of the guys, I had become quite friendly with. I would be sorry to see him go. We had spent night after night trying to communicate with each other. He was from some far off Provence and his dialect was nothing that I had heard before. He had no Cantonese and the only English he had was pronounced with such a lisp that he spat every time he tried to say
"Fuck you"!!
I went to help him pack, and wham I was thrown across the cell. I had taken my eyes off them for 5 seconds and that had given them

enough time. 917373 had kicked me in the back as I had bent down to help my friend. Stupid of me, so stupid. I had let my guard down for seconds and now I was in the fight for my life. I knew exactly what was happening and managed to somehow throw myself long ways and sideways over a bed so that I almost landed on my feet facing my attackers but as I raised my head and I saw the razor in the other guy's hand, wham again 9187373 kicked me straight under the chin. I fell backwards, my neck felt like it had nearly snapped but somewhere deep inside me my body was starting to fight back, they would not kill me. Adrenaline started pumping and I acknowledged it just as a toothbrush with the razor stuck into the handle swept through the air towards my face I managed to kick out and take the guys legs. And then I was up. I leapt towards 917137733 and head-butted him straight in the chest, he let out a huge
"Ugh"
Sound as I connected, but I didn't stop, I leapt to my left just in time to once again miss a swing from the other guy. I jumped over a bed but caught my foot in someone blankets and went down between two beds really hard.
"You are not going to get me"
I was screaming inside my head. Then they were both on top of me. The blows were raining down; I didn't try to defend myself I just tried to get away from them. I was waiting for that ice feeling across my skin. Then the thick warm feeling of blood surging out of the sliced conduits. I could have already been slashed, I didn't know, I just knew that I was going to fight to the end. I had punch after punch aimed at my side, I'm sure I felt a knife going in and out of me. I relaxed and let them tire themselves out, taking the punches but trying to get my strength and breath back. Once I felt ready I thrust myself up and forward and swung around catching one of them right in the stomach. As he crumpled I fell back but managed to kick out and caught the other guy. I bounced off the wall and jumped up and landed fully on one of the guy's chests. Then the cell door opened and 3 guards came running in. I was bent over, panting when they reached us. I was rugby tackled to the ground but smiled when it was happening. I didn't know my injuries but I knew it was over. As I lay there on the ground with the guards hitting the final bits of energy and life out of me, I suddenly felt like I was transcending the whole scene. The pain and fear left me and I suddenly felt a huge calmness

come all over me. We were all taken to solitary as it was late and we couldn't see

Chapter -36

Running the clock down

I headed down the stairs into the dark of Thingummy's, it was 10 o'clock by the time I arrived and the place was buzzing, but not with many people I knew. It didn't matter because the three amigos were at the bar. Curly-haired triad big brother the actor and his wife. Peter poured me a pint and I sat with them for a while. Curly once again told me to get off the gear. I told him my plan and he laughed and wished me good luck. Even actor and wife seemed to be fonder of me that night. My Lee was there, pissed as always and leering at anything in a skirt. I went over and sat with him, and he embarrassed me with a fondness that I hadn't expected. He spoke to me in his pissed Cantonese. I couldn't understand the words but I think I got the sentiment. He cared about me, he was worried about me. He was saying that I was killing myself and I had to stop, then he started crying. Peter came over and got him to stop as he was embarrassing himself. He stood up and staggered up the stairs. Probably to go and sit in the park and fall into one of his drunken sleep. There were a few younger kids from island school so I sat with them for a while until I got bored of them and headed towards Lan Kwai Fong. This is where the New Year magic happens. It was mobbed. So full of people that you could hardly move. But I was on a high so seemed to be able to just magically push my way through everybody. I reached Scotties and managed to get myself a pint. I downed that then managed to squeeze myself back out onto to the main road again. Just in time for the New Year clock to start ticking down from 10. When the clock hit 0 everybody went mental. Music was blazing people all around were cheering. Stranger embracing each other. I found myself caught up in the celebration of it all. Hugging and kissing strangers, shaking hands from one person to the next. I was bouncing with everyone else full of the possibilities that the next year holds for us. I turned and hugged the next person; it was Miss Daley my English teacher. She looked at me and then we embraced. She looked at me again

"Is it true that you are on heroin?"

I was quite taken aback. I really liked her as a teacher, my favourite. And full of the promises of tomorrow, brimming with the excitement of changing my life I still could not admit it to her

"No"

I said.

"But your pupils are really tiny"

So quickly I came up with what I thought was my way out as I stood looking at her but right behind her was a huge neon sign

"I'm looking directly into that sign, aren't I?"

And with that, I moved off. It was as if I had been caught in a huge lie, I had been caught in a big lie. At that very moment, my mood collapsed again. I walked away from her miserable with the realisation of who I really was. I was a junky and everybody knew it just by looking at me. I wasn't magically moving through the crowd I now started to see the looks on people's faces when I was coming toward them, they were moving out of my way. I repulsed them, I scared them. I stopped when I caught my reflection in a window. I turned and looked at myself. Hollow eyes, cheeks, pinpoint pupils, grey skin, greasy hair, face full of spots. I was a junky and I looked like one. I had lost so much weight as I just didn't eat anymore. The only reason that I was functioning was because of heroin. I couldn't remember the last time I ate. I had no appetite for it, but also no appetite for anything else. I was a ghost, a living ghost walking toward the grave. I may never find my grave though as who knows where I might die. I may just die somewhere and nobody would ever find me. My body would decompose and be eaten by the vermin that live in the alleyways along with myself. My body would be stripped by other junkies hoping to find something they could sell. Bodies decompose quickly here in the heat. That was it I was decomposing right in front of my eyes. I had to go somewhere to take a hit. I headed back up to the park where sure enough I found Mr Lee asleep on one of the park benches. I got my gear out and took a big hit. I sat back took a cigarette out and lay back staring at the black and orange sky.

Chapter Thirty-Seven

Pik Uk for Xmas and deportation hearing

It was with a sense of doom that I got up early and threw my blankets together. Had a shower in the cell toilet and washed my hair. After being in prison all this time I was devastated to be called back to Pik Uk for my deportation hearing during the Xmas holidays. At no point in my whole time in prison had I had so many friends? I was looking forward to the days of watching movies together, playing games, eating biscuits and chocolate with my friends. It was a time of joy and sometimes local charity groups would come in and sing carols not that we were that interested in the songs, more like we would be happy checking out the ladies that would be there, smiling at us and passing on their Christmas joy!!
Anyway, that wouldn't happen for me this year, however, I did have plenty of snacks for myself and books to read. I was told that I would only be gone for a couple of days so there was a possibility that I could be back for Xmas day, but I won't get my hopes up.

The day of my journey off the island had come at last. Having spent the last year here in this mosquito-filled swamp, I was looking forward to seeing the rest of the world again. What I wasn't looking forward to was the ferry crossing. That dark hold with urine, faeces and vomit swirling around wasn't high on my to-do list. But to be able to see Hong Kong again, even just a glimpse of its magnificence was enough to excite me.
I got up early with Ah Mun to get washed and to get all my stuff ready. Ah Moon gave me some shampoo and I also rinsed my hair with conditioner. I took my blanket s to the store and my other things to the reception office. We all had a good share of Ah Muns breakfast since he was going home; he had a chocolate bar and a carton of juice for his breakfast. I said goodbye to chocolate and win sun as they would be gone by the time I got back. I then went up to the workshop to wait. I was called out shortly after 9 am to go to the RO. I saw the S.P he wished me a
"Merry Xmas"
Which was nice of him, and then I went to the RO to find my clothes. A few other HK guys are transferring to Pik Uk today. I saw Ah Mun get ready to go home. His clothes were a bit weird but I said he

looked cool. So now he's going home to his mum to drink tea. It was all he went on about for months and months. He then said after tonight it's karaoke and fucking. 13 new prisoners came to Lai Sun today, amongst them was another Sikh. Poor chap he looks quite useless, totally out of his depth, he seems really shy and scared. Hess only got 6 months so he'll be out about the same time as me, hopefully. At 12 o'clock we were told to change our clothes. I had been given some new ones as the ones I was arrested in all that time ago were only good for the bin. They're ok, quite smart, chinos with a smart shirt. But the belt is too small to go round my skinny waist!! But amongst my stuff I found my old brown leather jacket, I had totally forgotten about it. The lining is a bit torn but I put it on anyway. Wow, it took me back. To be wearing proper clothes after so long is a weird feeling; it is as if you are getting dressed for the very first time. Everyone all of a sudden looks really different. But the guys who have been in the longest don't suit their clothes any more. It's weird the new guys look like they've just chosen what to wear but us old-timers look like we are wearing clothes that are too big for us. It shows you how much weight you lose in these prisons. And not just around your belly but all over. I managed to pick up a newspaper to read on the journey, and then we all picked up our belongings and were handcuffed. The big old handcuffs. Not the wee ones that most people would recognise but the big heavy ones that stop your hands being able to touch each other. They felt really heavy this time and looked almost too big on my withered arms. We went through the main gate and climbed onto one of the big trucks. In the back was a few old prisoners from the OAP prison and some form the drug treatment centre. One of them knew me, I don't know how and said "Hey gwai gi, you go home now".

I ignored him as I had been trained to do all these years, I just gave a smile. The old prisoners just sat there staring at this strange foreigner. One looked like he was going home. All dressed up in his court suit, with his brown paper bags full of his belongings. The suit looked pretty outdated, and he looked very frail and pale, I reckoned that this chap had done some serious time. He didn't look too happy. Sometimes you wonder if after being somewhere like this for 10 or even 20 years it would be best just to stay there at his age. The truck slowly set off down the hill; once you got 100 yards away for the steel fences the island was beautiful. Like a desert island, with palm trees, huge bushes with the biggest leaves you've ever seen, you could hear the jungle noises as you went past and the smells. If you close your eyes and were able to take yourself away you could imagine that you were alone in the jungle. I longed to feel nature. I hadn't touched a leaf since I had been inside. To walk barefoot on the grass is a constant dream you have when you are locked up. So many things you don't think about. Even getting out of prison for a little while gives you the opportunity to see a long distance. Normally you can only see a few metres in any given direction apart from up. The horizon in prison is the sky. We got off the truck and were taken into the visiting room just at the end of the jetty where the ferries would come. Where we waited for ages. It felt like ages, it maybe has been an hour, but waiting to be thrown into the hold of the ferry made time distort. We heard the ferry before we saw it. The old engines grinding through its gears as it slowly pulled towards the pier. We were ordered to get up and walked back into the sunshine. When I saw the ferry my heart sunk a bit more. The paint was peeling off its wooden slatted sides, held together with rust. Walking towards it you could start to smell it. It looked like a retired fishing boat with a main wooden structure and a flat deck behind it. As we climbed the ladder to get on board a large square lid was opened on the flat deck that was covering a black void below it. As we were ushered towards it the stench really hit you. It was hard not to gag at the waves of pungent stench that escaped like galloping horses from the hole. You could feel it on your skin. It smelt like years of accumulated sewerage, heated to just the right temperature in the hot sun to take it to the right level of lethal. Chemical weapons came to mind as I was moved closer and closer. Every prisoner had the same expression. This could have been the weapon of choice to get rid of the unwanted, a chamber of death that we all compliantly walked towards. There was a steep set of wooden steps leading down into the hole. Each prisoner had to contort their handcuffed bodies around at the top and take a step backwards with nothing to hold onto into the thick soup of nausea. With legs trembling it was my turn. As my foot reached the first step I thought I had leant back to far and for a moment found myself struggling not to fall backwards. "Hurry up "came the shout from the over caring guard whose job it was to make sure we all went down without complaining. You don't complain unless you want to be beaten, I had learnt that a long time ago. There were about 15 steps until I reached the bottom. I almost imagined I would step into some kind of sludge at the bottom, sinking up to my ankles in shit. But the floor was wooden. I let my eyes adjust to the darkness. There were a couple of dim light bulbs that were swaying with the ferry, shinning dim light over the insides. It was nothing but a cargo hold but we were the only cargo. Lines of wooden benches with prisoners sitting. If I could see properly their skin would have been a pale white in colour. I was taken to a bench and made to sit down. With relief, my handcuffs were removed. How could they possibly imagine handcuffing us in this shit hole? What would happen in an n emergency? We wouldn't be able to do anything with these heavy lumps of metal. Would have been against health and safety surely. But my relief was brief. There was a heavy metal chain running around the base of the benches that I didn't see in the darkness. It had numerous sets of the lighter police cuffs attached to it but with a longer set of links between each cuff. One cuff was snapped on to my wrist and I pulled up the long links and looked at them.

"So you go toilet "

Said the guard and pointed to one of two old paint buckets that used to be white. I had never been seasick before but with the stench, darkness, fear and soft swaying of the boat I could feel the bile rising in my throat, I felt dizzy but I had to calm myself down, the alternative was not pleasant. I checked my bladder and with a sense of doom, I realised that I would have to empty it within the hour. Not knowing how long the crossing would take I tried to not think about it. After what felt like a full prison sentence in time the last prisoner was cuffed and the guard went up the steps. We all looked up towards the square of light and grimaced in unison when we heard the hatch being pulled across the deck and over the hole. Then it became nearly pitch black, some of the others let out audible panic. Some were moaning already, one guy in front of me puked on the floor. Others shouted at him, but it didn't do any good as he continued to retch until it was dry. The engines started up with a thunderous roar which shook the whole compartment. On top of the stench that was already here came another of diesel fumes and the boat slowly pulled away from the pier. The movement intensified and with no line of sight to steady your inner ear, three others started to throw up. One tried to make it to the bucket but slipped on the liquid already on the floor and knocked the bucket over, its vile contents joining the pool party that was already there. I lifted my feet off the ground and onto the back of the bench in front of me, not very comfortable when all I could feel was my now heavy bladder. The guy who said hello to me on the truck called me over to share a cigarette. His name was Ah Yik and he said he knew me because he was a friend of Lennon's. We chatted until I eventually had to get up to use the toilet. I was thinking about it the whole time we were talking. Planning how I was going to do it without falling like so many of the others had done. The bucket must have been pretty full by now as there had been a steady stream of prisoners going up to it and either puking or pissing into it. It must have looked awful inside. So I made sure to not look into it. I got up and grabbed one of the wooden supports whilst looking down to make sure I wasn't standing in something slimy. I waited for the boat to roll a certain way and allowed the roll to take me to the next support next to the bucket, trying to look down but avoiding the scene of horror sloshing about in front of me. I had decided to aim as well as I could without caring too much if I missed. I just wanted to empty my bladder and not get any waste on my clothes. I realised that as soon as was possible the bottom of my shoes would have to be cleaned or I would be carrying the stench with me for hours to come. After completing my epic journey I sat back down to Ah Yik. He told me that Lennon was getting out next month. And as we were talking the tone of the engines changed and you could feel the boat settling a bit more in the water. The thrusters then came on so I knew we must have reached our destination. Wherever that may be. When it was my time to climb the stairs with the heavy handcuffs having been replaced, I felt a surge of excitement. I knew that I was about to step out into the light and have Hong Kong harbour as a view. As my head made it over the lip of the hold the sight took my breath away. Just like the first time I had taken in the view all those years ago. But maybe even more intense this time after where I had come from. It was like escaping from execution to arrive in paradise. It was intoxicating like the first hit of heroin. Tears came to my eyes as I soaked in the view. We were at HMS Tamar, and as I climbed up the stone steps to finally arrive on dry land, I swung my head left and right to see as much as I could. Beautiful. The memories all came flooding back. My bus stop was right outside, the pier that I had slept rough on when my father had thrown me out just along the harbour to my right. The pier that I had embarked on so many boat parties with friends, within touching distance. It was like someone finding so many memories in my brain and turning them into virtual reality so that I could enjoy them at the

deepest of sensory levels. The smells, sounds, sights all absolutely marvellous, almost worth spending a couple of years in prison for, well maybe not.
We were put onto a minibus and to my great delight drove to central first to drop someone off at Victoria prison, then on to Admiralty and the Supreme Court. I started to feel dizzy; everything was moving so fast, I wasn't used to it. I was trying to see everything but I had to close my eyes for a moment or two or I might have been sick. We went from Admiralty through Wan Chai and then through the tunnel to the mainland. I started to just let the sights filter past me as I could no longer concentrate on anything. I had been away from this world for so long, I didn't belong anymore. How could I ever adjust again? I had recently realised that I was losing my English. I hadn't spoken it properly for a couple of years now all I could do was speak broken Chinese, my dreams were in Chinese. After an hour we arrived at the Pik Uk gates. They weren't as imposing as I had remembered them. They seemed to even be smaller than before. I was actually excited about going inside. It was familiar, the buildings I would know, the guards, the staff, most of the prisoners. Although my time here had been terrible at the start, now I was a long-timer and my attitude had changed. I was part of the system, I wasn't fighting it anymore, and it was part of me. As soon as we got through the second set of gates Pik Uk opened up to me. I turned to the right and saw some familiar faces on the basketball court. Although prison protocol didn't allow me to wave and shout some pleasantry, I did move my head up and down and got a couple of responses. When I got to the medical room the guards there said hello to me with smiles. It was quite nice. We had picked up a few prisoners on route to Pik U. And they were quite amazed at this foreigner exchanging pleasantries with the guards. Even the searching didn't bother me anymore. In the waiting room, I was even given a fresh set of clothes. Clean and new. And even underwear and a t-shirt. Shit, I felt like a fucking film star. Pants!! Clean pants. I hadn't had pants for two years. They felt strange but extremely comforting at the same time. I could feel them the whole time I had them on. I was given new socks and a shiny pair of shoes. I was dressed to impress, well prison-style anyway. We were taken up to the blocks and out into our cells. Mine was filthy. These cells were used only for new prisoners before they were moved to their long term cells, so nobody ever cleaned them. Our dinner was brought to the cells and when mine came I asked the kitchen guy to

get me some cleaning stuff, soap and a rag to clean my cell. Ten minutes later he was back with what I need and some powder to scrub the toilet and sink. So after a cold and horrible dinner. The food here being terrible compared to Lai Sun; I spent the rest of the evening cleaning my cell. I was going to be here over Xmas so I might as well make it as nice as possible. It was cold in the cell so I made a sleeping bag out of the blankets I had been given. I had brought a book and some wafers with me so I spent the evening reading and eating biscuits. The noises were there all night, but for me, they were just background noise now. I thought back to the very first night I was here, possible on the very same landing, how terrified I was. How terrified must be some of the new guys tonight? There first time inside, possibly withdrawing from heroin, alcohol, home comforts. Not knowing what was going to happen, heads filled with terrifying thoughts of what happens to new prisoners. But I was an old prisoner and I put down my book and fell asleep with the light still on, the radio still playing and the screams, shouts and banging soothing me into a deep and peaceful sleep.

Chapter -37

Disco Bay

I didn't know what to do with myself. As my cigarette finished I decided to go and top up my supply of smack. So I took another line and then headed for my favourite 7/11 in Wan Chai. It took me about 30 minutes to get there where I bought 4 bags of smack to do me tonight and tomorrow then I headed to the basket ballpark to take some. I went to a shop to buy some more cigarettes then headed back towards central. The streets were full of happy people celebrating. Couples walking arm in arm full of the promise of happiness for the year ahead, groups of friends singing. I nearly bumped into many of them and as I did they all turned to wish me a happy new year, and I did the same, time after time this happened then the next time when I turned to a couple it was Joanne and mike.

"Hey guys, happy new year"

"Hey man, happy New Year dude, we're just heading to get some gear, wanna join"

I could have said that had just got some and was heading back to central but I said instead

"Why the fuck not"

And off we trundled together back to my favourite 7/11 so that they could buy some.

We all headed to the park to take a hit, they mainlined theirs and I accepted their offer of some of theirs as well. We all sat back fully stoned and probably sat there for a good hour together.

"Hey man you wanna come over to ours for New Year's Day"

Joanne asked.

"Sure why not, where you staying"

"We're over at disco bay, so we'll have to wait for the first ferry". It was already about 4 am now so we only had a couple of hours to kill. So we headed back into Lan Kwai Fong. The streets were still busy with people drunk enough to be staggering and shouting all the way up and down the narrow roads. We went inside a pub and got a

couple of drinks. I and Joanne sat talking whilst mike dozed off in a corner. She was really lovely for a junky. She was beautiful beneath the damage that the smack in her veins was doing to her. Long dark straight hair and an angular face that was dark and quite intoxicating that it sucked you in towards it. She had a husky voice and a way of moving that actually stirred parts of me that hadn't been stirred in months. She would often put her hand on my thigh when I said something that amused her and she sat with her hand round my shoulders occasionally playing with my hair. It was taking me back to a better time a year ago when I seemed to be able to attract attention from the most gorgeous of girls without ever trying. It eventually got to about 0530 so we roused mike and headed down towards the piers where the ferries would be starting soon to the outlying islands. The ferry to discovery bay was actually a hovercraft. But by the time we got on board I was so exhausted I fell asleep almost immediately and missed most of the excitement of the journey. I was woken by mike pushing at me and shaking at me to get up as we had arrived. We stumbled off the craft and into Disco Bay as it was called. The only petrol-driven vehicles in this exclusive enclave were the fire engines everything else was electric golf buggies. But as we didn't have one we had to stager up the road until we got to their apartment. It was in a group of unremarkable tower blocks. Everyone looks exactly the same. We rode the elevator up to the 5th floor and clambered into their sparse apartment. With only a sofa and other bits of pieces of furniture, it was comfortable enough and pretty clean for a junkie flat. Mike went straight to bed but Joanne and I decided to do some more gear together. As mike was the one who sorted their hits out and he had gone to bed Joanne was snorting her now just like me. We shared our equipment together and got high. She then sat there and stared at me. I knew what was coming and to be honest, didn't do anything to stop it. But I would only let it go so far. She injected drugs. That meant possible disease. I didn't say this to her but I had enough of my wits about me not to be seduced into intercourse with her. I had never screwed a junky and never would. I had far too much-unprotected sex with other girls but I drew the line at a junkie. So she pushed me back on to the couch and started hungrily snogging me. But I felt nothing. I followed the routine as if a team member on a factory production line. Kiss this side of the mouth for 1-minute change to the other side for another minute. Make the correct noises as she rubbed my cock. Move my hands over her *back and then spend an equal amount of time with the said hand under her shirt whilst playing with each nipple and give the adequate amount of squeezing to each breast for the correct time period. Okay here goes I'd better rub her fanny for a little bit too. So I moved my hand to her thighs and lo and behold she opened her legs, now there was a surprise, not! So I ran my hand up to her panties and did what was expected of me. She was delighted and I became an employee of the month. This went on for a little while until I managed to pull myself away for long enough to say I wanted to take another line. This went on for another hour or so. She was getting a little frustrated, but I was holding my own, so to speak. Finally, we heard a noise from the bedroom and out popped mike. Angry.*

"What the fuck have you guys been doing?"

"Nothing, just hanging out"

Shouted back, Joanne. I knew enough that this was a bad situation. I quickly grabbed my gear and as they were still screaming at each other I managed to sneak out of the apartment whilst there was a huge crash against a wall.

Fuck me that was close, I didn't wait for the elevator I just headed to the emergency exit and ran down the stairs. I headed back towards the harbour and thankfully caught a ferry within 10 minutes back to central. It was now midday but with nothing else to do, I went to my bench on Blake pier and looked out over the harbour. I spent hours there that day just staring at the busy harbour. Little boats going backwards and forwards. It was then I noticed a note on my makeshift bed. I t was from 2 of my friends who had come to visits me at "my place" the night before. I had missed them by about 5 minutes. Friends had come to see me on New Year's Eve and I had missed them and had a pretty miserable time. That brought me down again. I did have friends but I had spent the night by myself. Although with people, I was by myself. Joanne needed me for her own freaky reason. To fill a void in her life even though she had a home and a partner she was still so empty inside just like me. I got up and decided to go for a wander.

Chapter Thirty-Eight
The next day.

I was at first disorientated when I woke up. But as I looked around me I remembered where I was, then the familiar Pik Uk morning chorus filled the hallways. I got ready for breakfast and sat waiting patiently. I had no idea what my routine was going to be here, and I had to admit I was at a bit of a loss. Having followed the same daily routines for so long I found myself getting a bit fidgety. Time kept going, past my normal breakfast time, so now I was very hungry. And still, I sat there. All the other cells had been emptied; it felt like I was the last person here. Forgotten about? I didn't want to cause any issues. I would have probably starved to death rather than making any noise and start any problems here that may take me to places I dreaded to go to. So for the sake of keeping the peace, I sat there. I must have fallen asleep because I was woken by a guard banging the bars with his keys.

"Hei sun gwai gi, jo chaan "(get up foreigner devil, breakfast).

My cell was unlocked and I was walked down the stairs. I hadn't noticed yesterday but just at the entrance to the block, someone had built a small aviary. It was full of the brightest of birds. It was a strange sight; maybe something to do with Fung Shui but to see something like that here, in such a depressing place was weird. I was marched towards the dining hall, my stomach rumbling and full of butterflies at the same time. I had so many memories of this hall, most of them terrible. I steadied myself and got prepared, but just as we neared the dining hall another guard came and told me to stop. I wasn't allowed into the dining hall. I was still a security risk from my previous holiday here. So with that, I was turned around and marched straight back to my cell. But as soon as I got to it I was told to get out again. I was then marched to B hall and put into a different cell. It was stinking. I was told to wait. I did. Not much else you can do whilst locked in a tiny cell in a high-security prison is there. Another hour or so passed before my breakfast was brought, cold and miserable. The rice was awful and the fish heads were almost inedible. But I had to eat, I had no choice, if I didn't eat them I may not get anything else for 7 or 8 hours as I didn't know what if anything would be brought for lunch. If it was the white congee I wouldn't eat it, but there was no knowing if it would be the green congee either. I ate everything on the plate with grim determination.

This was a bad start. If this is where they are going to keep me whilst I am here it is going to be a difficult stay. Xmas was going to be depressing. Lunch came and it was white congee so I said no, glad that I had forced down the old fish heads earlier. Not long after I was taken out of my cell and taken another larger cell. It was a corner cell in the area where un-sentenced prisoners were kept. It had barred windows the length of one side so gave a pleasant vista of the huge perimeter wall and the cat A's hall, where I had spent some unpleasant time previously. As I was enjoying the view the cell door opened and a TV and a trolley were pushed into the cell. I asked the guard if I could watch it and how long I could; he said do what you want. I nearly jumped up for joy. I plugged it in and although snow filled the screen I was undeterred. Ten minutes of fiddling went by and I eventually got it tuned in. There were only a couple of English channels so I settled for European football for a while. I then fiddled again and found a movie channel with "Home alone "just starting. I hadn't seen it before so I sat down and laughed out loud for the duration. It was like I had my own little palace, I could get used to this. Bring me every day, serve me breakfast lunch and dinner and let me watch TV all day. This trip to Pik Uk was looking better and better. Okay so I was going to miss all the Xmas celebrations but I imagine on Xmas day there should be some good TV to watch. After dinner, I was taken for a shower and back to my cell. After a shaky start, it had been a great day. I was happy, content, looking forward to tomorrow.

Next day
Today they got everything it the right order. I was taken to B Hall where breakfast was delivered on time and still warm. The food was still as bad but because it was warm it was more palatable. How can they make the rice so bad and what the hell did they do to the fish heads? Lai Suns breakfast was almost 5 stars compared to this shit. Anyway, I sat down and stuck the TV on. After about an hour a guard came in and told me that I had to work when I was here. He gave me a pile of paper that had folds in it, a pot of glue and was told to make envelopes. I did this whilst watching the TV. At lunchtime, another prisoner was brought in. He was a mainlander, II, looked frightened and wouldn't talk to me. He kept running to the toilet for a piss; don't know what the matter was with him. Later we were told that we had to do education in the afternoon. I asked what it was and a trolley full

of books was wheeled in. So education was read a book. Perfect, I had no complaints. I managed to find an ole Robert Ludlum book and sat on my plastic chair and read away until dinner time. My back was a bit painful from sitting all day so I asked the guard when we would be getting exercise, he told me he'd ask.

We had to fold envelopes all morning again until lunchtime. This time I went to have a shower first, and I took my time in the burning hot water. Well, I am going to court tomorrow so I needed to be shiny and bright, nothing to do with annoying the other two. But when they got back they said their shower was hot too, lucky fuckers. The TV had been put on when I went for a shower so when I came back and they went I turned it to the English channel when they came back from the shower they went to change the channel, I jumped up and told them that I was watching it today as they watched yesterday. The newest one came up to me and told to fuck off as there were two of them and only one of me. I pulled myself to full height and told him to fuck off and pushed him away from me. He fell backwards over a chair and hit the ground. And just my luck that a guard saw me do it. The alarm went off and a pile of guards came in and grabbed me, they slammed me to the floor, and helped my sore back by giving it a good old truncheon massage. I was then dragged to see the governor. Two days before Xmas, here we go. The governor wasn't available so when I went in it was the deputy governor, someone I hadn't met before.
"I've heard about you "
He said.
"You don't play by the rules, do you want to be in solitary all Xmas?"
"No sir ".
" you go court tomorrow, but now you go to solitary until I think what to do to you "
I was marched back to a -hall and was taken downstairs this time, into the dungeons. The corridor was dark as it was below ground level, although there were windows that gave me a view of B-hall. I was pushed into the bare cell, told to strip and was left there standing in my pants and t-shirt, so grateful that I had them. That night I was given a cold dinner and only two sheets and no pillow. It was going to be a cold night.

Chapter -38
Begging

The next morning I woke up feeling like shit. I had no get up and go and was running low on smack again. So I took a line and went to see if I could find Lennon. I had no joy so I decided to set up my begging station next to the star ferry in Tsim Tsa Tsui. I just sat there that day, not putting much effort into it. The thought again came to me that I wanted to escape; it was now only a few days to my 18th birthday. It was then I thought about killing myself instead. It would be easy. If I couldn't escape and there was no one around who wanted to or be able to help me it would be better off if I just died. I started thinking how I could do it. Sitting there at the ferry terminal with the while of Hong Kong running around me I was lost in my thoughts of how to kill myself. I saw 2 ways of doing it. One spectacular and one lonely. I could take a load of smack, head up to lion rock and just simply jump off screaming something awesome as I did it. I could just get a syringe and shoot an enormous amount of smack into my veins and do it quietly that way, either leaving my body somewhere it could be found or going deep into the jungle where I would never be found. The thing was I didn't want any pain but I would like to experience it. Why not, we experience everything wise in life why shouldn't we be allowed to experience our own death. My life had been interesting enough that if I was going to end it myself it should be something cool. Maybe the coolest thing that had ever done. Have people talking about it forever. Not being a forgotten junky that people would remember every so often in conversation when some other junky died.

I didn't even say thank you to the countless people who were putting money into my box after reading my fake sob story sign that I had. Telling people that my whole family had died in a car crash and I was trying to get enough money to go home to Scotland. It worked, and I made lots of money from it. I didn't notice the businessmen, the young people, the old aunties and uncles putting money in the box. The locals and the foreigners. I didn't notice this English family who had read my sign and then wandered a little way off to stand huddled together, pointing towards me talking quietly together. I was in the middle of another spectacular suicide when

"Hi, there".

I looked up into the faces of four people looking at me. They were all squatting down and smiling at me.

"Do you really want to go home?"

"Yes"

I said

"It's nearly my 18th birthday and I want to leave this place".

"If we helped you go, would you go?"

"Do you have a passport"

"Yes I do"

"Is it valid?"

"Yes".

"Give us a minute will you please".

I sat there wondering what was going on. I was pretty smashed and couldn't really focus very well. Maybe they would give me a ton of money that would help me get sorted out. They came back over and said

" we have decided that we will help you"

"We will buy you a flight to London straight away"

I burst into tears. It was the first emotion I had experienced for a long time, the first real emotion. The tears were rolling down my cheeks and onto the ground.

"What"

I said through the snotters that were dripping out of my nose.

"We will go to a travel agent and get you the first flight we can".

"Where can we find you later?"

"You can find me here"

"Okay we will try and get you on the same flight as us, we fly back tomorrow, would that be okay for you, can you get everything ready by then"

"Yes, yes I can"

"We will need your passport to buy the ticket"

I searched through my bag and found my passport. I took it everywhere with me.

"Here take it"

"Right we will come back here tonight, by the latest 5 or 6 o'clock, will you be here?"

"Yes, I'll be here".

And with that, they were off. Shit, this was it I was leaving, I was leaving tomorrow. Or maybe not, maybe they wouldn't come back and I had lost my passport. But no they seemed totally genuine. Oh my god. I had a lot to do. I would need to get all my shit together. Need to say goodbye to friends and need to get some gear so that I could survive the flight and to last me until I got help back in the UK.

Chapter Thirty-Nine
Supreme Court day trip

As soon as the radio came on I got up. It wasn't difficult as I had barely slept last night. I was shivering cold with only a hard plastic bed and two sheets. I lay on the hard surface and tried my best to make the two sheets as thick as possible by folding them, but it never worked. I tried to pull myself into a ball to keep warm but it was just awful. I got washed as well as I could with the freezing water from the tap. I didn't have any soap or toothbrush or toothpaste so I could only use my finger to try and clean my teeth. Not the way I wanted to present myself at the Supreme Court. I couldn't even shave so I looked like shit, even though there was no way for me to see how I actually looked. I had planned to have a book with me and some biscuits as I knew that I would be at the court for a long time. But because of the fight, I had nothing. I was taken from my cell early to go to the reception office. It was cold and foggy this morning. The morning light gave the whole place an eerie feeling just as it was 2 years ago when I first arrived. Now I was glad I brought my tatty old leather jacket. I slipped it on and hugged its warmth. Once we were all dressed, I and all the others going to court, we were taken up to the dining hall. I didn't have the same trepidation as I had the first day; I was just hungry and new that I would go straight to a table where our breakfast would have already been placed for us. We wolfed down the haute cuisine. Two of the guys across from me looked like they had just come in the night before and were in the throes of heroin withdrawal. They couldn't eat, so when no guard was looking I reached over and grabbed their fish heads. They looked at me with open eyes but said nothing; I waited for them to put down their spoons and then helped myself to the rest of their rice too. The irony. We were taken back to the RO and made to stand in line outside. I was a little bothered by the cold but there were a few guys who had come in during the summer months and were standing there in shorts and t-shirts shivering, they must have been freezing. And they looked it, their legs turning blue. Obviously, no-one in Hong Kong cared for them or they would have had clothing brought in for them. So they stood there shivering. There were two other guys going with me to the Supreme Court. They looked really rough guys, proper triad tattoos. The Supreme Court was for people getting long sentences, and people like me getting deported. So they were staring down the face of a double-figure sentence and being so close to the handover to china that was frightening. We were all cuffed and led to our transport. We were put into the ultra-secure bus that was only used for serious criminals. The bus has a central corridor with separate boxes with solid closed doors running down each side. I was put into one and sat on the tiny wooden bench, having to sit at an angle because my knees were hard up against the wall in front of me. There was only a very narrow slit of a window to give you light. The walls were covered in gang-related graffiti and it stank of urine and vomit. This wasn't the first time I had been in one but there was no getting used to it. The journey was uncomfortable and I had barely any view out the window because some idiot had melted some of the plastic on the window and some others have dug into the plastic so it was like looking through frosted glass. We eventually reached the Supreme Court on Queensway and were driven into the basement level. We were taken off the bus one by one and taken into a smoky reception office. The staff there were actually pretty friendly. We had our cuffs taken off and put into holding cells. It was pretty comfortable there and I would have been happy to stay there all day. Unfortunately, we were soon taken out and to the proper holding cells. We were led down a tight corridor that you could barely keep your shoulders straight it was so tight. At the end was a thick door that the guard struggled to pull open after he had unlocked the heavy bolts. We were then in what anyone would call a proper dungeon. I had no idea how old these cells were but they looked like something from the dark ages. The corridor had cells off each side. It was so dark inside each cell that you couldn't see much more than a foot inside each one. Each had a prisoner peering through the bars; one looked empty only for a face to suddenly appear at the bars. Some of these guys looked like they had been locked in there for years. When we reached my cell I was stopped and the guard opened the door and pushed me inside. It was dark; it took a short while for my eyes to adjust to the darkness. It was huge inside; you could quite easily fit 30 prisoners inside. But there was only me. No fixtures or fittings, unclean for decades. The toilet was in the corner looking at me with the faces of a billion bacteria unknown to science. Across from me, there was another prisoner, an older one. He had been here many times as he asked me to look for a match that had been hidden in the cell by a friend sometime before. He offered me a cigarette if I found it for him. So I began the search.

He told me it would be near the bars. The whole front of the cell was barred, from floor to ceiling and about 3 metres long. I started at one end and checked every bar but couldn't find it. I told him there was nothing there. He said to check the rest of the cell. I said I would check one last time. So I went around the whole-cell looking for this elusive match. T was so dark I had to use my hands until eventually, I found it hidden against the wall in the corner in a small gap between the floor concrete and the wall. I went to the front and waited for the officer to finish his walk up and down the hall doing his 15-minute check, and then I threw the match over to my dungeon companion. He then said that there was something else, but I couldn't make out what he was saying. He had to whisper but I couldn't make it out. Anyway, I had a look and eventually, I found a small piece of match striking paper. I had a small piece of tissue paper in my pocket so I wrapped the striking strip into it so that I could throw it across. He caught it and quickly took out a cigarette. He struck the match but almost immediately it spluttered and died. It must have been damp from being left in the cell. Shit, what could we do? I then heard some voices down the corridor a few cells away and they were talking English. So I called down to them and asked if they had a light and they said yes. I asked them to throw it down the matches down but they thought I would steal them. So the cigarette was thrown to the guy in the next cell to me because they were in the cell next to him. The cigarette was lit; each took a puff until it was returned to the guy opposite. He smoked away for a while then threw the rest to me. But when he threw the end broke off, I had to quickly get down and grab it with my hand and bend down to relight the remaining cigarette off of it. All of this was witnessed by a guard but he just laughed and said nothing. I sat back in the darkness of the cell and relished the last few puffs of the cigarettes. It made me feel high, so I dozed in my highness for a while. About 30 minutes later we went through the whole thing again with me ending up with the cigarette again but without the dramatics. I started chatting to the cigarette provider across from me. He's 19 and waiting to be sentenced for a robbery he did where he tied some people up. He gets sentenced on the 31st of December and reckons he'll get over 10 years. He said all this matter of. Shit, I had forgotten all that time ago waiting for my sentence, I wasn't as cool as him and I thought I would be getting under 10 years. Just after he had finished telling me his story I was called to go up to court. Probably the first time I didn't care about going to court. I was taken up to court 10 with a guy from Pakistan. He was there for the same thing after serving 2 years in Stanley prison. He didn't want to be deported but knew he had little chance of staying. I went in first at 10 am. I sat down in the court and looked around me. I was thinking of all the lost souls and lives that this court represented. It had a real sad energy about it. But maybe that was just how I was feeling. Sad that my life had come to this. Sad at this young age to be in the position to be deported out of a British colony. I then realised that my legs were knocking together. I kept reminding myself that there was nothing to worry about; they are not going to extend my sentence or give me shit for anything. It didn't work. It was only when we were told to stand for justice Bockhary to come in and then told to sit down again that I felt better. The hearing started. Someone read the s out about the deportation order. While they were doing that I looked around the court again. There was nobody there. Not even Mr Forse this time. I guess no-one knew that I was here. Just then justice Bockhary asks me to stand. He looked at me and said

"You're not going to appeal against the deportation are you?"

"No your honour "

I replied quickly.

"Good "

He said.

He was just about to get up and leave when I pulled my courage up from somewhere, stood up and cleared my throat. The power that the court had over me was almost physical; I could feel it warning me,

"Don't do it "

But me being me I did.

"Your honour, I have three questions ".

I couldn't quite believe how difficult it was for me to interrupt him, me a lowly criminal and him a high court judge. He smiled and said

"Fine, no problem at all ".

So I asked him the three questions I had rehearsed.

"Will my flights be paid to Scotland, when would I transfer to Victoria prison and when I get to the UK will I be free?"

He put all my questions to the immigration officer. He had taken my questions seriously and had set aside some of his busy schedules for me. I started to feel a little less of a number and a little more human. Just the simple of being listened to by someone so important, maybe I feel important again. It was an important step towards being a free man again. The immigration officer gave him the answers and I thought that would be it. But oh no, this caring man started to put points forward on my behalf, he was fighting for my rights when during the last couple of years I thought I had none. He argued that I had to be given my full fare to Scotland as that was where my family was. He said that I should be put on the very first flight possible to the UK, even if it meant an earlier transfer. He also stipulated that on my release I had completed my sentence so the immigration and police in the UK will not be given any information on me and that I wouldn't have to wear an electronic tag around my ankle for the remainder of my sentence. I hadn't even thought about that. Because I had some time off for good behaviour left, but only some, the remainder that I served outside would be under probation and I would have to wear a tag. But that was only if I was released in Hong Kong. Although it's a colony of the UK the criminal laws are slightly different. He then told the immigration officer to get all of the details of his determination to me as soon as possible. I thanked him immensely and was ushered out of the court. I think I was standing a few inches taller. I waited in the side room whilst the Pakistani guy went in for his hearing. After a short while, he came out with a smile on his face. It looks like he'll be able to stay. His wife is in Hong Kong and he has a job to go to. He was well chuffed as was I for him. We got back into the lift to go back down to the holding cells when he tried to give me a few cigarettes but the officers stopped him. I'm not free yet. When I was safely locked back in my dark cell an officer came down and struck up a conversation with me. I talked to him only because I thought if I was pleasant enough he would get me some cigarettes. He was a real pain, he talked with me for ages about why I was there, how long I had been in for, what it was like what would I do on release etc. etc. After about ten minutes I interrupted him and asked if he could get me some cigarettes and he laughed and said no, turned and walked off. So I went to the back of the cell, made a pillow out of my jacket and lay down for asleep. The other two guys from the cell in front of me and next to me came back down around 12 o'clock. We were served a sweet congee. I only ate it because I was hungry, it was pretty foul. The guy across from me produced another cigarette but as hard as we tried we couldn't get a light from anyone. He threw the cigarette over to me as he said because I was a foreigner I may have more luck getting alight. I heard the bottom door open and the prisoner who worked there

started collecting the mugs as he reached my cell and I passed him my mug I held onto it and asked him if he had a light. He was a really old guy so at first, I thought he hadn't heard me. He would have understood me as I spoke perfect prison Cantonese at this point. He carried on down the hall collecting mugs, then once he had collected the last one he went up to an officer and pointed at me whilst he spoke in a really quiet voice.
"Bastard is grassing me up to the guard "
I thought, then I saw the guard nod and the old guy shuffled towards me and held out a box of matches. He had asked the guard if it was ok to give me a light. When I saw the matches I nodded, using his other hand he made a signal for me to pass him the cigarette, I did so and he lit it for me. He passed it back to me and I moved back into the darkness to enjoy the smoke. I only took a few puffs before I threw it to the owner. Instead of finishing it himself he took the same amount of puffs I had and threw it back to me and told me to finish it. When I picked it up I tore half of the filter off of it so as to get a really good hit. I felt like I was floating so I lay down at the back of the cell and allowed myself to float off dreaming of my upcoming release. I heard his cell open and he was off to court again. I drifted off thinking of flying away from this hell that I was in. The grass between my toes, girls, as many cigarettes, as I wanted, sausages and beans washed down with an ice-cold beer. I woke up with his cell door opening and closing. And then it was time to go. They came and unlocked my cell and as I turned into the corridor I saw the clock at the end and it was 5 pm, I had slept under my tobacco-induced stupor for the whole afternoon. The officers who collected us were real bastards this time but the good news was that we were being transported in one of the old school buses. They were a lot more comfortable than the vans and had huge windows so that I could take in the view. I was handcuffed by myself and taken to halfway down the bus. The bus was already half full as they had picked prisoners up from the lower courts before they came for us. As soon as I sat down I was kicked in the arse. I looked around and saw one of my friends behind me. I laughed and was immediately chastised by one of the guards, my mate laughed too and got hit on the head, we then both laughed and the guard just walked away. The bus started and we were soon on admiralty. It was evening time so everything was lit up and there were Christmas lights everywhere, it was the most magical Christmas experience I had ever had. I normally hated Christmas but

this was just splendid. We drove right along admiralty which was so covered in Christmas light I was nearly blinded. Then through Wan Chai and to the tunnel, I then drifted off to sleep again. Huddled in my jacket feeling the imaginary sensation of freedom heading back towards Pik Uk. It was almost exactly 2 years ago that I had taken this journey for the first time. A compete wretch of a child. Dirty, scared, at the start of horrendous heroin withdrawals. 17 years old with no hope for the future, nothing to live for. An idiot who had thrown away every possibility that Hong Kong has to offer. A delinquent who had hurt family and friends. Someone whose friends crossed the street when they saw him coming, From begging on Nathan road to get money for drugs, for breaking the law without thinking of the pain and the consequences. I sat there now a changed man. I would make the same mistakes again, I had survived, so far, and I would continue to go from strength to strength. If I kept myself out of trouble I would free in a matter of months. No longer a teenager but a man. I just had to get over the next few days and get back to Lai Sun. It was just as we arrived back in Pik Uk that I remembered that I was in solitary. I was searched and got changed and was marched to the basement. Now I was cold. I didn't have the benefit of my leather jacket and the temperature had really dropped. When my cold dinner was brought t I asked if I could get some blankets as I was really cold. One was brought, only one, but it made a slight difference, but that night helped me realise that this nightmare wasn't quite over.

Chapter -39

Escape

I grabbed all the money out of my box and stuffed it into my pockets, jumped up and half ran to Chung king mansions. I ran straight to the back stairs and was taking them two at a time when I ran straight into Lennon.

"Diu lay low mo Gwai Gi, where the fuck you been, been looking every were for you, fuck you mother, come with me Gwai Gi".

We went back up the stairs and down an unlit corridor where a few knocks on the door got us our entrance.

"Where the fuck you been, never mind, here, sik yin"

So we chased a dragon together.

"Lennon I've got some mental news, a family said that they will buy me a ticket to the UK so that I can get clean, I leave tomorrow"

"That great news, you can take stuff for us"

"You take stuff for us then you can leave".

His tone of voice told me everything. The Chinese hate losing face, it is what will get you chopped up. For me to leave the gang I had to have a one-way ticket that looked like he had planned. So I would have to take some smack to the UK and when I had done that for him he would have gained points and I would be free. It was a no brainer. Perfect.

"We go meet these people together, what time you get the ticket?"

"5 o'clock at Star Ferry to Tsim Tsa Tsui"

"Okay I go with you, wait until you get ticket then we go get you stuff okay gwai gi?"

"Ok".

At 430 we left the mansions. Lennon had spent most of the time until then making phone calls, disappearing for 30 minutes at a time then reappearing again. Part of me was saying that it wouldn't happen.

They either wouldn't turn up or couldn't get me a ticket because there were none or the last minute tickets were too expensive. So when I was sitting there at the same place they had left me all those hours ago, with Lennon leaning on a lamppost with his back to the harbour and keeping an eye on all the comings and goings, they turned up with smiles on their faces. I stood up and welcomed them.

"We got you a ticket on the 5 pm flight to London Heathrow tomorrow night. The same flight as us."

"Thank you so much"

I said this time with less emotion as Lennon was watching.

"Can you get to the airport by yourself, do you have enough money?"

"Yes"

I said. And at that, they passed me over a bag. It was full of new clothes and trainers. The clothes that I wore for begging were quite frankly disgusting. I had made them like that to get more pity money. The trousers were old linen ones covered on stains that I had engineered. The coat was once pretty smart but every day I made sure I dragged it through a gutter or two to get that fresh, I just slept in a cesspit last night, odour to it. In the bag were a pair of jeans, a t-shirt and a jumper all from the Giordano shop in Ocean Terminal. I had walked past the shop many times but had never been in. a little like Benetton but slightly lower price. After thanks and more promises had been made to this amazing family that I would definitely be there tomorrow at the airport and at all times I could see Lennon in the background watching everything. When they left Lennon sauntered over and asked to see the ticket. There it was in its entire exciting format. 1700 BA flight Hong Kong to London Heathrow.

"Let's go"

He said and he turned towards Nathan Road. I followed him up the back stairs in the mansions and when he got to one door he knocked the special knock and we were let in.

"You wait here, I come back soon"

He then said something quickly to the other triads that were lounging about on the furniture that most would have thrown out. All I could catch was

"Gwai Gi"

And he was gone. One of the guys passed me over a tray full of smack and different utensils for the partaking of said substance. There could be worse places for me to be. So I tucked into the goodies, lay back and listened to the young triads from Hong Kong, not understanding what they were saying but enjoying the guttural tones and flamboyant displays whilst they were recounting their last escapade of work, war or sex here in this colony of opportunity. I closed my eyes and thought back to all the adventures I had during my short time here and how it almost killed me. I was determined to return to the UK for my birthday but as soon as I had sorted myself out I was going to come back to Hong Kong as I truly believed that this was the place that I should be. I had seen how easy it had been to make legitimate money here and also illegitimate. But when I returned I was going to go straight. I had learned so much about how easy it is for a Gwai Gi to get a job here and it would only become easier with the 1997 handover looming large on the horizon. You would have to be crazy to stay here after that happened. The Chinese wouldn't just sit and honour the agreement it had with the UK, that wasn't their style as it would mean losing face to the UK. No, they would come in and rip up the place. Far too much money to be made. Why were so many Hong Kong Chinese trying to escape if the hand over was going to be straight forward? Anyway, that was a long time away. I would work up until then and then find somewhere else to go. Hopefully, I would have settled down by then with one of the Hong Kong lovelies that I had met when I had first come here. My god, coming from a life where no-one ever paid me any attention apart from when they were laughing at me getting beaten up by someone else to having all these amazing and gorgeous girls all around me, all of the time. It really was a head fuck. It was also my downfall. I had never had that kind of closeness with anyone before and I didn't know how to handle it. I thought that I had to keep making them like me by doing more and more silly things. I could not be out and about just in case they went off me. I wouldn't have been able to take the rejection. If I had been rejected it would mean once and for all I was correct, I am a horrible person that no one will ever like. These first few months had just been a blip and then people would see my full colours. It was a nightmare every day for me. At the time when I should have been the happiest in my life all I could think of was losing that happiness. And that had led me to where I was sitting now, waiting for a triad who had befriended me in Thingummy's and with veins full of a drug I had never heard of before waiting to escape somewhere that should have been heaven. I would have to say some goodbyes, especially to Rebecca. She had been so supportive of me. Every time I saw her I could see her love for me in her eyes. She cared for me and I just couldn't accept her help. I would have to call her. I got up to leave to make the phone call when the triad next to the door jumped up and shouted

"Cho die"

At me. I had no idea what he meant but I quickly learnt when he pointed at the seat I had just vacated, shouted

"Cho die"

Again and this time pointed at the seat. I was being held. I hadn't realised it until this point. I was not allowed to leave, I was being held against my will. Then I realised that Lennon had my ticket and my passport. Fuck, how stupid had I been? What did I really know of this guy? No, surely everything was fine and these young triads were just as keen as I had been to follow orders from Lennon. They were probably worried that if they let me leave something would happen and they would lose face and have to be dealt with, and [probably quite painfully. So I sat down to wait. I made a huge line and snorted it back not knowing how long I would be there. I drifted off to sleep and dreamt of my successful return to Hong Kong after getting myself sorted out.

Chapter Forty
Christmas Eve

I woke up early, the light just making it through the windows between where my cell was and b hall. I folded my sheets and blankets and managed to get washed in the cold water before the radio came on. I sat there wondering what was going to happen. The acting governor had said he would decide what was going to happen to me. I was on report or anything, yet. So I just sat there waiting. I thought about the events yesterday, the judge, the young guy in the cell opposite. He was staring down the very beginning of a ten-year sentence, that's what he thought anyway, and I was very nearly at the end of my sentence. So no matter what happened I would be going home in a few months then I realised it was Xmas eve. Of all the days to be sitting in solitary not knowing what was going to happen. I was gutted that I wasn't with my friends in Lai Sun; I had been looking forward to this Xmas more than any o had in the past I don't know how many years. Just then my breakfast was brought to me and disturbed my thoughts. It was awful as normal. I suppose that after a while in Pik Uk you would get used to the food just like I had got used to it in Lai Sun. After breakfast and with no information to be got on how long I would be spending here I sat on my bed and tried to meditate. I must have fallen asleep as the next thing I know there was a guard screaming at me to get up and that I wasn't allowed to sleep or even lie on the bed in solitary. So I went to the corner and pulled out the fibreglass chair and pulled it the front of the cell. I sat on it looking out onto B hall. I could see through a number of the windows in B hall, and could catch glimpses of the daily comings and goings. It was quite difficult and I had to squint to make things out, it must have been about a hundred yards from where I was sitting, but I could see a bunch of prisoners sitting on the floor watching TV I couldn't make out anything of what they were watching but I found myself mesmerized by the colours on the screen and the flickering images. Every time a negative thought came into my head I removed it straight away with thoughts about what I would be doing once I had been released. I refused the white congee for lunch and just sat there all day staring out to b hall. And that was all I did, I battled negative thoughts and stared at a far off vision.

25th December
Xmas the day to remember how lucky we are and to pray for the ones less fortunate than ourselves. I know I'm lucky. It may seem strange to hear me say this in current predicament, but I am lucky. I have food, clothes, somewhere to sleep and a family, they may be on the other side of the world but I know they love me. I just think of the poor people in Somalia, I am lucky. I will wake up tomorrow morning; I don't have to wonder if someone will kill me, whether I will have a home or food tomorrow. I don't have kids to worry about on a daily basis, will they come home, what is their future. This is the true meaning of Xmas. Today I tried something a bit crazy. In my mind, I called out to my mum
"Merry Xmas Mum".
I sat there on the stool for actually hours shouting out n mind as loud as possible
"Merry Xmas Mum".
I did it for so long I started getting a pain in my temples. I'll never know if it worked, but it was worth a try. When I did wake up this morning I actually woke up late, and not in a very Xmas mood. I had a stomach ache so after I had folded my blankets and sheets, brushed my teeth and threw water on my face I went for a shit. My bowels exploded, the stuff flew out at a high pressure. It was a liquid-like thick soup, and it stank. But it felt so much better afterwards. My breakfast was brought to me but I could hardly touch it. I left the fish and most of the rice. I could hear all the other prisoners leaving their cells to go and celebrate Xmas by watching film after film in the dining hall that they were allocated to. I remember the Xmas in Pik Uk before. Some religious group had come in and sang carols and handed out sweets to everyone. All the prisoners would have piles of crisps biscuits chocolate and cartoon of juice, they would all be sitting together of groups of friends and today everyone would be allowed to chat with each other quite freely. The guards would allow people to move to different tables as long as no one caused any trouble, but why would they cause trouble today, it was Xmas and everyone was in a good mood, apart from me. I sat on the chair next to the door and peered through all the bars that separated me form b hall and could see everyone sitting around the TV, probably watching some Jackie Chan or Andy Lau film. If I squinted really hard I could just make out what was on the screen, but it took do much effort I just gave up. I went to the toilet again and had another angry bowel

movement. I sat there until lunchtime, just sitting and thinking of my family. Wondering if they were getting together at my mum and dad's house. Then a guard came down the corridor and unlocked my door, I had to g and see the deputy governor. I hadn't realised how cold it was outside, but as soon as we left the cell block and the wind got me I was frozen to my bones. So I marched quickly and with wildly swinging arms to try and keep warm. When I got to his office had to stand outside for about 15 minutes. I was shivering with the cold. I started losing feeling in my feet and hands. But every time I went to try and warm them up the guard would shout at me to stop moving. When I started shivering violently he even shouted at me. For a split second, I considered talking back to him, but for once I managed to keep my trouble making trap shut. I was pretty worried about what might happen. What if they decided just to keep me here in Pik Uk until my release? Keep me in solitary again until they could finally get rid of me. I also was worried that he would be in such a bad mood because he had to work on Xmas and couldn't see his family that he would totally throw the book at me and give me a crazy sentence of a week in solitary thus meaning that I may not get back to Lai Sun either. But he smiled when I walked in.

"I have decided to be lenient with you, I know that you have had a really hard time adjusting to prison life and as its Xmas, I am going to allow you to rejoin the general population, but be under no doubts that if you cause trouble again I won't hold back in punishing you"

A smile filled my full face. I would get back in time to enjoy at least some of the mass cheer after all. I thanked him and backed out of the office bowing, I was taken directly back to b hall. There were three other prisoners there but not the one I had a fight with. So I sat with time just in time for the first film to come, "double impact ". It was okay. It was the film that I think Nik Charge said that he was in. but no matter how hard I looked in never saw him. It wasn't great but it did have a hot sex scene that warmed me up, lovely tits and body! Once it had finished we watched some Chinese shit. It had some subtitles so I could follow it a bit. But to be honest it was just great getting out of my cold cell and watching the TV with company, even though no one engaged me n any kind of chat. I just sat there myself, feeling quite content and looking forward to sinner which was always great at Xmas. It may be a long time to wait for a decent meal but this year it definitely didn't let us down. It was like all the best bits of meals throughout the year added with some stuff that we just never

get. We got a chicken wing, a boiled egg, and a sausage. Hadn't had one of them in over two years, and a meatball, along with the rice and vegetables I was so stuffed I started to thank the thunderous evacuation of my insides that had made lots of room for this feast. Once everything had been cleared away we went for an hour's exercise, this time no one wanted to go. We had just filled our bellies the last thing we wanted was exercise, and it was freezing outside. I remember last week when I was begging for exercise now I was begging to stay in. but it didn't matter and we had t go downstairs and out into the cold. I was pretty miserable when some prisoners walked past us. One was an old friend 80253,
"Gwai gi can you do something me? "
He called over,
"What"
I said,
"Suck ma boabie".
Aw man how I laughed. It was so out of nowhere, I was worried I was going to lose my dinner, I laughed so hard, it was the funniest thing that happened in ages. We then were taken back to our cells. I hadn't seen mine for a few days because I was in solitary and court, I was very happy to see all my things just as I had left them but also on everyone's beds there was a little packet from the HK bible society full of goodies. It had chocolate bars, marshmallows and biscuits so along with my other biscuits that I had kept n the cell for my court trip and the book that I had brought with me; I had a great little Xmas party to myself. Sometimes things have to get really bad for us to enjoy the simplest of pleasures in life and tonight I was happy and contented. It's amazing now how I realize that getting something so small can make me so happy. To think about how many prisoners the society had touched today some in a lot worse circumstance than me. They hopefully lifted their spirits and made life just that little bit better. That night was the highlight of the last two years. As I later lay in bed considering life, my mind drifted to what was happening in Scotland and at my parent's house. Being 8 hours behind Hong Kong the family would be starting to arrive. I didn't know whether my dad was home for this Xmas or away at sea. Would my older brother and his new wife be joining the family or staying with hers? And I had no idea about Chris. He was only 15 but if he was anything like me at 15 he would be out with friends somewhere. He would prefer to be somewhere else than be at home,

especially If dad was there. As I thought about it I really didn't know what was happening with my family. Any letters that I did get from my mum just covered basics and didn't go into any specific details. Although when I managed to write to her I always asked for details, they never came. From time to time I asked her to ask my brothers or even dad to write to me, but they never did. It just told me that no-one wanted to be in touch with me. I wonder if there was an unspoken rule that my name was never to be mentioned, had my family decided to try and forget about me. Had I brought so much pain on the family that no matter what I did in the future they would never accept me back in? I decided that I had better write to my mum as soon as I got back to Lai Sun, just to let her know about the deportation hearing and what the judge had said. I didn't know when my release date actually was supposed to be. I was thinking with the time added on so far it must have been around February the 17th. It was one of those things that I didn't want to ask. And anyway maybe they would release me sooner as the judge said. Whether that would be a day, a week or even a month earlier, I had no idea and no real way to find out. The first I would find out was when I got called up to see the governor a month before my release. The guys called it
"See one month".
Literally meaning having your one-month meeting before discharge. It was always exciting when one of your friends was going to
"See one month"
Especially if they had been inside for a number of years. And although the judge asked for my flights to be paid to Scotland I didn't know what would happen when I got there. Would my family want to see me, would I be homeless having to go and stay in some hostel somewhere. Even if they wanted me to stay with them, would I want to? The adjustment from prison to home life didn't look like something that was going to be easy. And what was I going to do when I got released? Go to college, get a job? I had no idea. I hadn't really thought about it. I had only thought about girls and partying, to be honest, by now when I thought about a cold fear crept over my skin. The fear of freedom, I had become institutionalized.

Chapter -40

Ready for departure

It was 10 pm when Lennon finally got back. The door opened

"Let's go"

That was the demand and I staggered to my feet to follow him. We headed n foot towards Mong Kok and ducked inside a dai pai dong where we had tea and steamed rice with pork and Chinese veg. I was starving but I managed to actually eat something this time. Lennon spoke to me quietly

"Okay all arranged. Tomorrow I go to the airport with you. You take one case. When you get to London you are met by my friend. No problem"

"I want to say goodbye to some friends, go to Thingummy's tonight."

"Tonight no Thingummy's, we stay Chung King. Tomorrow say goodbye one friend, no time, no problem"

There was no point arguing with him. I said that I was going to call my friend and I went to the phone at the spice shop next door. I arranged to meet Rebecca at Pedder Street the next day at 12 o'clock that would give me plenty of time to get to the airport which only took under an hour to get to.

After we ate Lennon and I went back to the mansions. I lay down on the bed and drifted off really quickly, in my mind planning what I had to do tomorrow.

I woke with the early morning traffic. Lennon was still sleeping so I sneaked out of the room and down onto Nathan road. The light was still dusty from the early sun. I turned left and slowly walked down towards the harbour. Taking in the signs dotted around me maybe for the first time with effort. I walked passed my begging spot remembering the first day I had sat there, head down, embarrassed with my sign of fiction. I made a killing that day, my begging box runneth over. Was I looking at Hong Kong for the last time, it was a possibility. I had screwed it all up, a wave of the morose swept over me. A tear nearly came to my eye when I thought back over the last year. Eventually, I came to the harbour and as the first few boats of the day made their way around the anchored ships I wondered to myself if it would have been better never to come, to kill myself on purpose or by accident, or just to stay and die a slow drug-addicted death. I thought of my parents and my brother probably still sleeping over to the left in Happy Valley. I snorted when I thought of that name. It hadn't been very happy after all. The last person I had seen was my mum when she came down to my pier on Christmas eve and gave me HK$200. She didn't try and get me to come home, she didn't offer any advice or support she just left me and when she was out of sight I ran with my money to buy more drugs. I wouldn't tell them that I was going. They knew where I was and if they were bothered they could come down and see that I wasn't there anymore. At that, I remembered that I had left bags of my things on the pier. I hadn't had time to go back and get them. so I quickly ran down to the ferry and jump over the rail and went to the island. Before I got to my bench I could see that there was nothing there. The whole history of my stay in Hong Kong had vanished. All my photos and keepsakes were gone. I sat there for a while and realised that maybe it was supposed to be like that. It gutted me to lose all of my photos but I could always take more. I got the ferry back to Tsim Tsa Tsui and headed quickly back to Chung King. I had been away for about an hour but I got back to find Lennon still sleeping. I took another line of smack and started bagging up a few grams in some discarded drinking straws. I would have to stuff them up to my arse going through customs just in case. Let's be honest I looked like shit and stood out like the junky scum I was. I made 5 straws up and wrapped an elastic band around them then took a rubber, unwrapped it and stuck the straws inside. I wouldn't stuff them until I got to the airport. No point being uncomfortable all day. Lennon got up at ten and we went down to get some tea.

"We go Tuen Mun get bag then we go central, you see a friend then we go to the airport."

So off we went. This time we got a taxi. Tuen Mun isn't a pleasant place, well the parts that I usually went to weren't. we reached an apartment block and got out of the taxi. The flat we were going to was on the 9th floor but we had to go past three different groups of lads with combs in their hair first. Hand signals were made, pleasantries exchanged and finally, we got into the apartment. I had never seen so much smack in my life the place was full of it. Piled up

on the floor and getting processed on long tables. This was a sorting house for all the low-level dealers. They would come here and get their supply. There was no money anywhere; they never kept the 2 in the same place. I was told to sit with 10 pairs of untrusting eyes fixed onto me. whispers were being made
"Gwai gi, deu lai low mo"
between the workers, some with face masks on whilst they cut open bags, measured and filled the smack. They must have been out of their fasces as the room was full of dust from the smack. I was quite happy. Lennon came back into the room
"we go"
he was carrying a black suitcase like a Samsonite or something. We left, back through the hair comb brigade and back into a taxi that seemed to be waiting for us but was different from the last one.
"You got everything you need, you wanna buy anything"
"no I'm fine; I can get stuff at the airport"
"good good, this is your case you give to my friend in the UK; here is your passport and your ticket, keep safe."
"Okay, no problem"
we then sat in silence as the taxi drove us through the tunnel to the island. We got out of the taxi round the corner from Pedder Street. As I turned the corner I could see Rebecca standing there. Our eyes caught each other's and I almost ran to her. We embraced and I said "I'm leaving now. Lennon walked passed us and secreted himself into a side entrance to one of the office buildings, always watching, always watching.
"I have a ticket to leave tonight"
"I am so worried about you, are you okay"
"Yes"
I said and we embraced again. I didn't know if I would ever see her again and this made me saddest of all. I think deep down inside I knew that she just wanted to be my friend, but I couldn't do it. I couldn't get close to anyone, I couldn't be her friend, and for that, I was deeply sad.
"wait, before you go I want to give you this"
She started to twist a ring off her hand. It was her smiley face ring. With the eyes, nose and mouth cut into the metal. "Take this and never forget me"
I looked into her eyes and said thank you. I started to put the ring onto my finger………

Chapter Forty-One

Last day of the year
I thought to myself as soon as my eyes opened this morning. Time is a completely manufactured concept by man. To judge a day we wait for the earth to rotate on its continuous journey through the galaxy. The time on earth is only the time on earth. It doesn't speed up or slow down, that only happens in our minds. Although we created time we cannot control it, it controls us. We use it to grow crops, to specify a working day and to punish. We all have a certain number of heartbeats is this not a better way to judge our lives rather than how long we have done something, or how long we've been doing something. I read somewhere that time was the enemy of love, that we judge our lives by days and months and years when we should judge it by our laughter our joy and our fears. If I judged how long I had been in prison by the second part I would say ive been here for decades. My adrenal gland has been on active duty for the whole of my time here. Constantly pumping out the chemicals that have left me with heightened senses, always on edge, with a faster heartbeat meaning my days alive have probably been cut short. My days haven't been cut short with the slicing of a blade or the dreaded sharpened chopsticks so I still have time, time to do what? I think of the last year. That first day of this year finding a drowned rat in my toilet, and thinking what it symbolized. All in all, I feel the last year has been better than the first one. Yes, it's had its hardships, nightmares and near-death experiences but the year before, well it was a year of constant threat. Or should that be a perceived threat? For a lot of it was in my mind. I realise that now. Now that I can see clearly I realize that I had probably brought a lot of my problems on myself. That week with Lennon helped me to realise this. In Pik Uk, I was always restraining myself from my real reactions and lived in a made-up world. Here in Lai Sun, I have been able to let me be more like myself, not totally, but nearly. I've done mostly what ive wanted to do and also thought more about other people. The real test of who I am will come in just over one hundred days. The day I am released back into the society that I had lost before by my actions. It will be bittersweet. Returning to the place I loathed, the place that created the depression early on in childhood that stays with me today. Not Hong Kong where the first months were filled with love, fun and possibilities. I will have to go back to Scotland to rebuild. The place

where I felt tortured is the place that I am excited to be released into. No not excited, I am excited by the thought of release from this hell, but not on returning to the other place. That other place where my parents are, those parents who abandoned me here when I needed help the most. To a family that I haven't spoken to in years, who I have never heard from whilst I have been rotting these last years. So, no not excited about that.

So tonight is New Year's Eve. The last time I saw this time of year outside I was in Lang Kwai Fong. I didn't feel right, but I forced myself to be there. I bumped into many people that night, but nobody stayed around me long enough. The last memory I had was of my old English teacher outside Scotties saying how small my pupils were. She was obviously alluding to that I was using drugs. I told her that was because I was looking towards a bright light. And as she turned round to look at that light, I made my move and disappeared into the crowd. It was then I met up with the two from Lantau Island and had that mini-adventure with them. I regret not staying for the countdown to the new year but I had to escape my demons and get high.

Next week I will be down to double figures left to serve. I managed to get my hands on six business card sized calendars for the next year and I am now going to cross out every day back from next new year to maybe one month before when I think my release date will be. The crosses will start moving together. I know that the prison chat is that this can slow down your time by looking at the date every day it reminds you and the best thing to do is just try and forget what date it is, but we cannot control time, time will move psychologically quicker for me if I feel good about life, and having only 100 day to go makes me feel good, if only a little bit.

Chapter -41

Nicked

Wham. I was thrown against the wall.

"Get down get down, police police"

I head-butted the first guy, lashed out with my feet but then was grabbed from behind. I looked to see where Lennon was but he had disappeared. Bang I was punched in the face then the belly. I almost puked. I tried to get free but my legs were taken away from me. I landed with a huge crack on my back. In the background, I could hear Rebecca screaming but couldn't understand what she was saying. I tried to get up but fell back I then tried to kick the guy closest to me in the nuts but I caught his leg I then managed to get up a bit, leaned forward ready to attack again

"stop, police"

a badge was being thrust in my face by one hand and alongside it was a gun almost touching my face. I surrendered. I could have fought and gone out in style, but I didn't, I surrendered. I was immediately hoisted up and half carried and dragged to a car and thrown inside. A blanket was thrown over my head and my wrist s were handcuffed behind my back. Then they started beating me. the punches rained into my lower and then upper back. I would have shit myself if I want so full of smack and been constipated for months. The car took off extremely fast and I was being thrown about the back by the motion and by trying to escape some of the blows.

"We know you, we been looking for you long time"

"I don't know what you mean, I don't know anything"

I was shouting back. I nearly puked after one punch but managed to hold it together. For the whole journey, I thought I was going to be killed. I thought that it was a rival gang or someone I had caused to lose face. Maybe they were just pretending to be police so that they could take me and kill me. why the blanket over my head, why were they beating me so much. This was it, they would beat me so much that I wouldn't have any strength left to fight back and then they would take me out of the car, perhaps cut me a bit for fun before either shooting me or chopping me to pieces and feeding me to the fish or rats. The car stopped and I was dragged out by the feet on to the ground. With the blanket still over my head I was bounced off I don't know how many walls until I reached a room where I was told to sit down and finally had the blanket removed from my head. It was an interrogation room. They were police, thank fuck for that. They made me stand up and stripped all my clothes off me. I stood there shivering from cold and fright as they went through my pockets finding my ticket passport and 5 grams of heroin stuffed into a condom, fuckin great. What's this, where you get it?

"fuck off"

punch to the belly, well done

"where you get this"

I said nothing. All the time I had been with Lennon he always repeated the same thing to me

"keep your mouth"

meaning never talk. I had seen him at work; I had joined in some of it. I had seen what happened to people who broke the rules so I was definitely not going to do it. I had read enough books and watched enough crime shows to know that the worst of the worst were grasses. One night we were lying in Tsim Tsa Tsui park stoned when he told me all about the triad.

"Police, triad, business, triad, everyone triad. They say no, not possible but it true. You wanna do business you have to be a triad. Prison full of the triad. Some go there to work for big brother. If you go prison you no need to worry because triad there looks after you. But you no say anything, people who talk they die".

It didn't need any further explanation. The papers had stories about the triad all the time and how the local government was trying to stop corruption at every level. But you only had to walk around Hong Kong with your eyes open to see it all in front of you. The guys selling smack outside nearly every 7/11, triad. Walk down any road in Wan Chai and you would see them at different corners. Different groups within the several triad gangs had different uniforms and distinguishing behaviour including hand movements and even having a comb in their hair. Most of the time a foreigner would have no idea what was going on and would probably never get involved in anything. If you were in a pub in Wan Chai and started acting like an arse the local triads weren't going to come in and chop you up, the bar staff would just get you to leave, throw you out. However, if you were a different triad you would expect to have trouble and even more if it was your own turf that you were acting an arse on. It is all about keeping or losing face. If you do something that embarrasses someone you are for it the best thing you can do is meet with them and express your sorrow for the way you have acted by cutting off one of your fingers. This will take the immediate pressure off. I'm serious. Death by flying daggers is part of the triad motto and you get that by making someone in the family lose face.

So I kept my eyes down and said nothing.

"you deal with drugs?"

"Why you have like this?"

they were talking about my 5 individual grams in the condom.

"You sell drugs, you drug trafficker, you go prison 10 years"

Then they found my ticket and passport

"so you are drug smuggler, now you life in prison"

"tell us everything maybe you go home, you say nothing you never go home"

I kept my head down and said nothing. My wallet was next for examination where they found my rolled-up ten-dollar bill and my card for making my lines along with the mirror I couldn't really deny what they were for, but still, I said nothing. This went on for hours. I sat there with my head down, not looking at anyone. Different police came into the room shouted a few questions at me then left. I didn't answer anything. I was then taken down a corridor and into a big room with a metal cage in the middle, I was thrown inside, still only in my underpants, shaking with the cold, fear and now the beginnings of withdrawal. This was my only gauge of how long I had been there. I had been grabbed at midday and had taken my last line maybe 10 minutes before that. So now it must have been at least 4 hours as that is when the first worm of withdrawal would slowly start entering my body. Shivers at first, hunger for smack, slight aches and pains.

Then slowly all I could think of was another line. My body hungered for it like someone who had been starved for a day. I sat on the floor of my cage watching the police at a metal table fill in forms whilst looking at all my belongings eventually another few police came into the room. They chatted quietly to the police at the table then one walked up to the cage and said "we have been looking for you. Now we have you. You are wanted for a number of robberies, and now we have you. You should cooperate with us; it will be easier for you. Now tell me your name." I slowly looked up at him. Our eyes met, my heart wanted to speak to him, I saw kindness in his eyes and wanted to believe that he would help me and if I talked that this would be over quickly and I would get out. But I knew it was just an illusion. I had been caught, even if they couldn't get me on any other charges I had 5 individually wrapped grams of heroin which could only be described as me being a drug dealer. No matter what I said the evidence was there. So I said nothing. Question after question came. How old was I, where did I live, what was my name, where are your parents. At one point I was informed that someone was calling looking for me. this didn't sound like a trick, this I believed was Rebecca. But I couldn't say anything. I sat there thinking of her, what she had been through seeing that happen to me, but I couldn't do anything about it so I said nothing. And still, withdrawals crept through my body. It was as if my nervous system was being invaded. From my fingertips to my spine to my brain, I felt a pang of hunger and an ache start to descend into my bones. I had never had to go through withdrawal before; I had been close but always managed to get money to get high again. But this time I had no hope of that happening and no real knowledge of the hell that I was about to go through. Sometime in the evening, I was thrown some old clothes in my cage. They were stinking but warm, a blue t-shirt and an old pair of faded blue jeans that were too big for me and with a broken zipper. This whole time I had been handcuffed but now they took the thin police cuffs off. I rubbed my wrists but the freedom didn't last for long for as soon as I had the t-shirt on and jeans a new set of cuffs were clamped down on my wrists. These things were monstrosities weighed an absolute ton and stopped my hands get anywhere near each other. They had huge solid metal shields as if to stop you getting anywhere near the mechanism. I was told to get up and was hauled out of the cage where I had been for at least 5 if not 6 hours. I was taken up a dark set of stairs and then thrust into the light of what seemed to be the main police office with banks of desks piled high with papers. I walked passed one desk and sitting on it was a police gun in its holster. For a split second, I thought of grabbing it and being like Rambo, shooting everyone dead and making my escape so that I could go and buy some smack. I would risk my life right in that second to get some more smack. But that second passed and we moved past the table but that gun had burned a hole in my brain and I couldn't shake the vision of it out of my head. Maybe it was put there on purpose, maybe they had planned it and unbeknownst to me it was unloaded and there were 5 cops all with their guns at the ready to put 50 holes in me. As they said they had been looking for me for ages before they found me, had been questioning me for ages and I had said nothing I had caused them to lose face. I was taken into a small room with a desk and chairs. I was pushed into one and then my handcuffs were chained to the table. I imagine the table was chained to the ground or I could have lifted it up and done a runner. That would have been a funny sight seeing me running down the street with a table over my head searching for a 7/11. But the fun stopped immediately when the door opened again and my mum and dad walked in.

Chapter Forty-Two
A New Year

I saw a friend today. A friend from school. One of the nicest guys I have ever known. And what I saw him doing was a reflection of what a great guy he is. I wanted to write about how happy I am about it being today, a new year, and my last year inside, but I can't. Looking back 24 hours of what I wrote and thought about yesterday feels terrible. My own self absorbed thoughts about my own life were brought back down to the ground after I saw my friend. You see as it's a holiday today we weren't sent to the workshop, instead, we were taken to the dining hall, had breakfast and the TV was put on for us to watch. Today they didn't put a movie on, they put the news on. And then the horror. At the stroke of midnight in Lang Kwai Fong, when everyone heads towards the countdown clock, someone slipped on the wet cobblestones, slippery from the alcohol that had been lost in the jostling of hundreds if not thousands of party-goers. That one person started a domino effect, as the clock ticked down more and more revellers surged towards the clock, not wanting to miss the moment it finally got to zero and everyone would scream in delight. Last night the screams were different. 20 people wouldn't make it to the new year, their screams lost amongst the others. They said there were ten thousand people there last night. In such a tiny few streets. The news went to the rescue efforts right afterwards and that's when I saw Egil. Handsome, tall, blonde hair in usual style and dressed in a beautiful, white tuxedo, stepping over bodies and trying to help anyone that could be helped. I only saw him for a second or two but was immediately filled with pride that a friend of mine had jumped in to help. There were hundreds of people helping of course, not just him. But my eyes went to him. The sadness of the event brought me down to earth with a jolt. Here I am a prisoner on the first day of the year that I am due to be released. A day that should have been filled with joy. I chose not to think of myself today, I chose to think of the others. The others that had done no harm to anyone, those who were innocent and law-abiding. I thought of their families, suffering the not knowing. Trying to find loved ones in the chaos that followed. Today's paper only managed to get a small story about last night, but tomorrow it will be full. One other note about today's paper. My cigarette friend from the Supreme Court who thought he would get ten years, well he only got 5.

Chapter -42
Shame and terror

I became a kid again instantly. From gang banging to childish embarrassment, from heroin addiction to being ashamed. I didn't give them my parent's details because I probably didn't want to have this feeling of shame. They both stood there not exactly looking at me but I could see that my dad was raging. A plainclothes officer sat down and gave my parents his condolences. For fuck sake, seriously. So sorry Mr. and Mrs. for the shame your child has brought upon you. In that split second there was no denying it I was the one who had done wrong and any mitigating circumstances that could have been used would have been useless. I refused to talk, to say hello, to acknowledge them.

"We cannot question you without your parents being here as we now know that you are under 18 years old and seen as a minor"

Under 18 years old, was I still under 18 years old? In a couple of days that wouldn't be the case.

"you have to answer the charges that we put to you in front of your parents"

I said nothing. The charges were read out to me and I was given the charge sheets. But they were in Chinese. I couldn't read them. They pushed a statement in front of me that they asked me to sign, but I didn't know what it said. So I sat there and said nothing. All I could think about was the pain that was starting to enter my entire body. Every bone and joint was starting to ache. I couldn't get comfortable in the chair I was chained to. Each time I moved it felt that my arse was covered in bruises. My back was, I was sure, but I hadn't had any way of checking myself over for injuries sustained during my initial arrest and car journey. My focus came back into the room but very quickly dulled again. People were talking but it all seemed to be a distant rumble from outside the room. they were talking to me but I couldn't really hear them. This must have gone on for a couple of hours but those hours are nothing but a black hole to me. I was unchained from the desk. My parents left and then I was on my way down another flight of stairs. These ones were darker. I had gone passed a clock on the way to the stairs and was shocked to see that *it was nearly 10 pm. 10m hours had passed, I hadn't eaten, gone to the toilet or even had a cigarette never mind some smack for all this time. As we go further and further down the stairs it got darker and darker and the walls seemed to transform from normal painted ones to ones that were crumbling and damp. In the whole atmosphere was changing. It was humid, cold and dark. I laughed to myself and thought that it was as if I was getting taken down to a dungeon. I shouldn't have laughed because when the smell hit me realized I was. We were in the basement; I could hear water dripping, murmuring, sniffing, and moaning coming from all directions. It was pitch black. I could just make out bars in front of me as my feet splashed in foul-smelling water that had pooled on the broken concrete floor. I was stopped and a steel barred door was opened n front of me and I was pushed inside. It must have measured 6 foot by 6 foot and had nothing but a wooden bench along one set of bars that separated it from the other cells on each side. It stank of shit, piss and everything else. There could have been dying down there, I could smell it but couldn't see it. The door was clanged behind me and the key turned into the lock. This was is it, this is your new home forever, and then the light went out. In that dark cell, I discovered a new sort of pain. Every part of my body ached. I tossed and turned on that thin wooden bench, trying to find one part of my body that didn't feel pain. The weight of my skinny junky body pushed down through my skin and was welcomed by a dull ache with the bone closest to the surface. I was also sniffling, my nose was running, I felt that the worst fever ever had engulfed my body. On top of that, I was freezing cold and frightened. I couldn't do this, this was worse than any of the scenarios I had thought about when contemplating suicide. I was a miserable wretch and I lay there for what felt like an eternity before I heard distant steps echoing through the dungeon. A blanket was thrown at me and I grabbed the stinking and itchy item as if it was my saviour. It stank of the cell I was in, it ripped my skin with its harsh hairy fabric but it brought me some warmth. I did sleep that night. The darkness woke me up in the morning, no; I didn't know it was the morning. there was no natural light in this hell, but it seemed a bit lighter as if someone had switched on a light somewhere that I couldn't find the source. There were moaning and coughing, spluttering from the other cells but it was still so dark that I couldn't and wouldn't see much further than my own confinement.*

My cell opened and I was handcuffed again and taken upstairs, I could barely open my eyes, it could have been a dream because of how removed from it all I was. I ended up in the back of a police van, by myself, lying on the floor and was driven off somewhere. It was daylight but I daren't try and look out of the windows due to the pain in my eyes. I was now just a wretched animal suffering from some sort of fatal disease. Being driven off to slaughter. I no longer felt human every bump in the road caused me pain and delirium. The van stopped I was taken out and then found myself in another cell. This time I wasn't alone. The cell wasn't much bigger but it had what I could count as 10 others inside it. I found a bench at the back and tried to lie down. All the others in the cell were a lot older than me. some looked clean and fresh whilst another couple looked like down and outs, probably a lot like me. I looked around and finally, my eyes settled on a guy sitting right next to me. he was staring at me and smiling.

"you look like shit mate"

I was glad to hear English.

"uuughhuhg"

I think I managed.

"What's your name?"

I told him,

"What's yours"

I managed to muster the strength to ask "Gary".

"Where are we, Gary?"

"We're at, the western magistrate's court".

With that, he then settled into telling me his whole life story of recent months. I was quite glad because he seemed only interested in talking about himself and asked me no more questions. He had been living rough in Tsim Tsa Tsui park for the last few months

"you know you can always get a good meal out of the bins in the park" he went on, "sometimes I get cakes and all sorts of things like that, I eat like a king"

in all the time I had been homeless I had never once considered going through bins but this guy went on to tell me where all the best bins were.

"how old are you"

"I'm 17"

"shit you'll be sent to Pik Uk then, that's the worst place possible, hey I know what to do just pretend you are older than you can come with me to the adult prison, you get good food there and you can smoke, at Pik Uk you get fuck all and it's the most dangerous prison because of all the young triad trying to kill you"

"but even better why don't you do what I do and pretend you are crazy"

I don't think Gary had to try hard to get sent to Siu Lam,

"in the prison, you don't get a mattress and have to either sleep on the floor or hard plastic bed, in sui lam, which is the mental prison you get lovely white hospital clothes to wear and a lovely big hospital bed to sleep in. okay so they do fill you with drugs to control you but it's worth it"

"what do they give you?"

I asked somewhat interestedly.

"well, they give you a combination of water and oil injections that completely whack you out for hours. They could put a cigarette right in front of you and you can't even move. You shit yourself, piss yourself and can't move and do anything about it."

Wow sounds wonderful!

"You should do it, will make your time easier".

The one thing that this one-sided conversation gave me was hope. Hope because I wasn't as far gone as Gary. I still had enough of my old self left to know that not one part of what he said sounded like the road I wanted to travel. We hung around in that tiny cell for another hour or so. More prisoners were being shoved in every 30 minutes or so until there was barely standing room. fortunately, when it got to that point a few of us were called to the front of the cell and we were handcuffed then brought out one by one. Once I squeezed myself out of the sardine tin I was then introduced to something I never thought I would have to be. I was given ankle shackles which were then attached to a chain around my waist where my handcuffs were also attached. So totally restrained I was led by one guard up a steep and extremely narrow set of stairs. At the top was a narrow long corridor that already had a handful of prisoners squatted down against a wall. There was a guard with a gun, waving it backwards and forwards over the prisoners. I was pushed into the line and made to squat down with the others. This caused my whole body a load of pain that I had forgotten about during the storytelling from Gary. Every few minutes a door at the end of the corridor would open and one of the prisoners would be called forward and then disappear through the door. Where was this door leading to? I had no idea. When the first one disappeared I wondered what his fate was. I squatted there, leaning against the door staring at the door wondering what it led to. Then after a few minutes, the door opened again and he reappeared. He was taken back down the corridor and back down the stairs that we had come up earlier. I was starting to shake, from anxiety, from withdrawals, not only of heroin but of nicotine as well. Finally, my name was called I struggled to stand up and then started to totter, which is the best way to describe it in my leg irons towards the door. The anxiety was rising higher and higher inside me. I had no idea what I was about to walk into and I was scared. I got to the door, took a deep breath and walked through into the courtroom itself. A hundred people turned to look at me. I felt like I was on display and half expected boos to ring out around the room. Every face was foreign to me, I recognized no one. I slowly turned my head to the front of the court, passed the police, passed lots of people in suits sitting behind desks and then up to a large wooden structure with an old looking English guy sitting with his head in his hands at the top of it. He just sat there and stared at me. Someone started talking to my left I turned my head to hear one of the guys in suits talking about me and the charges that I had. It went so quickly I couldn't keep up with what he was saying and before I knew it the judge was saying "remanded for 2 weeks" and then I was grabbed by the shoulder, turned around and pushed out the open door behind me and back into the corridor from where I came. Back down the stairs *and back into the cell I had been in before. I lay down on the bench and waited for the next instalment of the horror.*

I waited all day as it must have been night when they finally started to empty our cell. We were taken a few at a time to the entrance that I had arrived that morning. This time we were put into a proper prison van and driven off into the night. We drove through central and towards Admiralty, I didn't realise it but I wouldn't be seeing much of this in the future. We turned right up a hill and came to the back of the supreme court, where we were decanted again into another cell. Now, this cell was enormous, the cell of your nightmares. Full of the truly bad of Hong Kong. In here were not just magistrate court prisoners but prisoners from every court with charges ranging from robbery to rape, murder, and serial murder. It was full of very angry people. I saw Gary heading off to a corner so I followed him, this time realising that although he may be a twat, a deranged twat, he knew things that I had no idea about. He had been through the system and I was small fry in here. Thankfully I wasn't there for long when my name was called and the cell gate opened and I was taken out and put onto another prison vehicle. I was led up to the back and sat down, another prisoner was sat beside me and we were handcuffed together. Still with leg jewellery on the ride was not the most comfortable I had ever been on. I tried to keep an eye on where we were going because a thought had been growing in my mind. What if I just escaped? Surely it would be possible. So I tried really hard to see where we were going but unfortunately after coming out the other side of the harbour tunnel I got completely lost.

Chapter Forty-Three
The Rapist

We found out that rapist was going to be released. He had kept it very quiet from all of us. I was approached by the top workshop guy and told that they were going to give him a leaving present and asked if I would like to join in. at the signal, the workshop officer went to his office and closed the door. We grabbed rapist and dragged him to a quiet corner, one guy was put on a watch and everyone else was told to mind their own business. I didn't know what was going to happen, but I had to join in or lose face. They got him onto the ground he seemed distant as if he realized that this may happen and that by his own guilt he may deserve it. He didn't make a sound, he didn't struggle like his victim, he shut his eyes and prepared for whatever his punishment was going to be. The big brother told us to hold him down and then little brother pulled down his trousers, he may not have known what was going to happen but his penis seemed to have a good idea as it tried to hide in his belly. I later learned that this is a common assault that happens to rapists. Little brother produced a sharpened piece of metal and slowly started to run it down the length of rapist dick. The blood welled up quickly, a rag was shoved in rapist's mouth as now he started to fight and shout, scream. More and more bloody lines were drawn down his circumcised dick. When there were lines running down its length all the way around, the big brother told him that from now on any time he gets a hard-on he will never forget. We all let go, he took the rag out of his mouth and covered his tattered manhood, he ran to the toilet where he was heard sobbing. After a while, he retreated to his corner and sat there for the rest of the day sobbing. The next day he was released. It played on my mind that night at how barbaric his punishment was, and was it justified. In our eyes it was. He had committed rape, the worst crime; I was friendly with some murderers as their crime didn't seem that bad, sometimes just an accident.

Chapter Forty-Four
Riot

Tensions had been rising over the last few weeks. There had been an influx of Il's from Fulam province. They had all been arrested together working somewhere in the New Territories. They had a big brother who seemed to think that he could take over the running of the prison. There had been a few fights; just one to ones recently but you could feel the atmosphere getting heavier. Something would break, and today it did. As I was nearing release I was making an effort to get up early each morning. I would spend half an hour working out before the radio came on and then have a toilet shower, even though it was really cold, it was a great start to the day. At breakfast there was an eerie silence, people weren't eating as normal. There were looks and hushed conversations. People were concentrating on the dining room rather than their food. Seh Yeh Gi was discharging today so as per convention he offered his food. No-one took it, so I ended up with two plates of rice. I was totally oblivious. We got to the workshop and did another workout. It was a little warmer at 28c so the workout made me sweat. Just then there was an uproar coming from another workshop. Gu Mo had gotten into a fight with a Fulam guy. Gu Mo had just got out of the hole for fighting; now he was going back down. At lunchtime, all the Hong Kong guys looked really fucked off. There was supposed to be football this afternoon but it was cancelled. I guess even the staff knew that the whole prison was on a knife-edge. I was working out in the workshop during the afternoon when Bun Ah Gi came up to me. He was one of the top Hong Kong guys. He took me aside.

"Gwai Gi, you a nearly released. You are our friend; you must do what I say."

"Do what."

I asked

"Today at the dining hall there will be a fight, but you must not join in."

This was a direct instruction to lose face. You can never not join in a fight your friends are involved in, but he continued.

"You have been a good friend and we ask you to help us by not fighting."

I wanted to complain, but by doing so I would be making Bun Ah Gi lose face. So I had to agree.

The fight wasn't just Hong Kong guys against Fulam, but also the Cheung Chau and Hoy Fung would join with the HK boys.
It was going to be huge.
Before dinner that night it was our turn to march. And boy it was tense. Anything could have happened at any time. We weren't searched as we left the workshop so I knew that lots of people would be armed. It did allow everyone to get into the correct positions to sit together at dinner. As we all marched into the dining hall I noticed that not one person gave their ID cards to go for a shower. I ended up sitting between Ah Tai and Ah Sum. We sat there, no-one talking and ate our dinner. Just as I was finishing the last of my rice, out of the corner of my eye, I saw Gwai Fu walking with a chair right through the middle of the dining room. Everyone froze. The officers just watched, nobody reacted. He reached the Fulam big brother's table and swung the chair with all his might down onto the big brothers head. BANG. Everyone jumped up. The HK guys, Cheung Chau and Hoy Fung all ran at the Fulam guys. My instinct made me jump up and start to run at them as well, but both of my arms were grabbed and I was hauled back towards the wall by Ah Tai and Ah Sum. They had been placed either side of me to do just that. They had been chosen not to fight but to stop me from getting involved. My heart sank as I was being restrained, it was absolute carnage. Chairs, tables, bodies were flying about. 100 prisoners with so much anger and hatred were going at it like it was the last fight that they would ever be in. I looked around and noticed that there were no officers to be seen inside the dining hall. The alarm then went off, even that sounded delayed. Normally all you have to do is stand up in the dining hall and the alarm would sound. The noise was deafening, the sight was intense. It was difficult to see what was happening, however, the HK boys and their team were definitely on top. The Fulam guys were completely outnumbered. They probably had two or three on each one. This fight had been meticulously planned. Down to every detail including the officers? But just then they came in, with full riot gear. They charged the fighters with shields and batons swinging. Those who saw them coming fled towards the walls, those too involved in what they were doing were mowed down and dragged off and beaten continuously by the officers. Then it was over. We were being screamed at to get against the walls, turn our backs and put our hands over our heads squatting down. The fighters who hadn't been caught ran towards the wall. Ah Ho and Ah Sum came and I tried to

shelter them next to me. Then the officers started to have their fun. I have never seen so much brutality, and will never see it again, it was sick and pointless. At one end of the dining hall, they had thrown the Fulam guys into a corner and all the rest had been dragged outside. You could hear the batons still making contact with flesh. The officers went around the wall pulling guys out that they thought had been involved in the fight, they then took them outside where they beaten and beaten. They dragged the fighters out one by one and gave it to them with batons and feet. Swearing, laughing and threatening. Guys who tried to hide were found and dragged out. Then one by one 6 or 7 officers started bringing the fighters back into the hall. They were thrown into the middle of the hall and the officers started beating them. If I bent my head I could see under my arm what was going on. I could see this small figure curled up into a ball with a group of heavily armoured men swing their batons relentlessly at them. It was traumatic to watch. I couldn't imagine what it would be like to be getting beaten like that. After a minute or two that poor soul would be dragged out and another dragged in. This went on for an hour. The officers said things like,
"I'm great", and
"Do you want to see the doctor?"
One guy went for an officer but he was beaten back. The officers started screaming come on come and smashed him repeatedly with his baton. Then they again moved amongst us at the back wall. Our heads were pulled into view by our hair to see our faces. I tried to cover Ah Ho but he was dragged out. He was beaten repeatedly on the lower back with a baton and was kicked, I don't know how many times in the kidneys. I felt sick; it made me shiver with rage. During the fight violence and force would have been justified to stop it but now whilst the fighters were sitting quietly on the ground to have 6 men beat them for a couple of minutes each had no justification apart for fulfilling the officer's lust for violence. The beatings went on for nearly two hours and we were made to sit there throughout all of it. If we moved or looked up we were threatened with the same violence. We were taken back to our cells at 7 pm. Our cell was practically empty, only a few HK guys were spared, all the rest were in the hole where I imagine the beatings would be continuing. Outside you could see the officers laughing and enjoying the aftermath. They would show each other how they beat the prisoners, even the super was laughing. Just when the lights went out at 10 pm

the alarm went off again, another fight. This won't be the end of it I'm sure; there will be repercussions over the next few weeks for sure. After lights out, we all sat together and had a few smokes whilst we went over the day's events. Later that night we heard helicopters coming to the island. They were either for badly injured prisoners or the police being brought in to investigate what happened. But we knew nothing, could only speculate. And we would know nothing for a long time to come. And we would never know everything. Had anyone died during the riot? Had the officers gone too far with anyone? All speculation, but not without merit.

Chapter Forty-Five
Post-Riot

The next morning we realised straight away what some of the repercussions would be.
The store guys were called for but the rest prison was on lockdown. Breakfast was eventually brought to our cell. So with store guys gone and the others in solitary, there was only
We ate it and talked. What we all came to was that this was going to last a while, but we had no idea how long. No one was telling us. When someone dared to ask and the officer who went by they were shouted at and ordered not to talk about it.
As we were on the ground floor, near all the admin offices we could hear things happening. After you've been in prison for such a long time as I had been, you get to know when things are different simply by the sounds. Normally everything is exactly the same so when there is the difference, you know. But then again it is amazing how little you actually did know. Because of the enforced silence of all prisoners, we weren't to know until days later and when the initial strictness began to soften, that the cell right next to us had been filled with all the Hong Kong guys who were involved in the riot. The six solitary/punishment huts were full. It was filled by the Fulam guys. No idea how many of them had been shoved into each of those tiny hothouses. It must have been dreadful. The conditions were unthinkable. But being a prison in Hong Kong all the HK boys were in relative comfort in a normal cell. OK, they were stuffed in, double the normal occupancy with no belongings but a normal cell that wasn't in the baking sun all day and they had a toilet and running water. A luxurious penthouse apartment compared to the huts.
After about 5 days we were allowed out in small groups to have a shower. We would hand in our ID badges and we would be called in groups. We were given a stern warning not to look at anyone, keep our heads down, and do exactly as we were told. There was to be absolutely no talking anywhere. Anyone who disobeyed this order, well, no-one really wanted to know what would happen.
By day 7 we were allowed out to exercise for an hour at a time. I n the yard we looked at the cell next to ours. A face would pop up now and again but be quickly told to get back from the door.
The first Monday after that first week we were to go back to our normal duties. So for the first time, the prisoners from all different

cells would congregate. The officer presence was massive. They were so on edge you were afraid to cough loudly.

But being a prison, the grapevine sprang into action. Stories came out about that first night from the larger cells upstairs. Fights were breaking out between any HK guys and any II guys, so all had been separated. Then fights were happening between II's from different provinces.

But most of all the main difference was that it was eerily quiet. At least 50 prisoners were missing, and most of the high ranking ones had gone. They had been taken off the island and back to Pik Uk.

Chapter Forty-Six
Dentist

All these months my only constant companion had been my toothache. It hadn't gone away, I had just got used to it. But today the dentist came and they remembered to call me. I was taken from the workshop down to the RO. There were about twenty other prisoners all with tooth problems. I wondered if my face was looking as petrified as theirs. We were marched up to the main gate and onto a waiting truck. We all clambered over the rail at the back and sat on the benches. Most of us staring at our feet. I was in mixed emotions. I was excited about getting my tooth removed but terrified of how it was going to be done. I had had removals when I was in Pik Uk; these were for smaller teeth at the front of my mouth. This time it was my third last molar. It was going to be an epic removal, I could just tell. We came to a halt and were shouted out of the truck. In front of us was a small overgrown pathway leading up a hill. The path went through some really thick and overgrown vegetation. When I turned to look at the guards with us they were double-handed and armed, so any thought of trying to escape would have been suicide. We were marched up the path, I let my hands move out from my sides and felt the leaves on either side of me. This was the first time in over two years that I had actually touched plants. It was exhilarating. I tried to close my eyes and imagine being alone, wondering where I wanted, engrossed in nature. At the end of the path was a long hut with many prisoners from all the prisons on the island squatting down in a line against the wall. And here we squatted too. As I was led to the end of the line I was able to take a quick look inside. Maybe I shouldn't have. At first, it looked like a barber. Lines of barber chairs with a person in a white coat standing over their next client. But there was no hair on the floor and the clients were screaming. On the walls, someone had decided that they would show off their collection of antique equipment. Only it may have been antique but it wasn't just for decoration. I squatted down with the others. There were 4 chairs in total so the turnaround was quick. As soon as one prisoner came out holding their face with blood running down their jaw, neck and onto their shirts, another was ordered to go in. One of the II's that I had become friendly with was a few in front of me. He was shitting himself. He had never had a tooth out before and he was shivering with fear. He was told to go in, but at first, refused. He received a friendly whack with the palm of the guard's hand and jumped up and scurried in. Although I was petrified I knew what the outcome would be, pain relief. As he had never been through it before he was only thinking of the immediate pain, not me thinking of the bliss and ability to eat properly again after 9 months. Another couple of wounded prisoners came out and I was called in. As soon I went in I could see that my II friend was still there in the chair. And he was bleeding. Not a little but furiously. The side of his face was covered in blood. It looked like he had been shot. As I stared in horror I was pushed down in my chair.

"Which one" the dentist barked.

I pointed, and he dove right in. I didn't see what he was using so just imagined it wasn't clean. He knelt on my chest and applied so much pressure to my tooth I thought my jaw would crack. But the crack I heard was the tooth coming out. The relief was instant. And so was the ejection from my chair. I have thrust a piece of tissue to put in my mouth to help with the blood and was out the door in moments, but not before I turned round to see my friend with three people around him and an ever-increasing puddle of blood on his shoulder. As soon as I was out the door I was marched down the path and told to get in the truck and wait. We waited and waited, but he never came. Eventually, we left without him and headed back to prison.

It was another few days later that he finally appeared. He had been admitted into the hospital because he had lost so much blood. It seems his tooth broke and ruptured something. He still had some tooth left in his jaw, but of course, would have to wait until his gum had healed and another 6 months before he could see the dentist again. A huge laugh went out when exclaimed

"That fucker isn't going anywhere near my face again. I go home before 6 months and use a knife to fix it myself"

Then all of a sudden one day whilst I was in the workshop I was called to "see one month".

I couldn't believe it. I had no idea. I looked at my friends who all stared at me. After what seemed like an eternity one of them came up and hugged me. It was the first hug since seeing Lennon. I was going home. I was leaving in one month. I was taken to the RO, not quite believing what was happening. I tell you I was almost crying whilst I sat there waiting to see the governor. My number was called and I was marched straight in to see him. I had the biggest smile, I was ecstatic. He brought me straight down to earth, with a crash.

"So you want to happen to you what happened to Mahmood?" He said.

"That won't happen Sir" I replied confidently.

He sat there and nodded his head.

"No, I don't think it will."

"You have done well, at the start you had many problems but now I see that you are doing well. You need to find a job when you are released and stay away from the drugs, ok?"

"Yes, sir" I almost shouted.

With that, I was dismissed.

When I returned to the workshop I decided that I would go for asleep. I wanted to dream about the future and not have to talk to anyone and share it. The future was mine, no-one else's. I found a quiet spot under the stairs and curled up for asleep. I didn't dream about the future, I actually dreamed about the past, a very happy day in the past. I dreamed about the day I took Anne-Marie, Pedro and Emma for lunch at the Hilton Hotel. I used the voucher that Rachel and I had won at the school dance. After we had split up, Rachel had very kindly given the voucher to me. I miss those friends dearly. I hadn't been a good friend to them, and that made me very sad. Anne-Marie was someone very special to me. Unfortunately, I wasn't able to return to her the care she had shown me. It was the wrong time for us. I cared for her so much, but I couldn't handle life at that time. And Pedro, well the less said the better. He was a great guy but I wasn't great to him either. Hey, I deserved whatever happened to me. And if he had a plan that night behind Inn Place, well good on him, I deserved that too. Emma, lovely Emma. I will always remember the walks to school, the hours we used to talk on the phone at night. We were always just friends, the hours were spent talking about boys and girls that we both fancied, and I seem to remember. The day that I realised how bad I had got was when I saw her and Lucy in Causeway bay and they hid from me. To get to such a low point in life is devastating. It was at that point I just gave up. I loathed myself just as much as they loathed me, their ex-friend, their junkie ex-friend.

Chex-friendly Seven

The End

Slowly, each day passed. I tried to keep to my routine, tried to not think of the upcoming reality of eviction from one home to another that I had previously been kicked out of. But, I was getting out. No matter what the future holds for me, I was getting out. I have a messed up personality, that's for sure, and for whatever reason, I end up in the shit all the time. I couldn't just do my time quietly could I? No-no-no. I did hard time, but that was my problem, my choice. When there were only a few days to go I was shown my flight ticket. I wouldn't be getting out early, but to see my details on the voucher with the date and time of my flight were quite something. My flight was on the day of my release. It was official. All I had to do now was not get into any fights. Don't let anyone do to me what had been done to Mahmood, by me.

Chapter Forty-Eight
Release

I estimate that I roughly got two hours of sleep last night. I spent most of the time reading, eating, smoking and eating. Kong Yue from the store had given me a few smokes as it was my last night. I tried to offer to share them but they wouldn't allow it. So I spent my last evening smoking cigarettes in a cell of 13 prisoners not sharing with anyone. As soon as the radio went on this morning I had a shower during which I washed my hair a couple of times. Ah Tai leant me his shaver, so I made myself clean and smooth. It meant that didn't have to waste time with the terrible shaver in the workshop. I threw my blankets together for the last time, not having to fold them perfectly like so many hundreds of mornings previously. I took them to the store and said goodbye to the store guys. I then picked up all my belongings and took them to the reception office. Don't know why I was holding on to so much stuff. But it was mine and all I had. I was feeling so happy. It was a happiness that I had never experienced in my whole life before. Breakfast this morning was B hall. 490 had lost a meatball to me so he passed it through the tables but just as it got to me, an officer approached our table. The meatball was quickly hidden from view. The officer came and stood over me.
"So you go home today"
"Yes"
I said, trying to be as blunt as possible so that I could get my precious meatball.
"Where you go"
"UK"
I told him.
"What you do when you get out?"
"For fuck sake"
I thought to myself. All the months I've been in here and now you decide to chat with me. No officer had ever just had a conversation with me. It was a sign of how institutionalized I had become. All I could think of was my meatball. All thoughts and wanting to discuss my release had gone. I just wanted my fucking meatball!
He finally left and the, now cold meatball was finally passed. After breakfast, we went up to the workshops where I brought out my hidden packet of biscuits as per prison rules and diligently passed them out to my friends. I then went to sit with Chi Kin and gave him a

chocolate bar that I had bought and saved for him. We sat chatting for a while and at 10 am,
"90760"
Was shouted from the workshop door.
This was it, the time had come. I went and said goodbye to everyone, trying not to make such a big deal out of it as they all had a hard time to do. All these friends that I had made over the last few months after the Mahmood fight. What good friends they had become. They were some of the best friends I had ever had, at a time of danger and depression. It is said that the best friends you can ever make are in prison. I'm not too sure about that, because realistically we would all stab each other in the back when it came to it. But I will miss them all. I wished them I quick release and a fabulous future. When I had come to prison I had little Chinese. The first year I just listened but now I could talk with them and I was able to tell them everything with heartfelt sincerity in Chinese. I was taken to the governor's office. Not much was said between us. All he said was that he wished me well and suggested I sign back up with the Navy when I got home. Yes sir, right away sir!
Then it was to the reception office. There was a load of paperwork that I had to sign. My release papers were checked, signed, and then given to me. My personal belongings, kept all this time, were checked and then signed for, but I wasn't given them just yet.
I was sent into the waiting room, to, well, wait. And that I did, I sat there for 4 hours waiting. Funny, but they were the quickest 4 hours of my sentence. Finally, at 2 pm I was told to change into my street clothes. They felt really good to put on. A bit strange, but good. I don't know if it made me feel more human, not yet anyway. Technically I was still in prison so still felt a prisoner. I knew what was coming up but I was unable to feel much difference in myself. At 2.30 I was taken out of the reception office, through the yard where I looked up and managed to wave to some friends in the workshop window. Up the steps to the main gate. The gate swung open and I walked out to the sun shining. It wasn't like you see in the films. The most important reason for that was because I was actually still on a prison island, so technically the whole island was a prison, so this wasn't freedom, not yet anyway. There was a truck waiting at the end of the path to the gate. I climbed up over the back rail and sat down onto the wooden benches clutching my paper bag. In the bad were a packet of wafers, my letters, my songbook and the diary that

this is taken from. There were some old codger prisoners on the truck who all just stared at me. We started off up the hill past the hospital where I had spent those days with Lennon, then down the hill towards the pier. This next bit I wasn't looking forward to. The ferry journey had always been horrendous but this time I was worried about the state that my clothes would get in. but this time instead of being put down in the hold with all the other prisoners I was taken upstairs, unshackled, to a room by myself. I had a comfortable chair and a window. As the ferry set off I managed to catch a glimpse back to Hei Ling Chau. How I had managed to survive that place I don't know. It was not the same survival that I had managed in Pik Uk, it was different. I think on two occasions my life was seriously in jeopardy here at the hands of others. And then I thought about the bravery during the riot of the two guys sat next to me to stop me fighting. If that hadn't of happened I wouldn't be going home just now. I would have had at least another 6 months on to my sentence and a beaten body, at worst, well who knows?

The ferry turned into the famously busy Hong Kong shipping lanes. I stared out at all these ships going backwards and forwards. Seeing the real world again and knowing that I was to part of it again soon. We docked at HMS Tamar and were transferred into a bus, like the one I had gone in that first day to Pik Uk, an old school bus. But this time I wasn't shackled. I had handcuffs on but my ankles were free to do whatever they wanted. We drove through the narrow streets of Central district on route to Victoria Prison. It was at this moment that I realised that I didn't really know where I was going afterwards. I knew I had a ticket to Heathrow but after that, I had no idea where I was going. What would I do in London, would I try to get back to Glasgow or would I just stay in London and try to make a life for myself. I had been given no indication whatsoever what would happen. We arrived at Victoria's impressive gates and were taken off the bus and inside. We were made to squat down in lines. This was going to be difficult. I hated squatting, ever since my knee problems squatting had always been difficult. It was painful and uncomfortable. I had to shift my weight from one leg to another every 5 minutes or so. I had no idea how long it was going to last this time, I was worried. It would take just one overzealous officer to turn on me and I could have time added on to my sentence. This thought had just started in my mind when I saw a guy in civvies walking up to an officer show him something and point at me. I was told to get up and

he introduced himself as an immigration officer and that he was here to take me to the airport. We went over to the main desk where lay a bag of my personal belongings. It was just given straight to me, so I took it.
He then turned to me and said,
"Are you going to give me any trouble?"
"No"
I said,
"I just want to go home"
"If you give me no trouble, no cuffs, understand?"
I nodded to him; he then turned his back and walked towards the main gate.
The gate opened and the sun shone onto me. This time as I stepped out into the street I truly felt free. Stepping out onto the streets without handcuffs is a truly different experience. He walked down the road a little to a minibus; he opened the back door and told me to get in. As I was sitting down I turned around and saw one guy in sunglasses at the top of the street start walking toward the minibus, then I looked around and saw 2 more plainclothes guys at different street corners start to come as well. Positioned ready for if I made a run for it. Packing enough weaponry to bring down an elephant as well I saw as they took out their assortment of guns and put them in a box at the front. Wow, thank goodness that never crossed my mind. The van sped off towards the airport, and then I remembered the new bag that I had in my hands. My watch was the first thing that I put on, then my sunglasses and then I found my funny little skull earring which I decided not to put on. My bank cards, HK Id card and other bits and pieces were in this bag. The time was now about 5 pm, the light was fading and as we drove through the streets the neon signs started coming on. We arrived at the airport an hour later. I looked at my watch. It was funny. Here I was able to put my watch on to tell the time on the day when time stopped having meaning for me. I want counting days, weeks or months anymore. Walking into the airport the immigration guy asked me if I had the HK$150 for departure tax. I just laughed at him and said no. What was he going to do, not deport me because I didn't pay my tax?! I was then taken to the deportee departure lounge. It looked like a business class lounge with large sofas and televisions dotted around it. Pretty luxurious to what I had been used to. I was taken to the reception desk which had police and immigration officers at it. The guy who

had brought me here signed my paperwork and then was gone. I was told to sit and wait. There were a number of other deportees dotted around the room. Somewhere smoking, some sleeping on the sofa. I joined the group watching the TV. Everyone else was African in appearance I was the only white guy. They paid me little attention for the first hour or so but then one asked me if I wanted a smoke. So I wandered over and joined them. I was handed a Benson and Hedges, had it lit and then sat down. They asked me about myself, I told them where I had been and where I was going. They paid little attention to my lame story; they all had more exciting and important ones to tell. To be honest I became quite tired at one point and took myself off for a lie-down. At 1030 I was woken up and told it was time to go. This was it; I was going to make it after all. For a while, I thought of all the things that could go wrong, what could keep me here. Police spotting me and realising that I was wanted for another crime that they tried me for. The plane breaks down, the law changing. Something was going to happen, but it didn't. I was taken by two immigration guys down a couple of corridors and then came out at the door where the bus that took people to the plane was waiting. I was the only one on it. It appeared that they had kept me to the very last. All the other passengers were already on board. As the bus neared the plane I saw I was flying British Airways, on a 747. That was exciting enough! We climbed the stairs to the plane where we were met by the head steward. One of the immigration guys handed him my passport.
"You'll get this back when we land in London"
The steward said.
I was handed my boarding card and I walked up to economy class and found my seat. I had been given a window seat with the middle seat empty and a fat Chinese guy in the aisle seat. He got up and let me squeeze past him into my place. I sat there, put my seat belt on and grasped my paper bag in my lap. Staring out of the window I realised I was leaving. I was looking out to Honk Kong for the last time. Their years that had just gone past were some of the most extraordinary that anyone could ever face. From parties on yachts, sex with beautiful girls. Some of the most amazing girlfriends and other friends. Working in weird in wonderful offices to living in the streets with heroin being my only companion. The crimes committed and the ones that thankfully never happened. The engines began to rumble and we started to hurl down this thin strip of land that we had

stared at from the top of Island school whilst smoking, looking over the amazing Hong Kong harbour with all its lights and promise. The front wheels lifted and I headed to freedom, still not knowing what that freedom would contain. It must have been the most enjoyable take-off of my life.

Epilogue

I sat there, not moving, clutching my brown bag of all my possessions tightly between my hands. The seat belt sign dinged and went off and others started to move around. I settled back in my seat. For a strange few moments, I didn't want to relax in case the plane was forced to turn around and go back. I wasn't free until that seat belt sign went off. For the next hour, I sat totally still, just as I had been trained to do over the last few years. Even if I needed the toilet I wouldn't go, I didn't know what the rules were. I was thirsty but didn't ask for a drink. I just sat on the most comfortable seat I could remember and stared right in front of me, not daring to turn my head either way and become involved in a conversation with anyone. Here I was, free, but still scared. I was scared that I couldn't speak English. I was scared that everyone was looking at me and knew who I was. I was looking forward and saw two of the cabin crew standing and looking at me whilst talking quietly to each other. What were they talking about? They knew I was a criminal; they were planning how to deal with me. I felt a surge of adrenalin, I was ready to run, but where could I run to. One of them started to walk towards me, I could feel sweat starting to run down my temples, my heart started to race, I was starting to have a panic attack, and I was trapped. She reached my row, and I pretended not to see her, I kept looking forward. She leant in towards me.

"Excuse me sir," she said,

Heart, nearly bursting, every cell telling me to run, I turned to her and said,

"Yes"

"Can you come with me please, and bring your things"

Being institutionalized, I obeyed the direct order.

The big Chinese guy next to me got up and I squeezed past him. She started to walk towards the front of the plane.

"She's taking me to the cockpit," I thought

"Why?"

We walked through business class and then she stopped.

"Please take a seat, sir, is there anything I can get for you?"

I looked at the seat she was pointing to. I couldn't believe it. Tears started to form in my eyes. I was being upgraded. I looked at her with watery eyes, and she smiled at me. I could have burst into tears and hugged her right there and then. I sat down and thanked her. In that act of such kindness, she had turned me from a number, YP90760, into a human being. I was now a free man again.
"Some water please"
"Certainly sir," she said
And she turned to get me my drink.

Epilogue

24 years later

I got through immigration. My friends, who had accompanied me by sheer chance, cheered when they saw that I was back in Hong Kong for the first time since I had been deported. We lived in the same village. They were travelling to Canada for a holiday and happened to be on the fight from Goa to Mumbai and then from Mumbai to Hong Kong. A total coincidence but a handy one as it helped me with my stress that travelling alone may have shot up and got me acting all strange and Autistic.

We shared a coffee together once we had picked up our luggage. They headed off to get a taxi to their hotel and I went and got the airport express train to Central. We promised to meet up again together in a couple of days before they headed to Canada.

I had never seen his airport before, formed out of two adjacent islands and lots of reclaimed land. The infrastructure was massive. I had to rub my eyes to take it all in. It was still obviously Hong Kong but it had changed so much. I started to worry that I wouldn't recognize anything, but as I climbed out of the darkness of the new Central terminus I was greeted with the past. The past I knew so well. As looking upwards is how you recognize Hong Kong. I found a tram stop heading in the direction of Happy Valley and took in the view.

As I travelled along on the tram towards my Airbnb accommodation I went back in time. Especially when the tram got to Admiralty, I saw the road leading to the Supreme Court and the years disappeared, the buildings morphed back to what they had been when I was last there. My plan was to check into my room and go for something to eat before I got a taxi up to Island School. I was back for the 50th-anniversary celebrations. I was scared; I didn't know how I would be received. I had caused so much pain all those years ago and didn't know if I would be met with hostility or what. The main party was tomorrow night, but tonight there was a party at the school and I had volunteered to help out getting things set up. From doing this I could firstly gauge if there were bad feelings and therefore forgo the parties altogether. It would maybe also paint me in something of a good light because I had volunteered to help. I really didn't know what I was thinking. But as soon as I had checked in, changed out of my travelling clothes, I was off. It was like I was on total autopilot. Here I was walking the streets of happy valley, causeway bay and

Wan Chai. It was different but the same. I knew exactly which direction to go and found myself walking all the way towards the school. My anxiety had caused my stomach to close into a rock. That rock had been there for all these years. It was the rock of guilt. It was heavy and had weighed heavily on me my whole life since Hong Kong part one. Now in Hong Kong part two, it made its presence known again. As I carried the rock and myself up the hills towards the school I felt sick. It wasn't the heat as it was colder than India where I now lived; it was the fear of rejection. The rejection would have been totally understandable. But then maybe there would be nobody there that would actually know me to be able to reject me. But maybe there had been a memo put out that I wasn't allowed back in the school just like I thought would have happened at immigration. I found the pathway up to the school that we used to hang out in and smoke cigarettes before we went down to McDonald's and then I was there. Standing at the back steps of the school, the steps that led to the zoo. I thought about taking this entrance, to sneak in the back so as missing out of the main entrance and the possibility of being knocked back as a persona non grata. But I decided that I would be brave and walk to the front. The street was eerily quiet for that time of day. I thought there would be a buzz of activity but I was the only one there. As I walked up to the main gate I stopped and looked at the sign for the school on the large curved white wall that encased the school. I thought of the outdoor poll situated behind it and the fun we used to have there. I took a deep breath; I would be at the main gate in one minute. I took the next uneasy step forward and kept walking. What happened next couldn't be true. Through all the years hours and minutes for this to happen now, well improbable. All of a sudden I wasn't alone on that street. The haunting noise of hundreds of students running out of school at the end of the day to climb onto their school bus which would have been parked where I was walking past, fading into history yet again. A lone figure came round the corner, although I'm short-sighted and I wasn't wearing my glasses I knew exactly who it was. At this distance, he hadn't changed. And as he walked he slowly looked up, I had stopped mid-step but then continued. I had thought and processed this moment hundreds of times. But none of them happened like this. He was also slowly starting to realise who he was now approaching and he started walking straight towards me. At that moment the last 24 years of self-doubt fell away from me. His face told me everything that I

needed to know. He smiled at me in disbelief; he was more than pleased to see me. We kept walking towards each other and as we met we hugged tighter than I could have imagined. There were tears in both our eyes. I told him how sorry I was for everything, how terribly sorry I was for causing so much trouble when I was a kid. Chris Forse looked me in the eyes and said,
"Come with me, I've told so many people about you and they are all dying to meet you".

Final Thoughts

It was that night at the Island School party whilst I was standing in the middle of the playground after I had just chatted with Chris Forse again that I felt something fall. To describe it to you it felt like a round, solid ball about a foot in diameter. It fell from my stomach and hit the ground hard and I suddenly felt a complete uplifting, a change. I had been carrying that weight for 26 years. For 26 years that ball had weighed me down. It helped to form my decision making, my life choices. But most of all it held me down. It was a ball of self-hatred. And when it fell I understood. I understood why things had happened and why they kept happening. Why my life always felt like a battle even though I knew my soul was a good one. Maybe that was my destiny, to understand. It was that understanding that let me write this book as honestly as possible without pointing blame, without over analysing.

Now that this book is out of the way I have so much more space in my head. Space to look at my life and see how I can use the lessons that I have learnt to hopefully help others.

There is always a reason behind the behaviour. Unless you find out what that is you will judge people for their reactions and not for who they truly are.

Never let your ego get in the way of giving someone a little hope.

If you have hope you have a chance.

What I did with that hope

After years of poor mental health and readjustment to the outside world where I had to relearn English, I finally found my calling. And that is helping others. I worked in Criminal Justice for some years, helping prisoners coming towards the end of their sentence prepare to move back into the community. After being made redundant I went to Glasgow and Strathclyde Universities simultaneity. At Glasgow, I completed my COCSA Counseling and at Strathclyde, I was allowed onto the new Autism MSc. Unfortunately, it was uncertificated as I didn't have a degree but they let me on after many conversations because of my diagnosis and determination.

I was also a volunteer member of The Scottish Children's Panel, which is Scotlands unique court system for children who have broken the law or have had laws broken against them. I was the first openly autistic, ex-prisoner and drug addict to sit on these cases.

I was diagnosed with Asperger Syndrome after prison which is an autistic spectrum disorder. During the course at Strathclyde, I discovered so much about myself that now made total sense.

I have now cousins, nieces and nephews all diagnosed and my two amazing boys, although not clinically diagnosed as yet, are also on the spectrum.

I lived in India for a number of years had so many amazing experiences and opportunities. Due to my criminal record and other rules and regulations, my employment opportunities in the UK are limited but in India, they take you on for your skills.

I have volunteered with NGO's who work with autistic kids. Have held workshops, presentation, attended conferences and held training all over India, Nepal and Sri Lanka. For one year I was also asked to be Principal at an international School! Now that was a year I will never forget. It was one of the most fulfilling things I had ever done. I sometimes even took lessons when a teacher was absent. I found that I had a passion for teaching and put all of my own personal experience into making sure that the students were all taken care of. I am still in touch with many of those students and their families and follow their progress. After I have taught at a couple of other schools. An Indian one and an international Cambridge school where I taught from P1 to A-Level economics.

But the most rewarding work was in the field of autism.

I helped organise and hold one of Indias first Autism Awareness events. I have trained many mainstream teachers on how to work with autistic students. Placing students into schools who were frightened of the word autism. I have trained professionals from Bangalore to Delhi. Psychiatrist, psychologists, universities. I helped in the development of schools for autistic kids in India and Nepal. I would like to continue this work if possible.
But now I have returned to Scotland as my children need to come and live in their native land for a while and go to school.
So what will I do next?
Watch This Space.

Printed in Great
Britain
by Amazon